MEASURING UP
Challenges Minorities Face
in Educational Assessment

Evaluation in Education and Human Services

Editors:
George F. Madaus, Boston College,
  Chestnut Hill, Massachusetts, U.S.A.
Daniel L. Stufflebeam, Western Michigan
  University, Kalamazoo, Michigan, U.S.A.

Other books in the series:

Ayers, J. and Berney, M.:
  A Practical Guide to Teacher Education Evaluation
Hambleton, R. and Zaal, J.:
  Advances in Educational and Psychological Testing
Gifford, B. and O'Connor, M.:
  Changing Assessments
Gifford, B.:
  Policy Perspectives on Educational Testing
Basarab, D. and Root, D.:
  The Training Evaluation Process
Haney, W.M., Madaus, G.F. and Lyons, R.:
  The Fractured Marketplace for Standardized Testing
Wing, L.C. and Gifford, B.:
  Policy Issues in Employment Testing
Gable, R.E.:
  Instrument Development in the Affective Domain (2nd Edition)
Kremer-Hayon, L.:
  Teacher Self-Evaluation
Payne, David A.:
  Designing Educational Project and Program Evaluations
Oakland T. and Hambleton, R.:
  International Perspectives on Academic Assessment
Nettles, M.T. and Nettles, A.L.:
  Equity and Excellence in Educational Testing and Assessment
Shinkfield, A.J. and Stufflebeam, D.L.:
  Teacher Evaluation: Guide to Effective Practice
Birenbaum, M. and Dochy, Filip J.R.C.:
  *Alternatives in Assessment of Achievements, Learning
  Processes and Prior Knowledge*
Mulder, M., Nijhof, W.J., Brinkerhoff, R.O.:
  Corporate Training for Effective Performance
Britton, E.D. and Raizen, S.A.:
  Examining the Examinations
Candoli, C., Cullen, K. and Stufflebeam, D.:
  Superintendent Performance Evaluation
Brown, S.M. and Seidner, C.J.:
  Evaluating Corporate Training: Models and Issues
Osterlind, S.:
  Constructing Test Items (Second Edition)

MEASURING UP
Challenges Minorities Face
in Educational Assessment

edited by

Arie L. Nettles
Michael T. Nettles

University of Michigan

EVALUATION IN EDUCATIONAL AND HUMAN SERVICES

KLUWER ACADEMIC PUBLISHERS
Boston / Dordrecht / London

Distributors for North, Central and South America:
Kluwer Academic Publishers
101 Philip Drive
Assinippi Park
Norwell, Massachusetts 02061 USA
Telephone (781) 871-6600
Fax (781) 871-6528
E-Mail <kluwer@wkap.com>

Distributors for all other countries:
Kluwer Academic Publishers Group
Distribution Centre
Post Office Box 322
3300 AH Dordrecht, THE NETHERLANDS
Telephone 31 78 6392 392
Fax 31 78 6546 474
E-Mail <services@wkap.nl>

 Electronic Services <http://www.wkap.nl>

Library of Congress Cataloging-in-Publication Data
Measuring up : challenges minorities face in educational assessment /
    edited by Arie L. Nettles, Michael T. Nettles.
        p. cm. -- (Evaluation in education and human services)
    Includes index.
    ISBN 0-7923-8401-6 (alk. paper)
    1. Educational tests and measurements--Social aspects--United
States. 2. Minority students--Rating of--United States. 3. Test
bias--United States. 4. Educational equalization--United States.
I. Nettles, Arie L. II. Nettles, Michael T., 1955-   .
III. Series.
LB3051.M4627   1999
371.26'01'3--dc21   99-12925
                                                     CIP

Printed on acid-free paper.
Printed in the United States of America

Dedication

To Ana Simone Nettles, age 11

Sabin Alexia Nettles, age 7

Aidan Selima Nettles, age 3

Our three lovely hearts, partners and children,

And

To all the other youngsters

in American schools who are striving

to measure up to the nation's evolving standards.

Contents

Contributing Authors

Zenaida Aguirre-Muñoz
Research Associate
National Center for Research on Evaluation, Standards, and Student Testing (CRESST)

Elizabeth Badger
Director of Instructional Assessment Initiatives
The College Board

Eva L. Baker
Professor
Director, Center for the Study of Education
Co-Director, National Center for Research on Evaluation, Standards, and Student
Testing (CRESST)

Joan Baratz-Snowden
Deputy Director
Educational Issues Department
American Federation of Teachers

Kimberly Gene Browning
Social Science Research Associate and Adjunct Lecturer
School of Social Work
University of Michigan

Nancy S. Cole
President
Educational Testing Service

Kimberley C. Edelin
Research Scientist
Frederick D. Patterson Research Institute

Edmund W. Gordon
John M. Musser Professor of Psychology, Emeritus
Yale University
Distinguished Professor of Educational Psychology
The City University of New York
Visiting Scholar
The College Board

Anastasia Raczek,
Boston College

Mark D. Reckase
Professor of Education
Michigan State University
*formerly of ACT, Inc. when the paper was written

Edward D. Roeber
Project Director
State Collaborative Assessment and Student Standards
Council of Chief State School Officers

Edward A. Silver
Professor
School of Education
 Instruction and Learning
University of Pittsburgh

Donald Stewart
President
The College Board

Sally Thomas
Professor
Institute of Education
Univesity of London

Catherine Welch
Director of Performance Assessment Center
ACT Inc.

MEASURING UP:
Challenges Minorities Face
In Educational Assessment

Preface

On May 13 and 14, 1996, the University of Michigan School of Education convened the second National Symposium on Equity and Educational Testing and Assessment with support from the Ford Foundation. Held in Washington, D.C., the symposium brought together 112 leading government and foundation officials, scholars, test and assessment developers, educators, and other users of tests who are leading assessment and reform initiatives in the United States. The purpose was to gain greater understanding of contemporary issues in the context of educational reforms that are underway throughout the nation. Several leading assessment experts were commissioned to write papers that were distributed to the participants in the symposium. This book is comprised of a selection of those commissioned papers.

Like the symposium, this book is a product of the Ford Foundation's long-standing interest in increasing public understanding of the equity dimensions of testing and assessment in our nation's educational system. Between 1987 and 1993, the Foundation provided leading support to launch a National Commission on Testing and Public Policy. The Commission revealed an urgent need to bring testing policies into line with our society's goal of expanding opportunities and enhancing human development. During the initial phase of the Foundation's efforts to address this issue, its grandees demonstrated the growing impact of standardized tests and assessment tools as the principal screening and sorting mechanisms for placing students in specific learning environments from an early age, and thus, in determining ultimate educational opportunities. Further investigations revealed biases in the development and use of tests that have contributed to the disproportionate exclusion of racial and ethnic minorities from advanced courses and post-secondary opportunities.

The Foundation's efforts to broaden educational opportunities for all students have focused on four main areas: (1) increasing knowledge about issues of equity in testing; (2) encouraging good practice among those who develop and employ such tests; (3) generating public awareness of the uses and misuses of tests; and (4) affecting the policy environment to encourage unbiased testing and assessments. The Foundation's major partners in these efforts have included researchers in universities such as Boston College and the University of Michigan; national organizations such as the College Board, the Educational Testing Service, the Council of Chief State School Officers, and the RAND Corporation; advocacy organizations such as the Mexican American Legal Defense and Educational Fund (MALDEF), FairTest and the National Coalition of Advocates for Students; and a broad group within the donor community including the Pew Charitable Trusts and the MacArthur Foundation.

Today, the debate over academic assessment continues to intensify. Some local jurisdictions have made high school graduation contingent on passing "minimum-competency" tests; others are seeing a resurgence in the use of tests as a requirement for advancing between grades; and several have begun to base educators' pay on the results of students' test scores. Such actions are taking place against a changed landscape that includes demographic changes in U.S. population, devolution of authority to the state level, scaling back of affirmative action, legal mandates to test previously excluded students, the possibility of voluntary national testing, and the growing use of computer testing. These developments, among others, have opened a plethora of technical, equity, and validity issues that are being inadequately addressed. At the same time, an institutional capacity for independently evaluating test programs, monitoring their use, and developing appropriate accountability mechanisms, remains insufficient. As one step toward responding to these challenges, the Foundation has recently awarded a grant to Boston College's Center for the Study of Testing, Evaluation and Educational Policy to assist in developing a permanent National Commission on Testing and Public Policy.

Throughout all of the Foundation's concerted efforts to address the issue of equity in testing and assessment, it has sought to encourage a wide-ranging dialogue on this topic among a broad cross-section of researchers, practitioners, and other advocates in the field. Recognizing that education paths are all too often charted by the use of "high-stakes" tests that inadequately measure student capacities, the Foundation views this publication – aimed at enriching individual perspectives and identifying areas of consensus – as an important step in that process.

Janice Petrovich

Director
Education, Knowledge and Religion Unit
of the Education, Media, Arts and Culture program,
Ford Foundation

Acknowledgements

In March, 1993, the Ford Foundation, together with the University of Michigan School of Education, convened the first national symposium on Equity and Educational Testing and Assessment. The purpose was to gain greater understanding of contemporary equity issues in educational testing and assessment, and to examine these issues in the context of the educational reforms that were underway throughout the nation. The culmination of this effort was the book *Equity and Excellence in Educational Testing and Assessment* (1995). Due to the continued progressive initiatives on behalf of both of these two organizations, a second symposium was convened in May 1996. In the spirit of identifying and addressing some of the challenges faced by many Americans in their pursuit of high quality education and training, we present Measuring Up: Challenges Minorities Face in Educational Assessment.

This book has involved the extraordinary efforts of many people. We are very appreciative of Alison Bernstein, Vice President of the Ford Foundation, Janice Petrovich, Associate Division Director for Education, Media, and Culture, and Susan Berresford, President of the Ford Foundation, for their support of the nation symposium and intellectual contribution to thinking about the important issues and challenges facing disadvantaged people who are striving to achieve in America. To Susan MacKenzie, our editorial assistant, we are fortunate to have your talents and careful attention to details as we completed this publication. To our staff at the University of Michigan and other assistants that worked with us for the past eight years to conduct two national symposiums and produce two edited volumes, thank you. They include Michael McLendon, Katherine Erdman, Sirkka Kaufman, Chris Eldred, Kathy Gilbert, Tammy Benshoof, Amanda Eldred, Cynthia Hudgins, Lisa McRipley, Catherine Millett, Daniel Patton, Jilo Williams, Tara Young, Daniel Carchidi, and Philip Knutel. Many thanks to all symposium participants and contributors these past eight years who include Joseph Aguerrebere, Zenaida Aguirre-Muñoz, Verna Allen, Gordon Ambach, the late Greg Anrig, Beth Bader, Elizabeth Badger, Joan Baratz-Snowden, Adrienne Bailey, Eva Baker, Mary A. Barr, Pamela Becker, Edgar Beckham, Mike Biance, Mary V. Bicouvaris, Shelia Biddle, Eve M. Bither, Henry Braun, Cynthia G. Brown, Kimberly G. Browning, Dale Carlson, Ruben Carriedo, Linda Carstens, Jacqueline Leong Cheong, Donald L. Clark, Beverly Cole, Nancy Cole, Elizabeth Coleman, Eric Cooper, Christopher T. Cross, Linda Darling-Hammond, Marsha Delain, The Honorable Wilhelmina R. Delco, Elizabeth Dickey, Austin Doherty, Anne Dowling, Carol Anne Dwyer, Kimberley C. Edelin, Don Edwards, Emerson J. Elliott, Stephen Elliott, Anita Estel, Howard T. Everson, Richard L. Ferguson, Michael J. Feuer, Ray Fields, Chester E. Finn, Joan First, David Florio, Pascal D. Forgione, The Honorable William Ford, Howard Fuller, Lloyd Garrison, Peter H. Gerber, Edmund W. Gordon, William H. Gray III, Vincent Greaney, Ruth Grimes-Crump, Lani Gunier, Marilyn L. Hala, Walter Haney, Anita Harewood, Andrew J. Hartman, Mary Hatwood Futrell, The

Honorable Augustus F. Hawkins, Kati Haycock, Haven Henderson, Antonia Hernandez, Jay Heubert, Judith Heumann, Philip David Hirschy, Mallery Hobbs, Hodgson School of Delaware, H. D. Hoover, Eleanor Z. Horne, Judy R. Jablon, Richard M. Jaeger, The Honorable James M. Jeffords, Yolanda Jenkins, John F. Jennings, Christine Johnson, Sylvia Johnson, Elaine R. Jones, Cheryl Kane, Albert Kauffman, Kenneth Kimerling, Daniel M. Koretz, The Honorable Madeleine Kunin, Suzanne Lane, Archie E. Lapointe, Valerie Lee, Joanee Lenkhe, Reneé S. Lerche, Robert Linn, Dennis L. Loftus, Karen Lowery, George F. Madaus, Bruno V. Manno, Samuel M. Matsa, Shirley McBay, Phyllis P. McClure, Marilyn McConachie, Erica Y. McEachin, C. Kent McGuire, Floretta D. McKenzie, Ronee McLaughlin, Deborah W. Meier, Samuel J. Meisels, Ann Meyer, Cecil G. Miskel, Ruth Mitchell, Arnold L. Mitchem, Donald R. Moore, Shirley Mow, Ina V. S. Mullis, Mark D. Musick, Eric Nadelstern, Deborah Nance, D. Monty Neill, Regena F. Nelson, Ruben Olivarez, Paul M. Ostergard, Deborah C. Peek-Brown, Laura W. Perna, Marvin W. Peterson, John Powell, Hugh B. Price, Puyallup School of Washington State, Anastasia Raczek, Rafael Ramirez, Paul A. Ramsey, William T. Randall, Diane Ravitch, Sean F. Reardon, Mark D. Reckase, Edward F. Reidy Jr., Daniel Reschly, Daniel P. Resnick, Lauren Resnick, Rodney Riffel, Sharon Robinson, Edward D. Roeber, Maryanne Roesch, Waldemar Rojas, The Honorable Roy Romer, Sophie Sa, Thomas H. Saterfiel, Raymond C. Scheppach, Cinthia H. Schuman, Robert B. Schwartz, Ramsay W. Selden, Robert F. Sexton, Richard Seymour, Sharif Shakrani, Jerome M. Shaw, Theodore M. Shaw, Edward A. Silver, Warren Simmons, Diane Smolen, Conrad Snowden, Robert J. Solomon, Floraline I. Stevens, Donald Stewart, Daniel Stufflebeam, David Tatel, Sally Thomas, Stuart A. Tonemah, Susan Traiman, Roy Truby, Mary Lynn Walker, Catherine Welch, Susan Wilhelm, Wayne C. Winborne, Linda F. Winfield, Thomas R. Wolanin, Dennis Palmer-Wolf, Pamela Zappardino, Bob Zelnick, L. Steven Zwerling.

We raise the banner of equity once more so that policy makers, educators, researchers, and families gain more awareness about the pressing uses of equity and testing. It is our hope that we continue to vigorously attack the unfairness and the inappropriate uses of assessment instruments and practices that should be seen as beneficial to all.

Arie L. Nettles

Michael T. Nettles

1 Issuing the Challenge

Arie L. Nettles
Michael T. Nettles

Throughout the past two decades we have been worrying about the challenges that American families face in preparing to learn, work and live high quality lives in a new society. The new society is more diverse, technological, faster paced and global. Our work has centered primarily upon educational performance and achievement. The nation has made extraordinary efforts over the past two decades to focus the spotlight on education as the principal vehicle to peace, prosperity and the preservation of power and culture. We now have national educational goals to guide us and assessments for measuring our progress along the way. These assessments provide the states and the nation as a whole with an educational barometer of the general citizenry. On the horizon are new national tests that purport to tell us as individuals how well we are achieving national standards, and even how well we fare in the international marketplace of knowledge and skill acquisition. When the national test is finalized and in place, each American family will have access to information about both the educational standards and tools to know how each one of us is measuring up.

Many issues related to fairness, equity, and appropriate use are apparent, yet are not being sufficiently addressed. Our effort in this publication is to raise the banner of equity yet again so that policymakers, educators, researchers, and families gain more awareness about the pressing issues of equity in the context of educational assessment. We hope that this will equip us to more vigorously attack the unfairness and inappropriate uses of instruments that should be beneficial to everyone.

The principal concerns are the differential performance by race and social class, and how educational tests can be used as barriers to progress. It is our hope assessments can instead prompt leaders to correct deficiencies that are identified by our assessments, rather than using them in punitive ways to prevent students from enrolling in high quality academic courses in elementary and secondary schools, or to deny admission into the highest quality undergraduate, graduate and professional schools.

Here are some of the facts that give us great concern – facts that we have been devoting much of our lives to addressing. According to Nettles and Perna (1998), in their statement of facts about racial inequality in educational testing, one of the most visible and pronounced areas of difference between African Americans and Whites is their standardized educational testing scores. These differences represent one of the nation's greatest educational challenges to equality of access and achievement. Differences in the test scores of African Americans and Whites are revealed at the earliest grade levels and they persist throughout the subsequent years of formal education. The following are just a few illustrations of the gaps that can be observed in some of the nation's most prominent assessments.

• African American and White preschoolers achieve similar scores on tests of motor and social development (100.0 versus 102.6) and verbal memory (96.2 versus 97.7), but African American preschoolers score much lower than Whites on tests of vocabulary (74.6 versus 98.2).

• Only 9% of African American 4th graders achieve scores at or above the proficient level on the NAEP reading test, compared with 37% of Whites.

• One-half (48%) of African Americans score below the basic level on the NAEP 12th grade reading test, compared with 19% of Whites.

• Only 4% of African American, but 17% of White, 8th graders achieve scores at or above proficient on the NAEP history test.

• Two-thirds (66%) of African Americans, but only 19% of Whites, score below basic on the 4th grade NAEP geography assessment.

• Only 24% of African American 4th graders score at or above the basic level on the NAEP mathematics assessment, compared with 72% of Whites.

• Two-thirds (66%) of African American twelfth graders score below basic on the NAEP mathematics assessment, compared with only 28% of Whites.

• Only one-third of African Americans who take an Advanced Placement examination receive a passing score, compared with about two-thirds of Whites.

• Average scores on the SAT are about 100 points lower for African Americans than for Whites on both the verbal (434 for African Americans versus 526 for Whites) and quantitative components (423 versus 625).

• African Americans average 17.1 on the ACT, whereas Whites average 21.5.

• African Americans score about 100 points lower than Whites on the verbal, quantitative, and analytic components of the Graduate Record Examination (GRE).

• Average scores are also lower for African Americans than for Whites on the Law School Admissions Test (LSAT) (142.6 for African Americans versus 153.7 for Whites in 1995).

The media, policymakers, educators, and the general public need to recognize not only that these gaps exist, but also that more serious societal problems provide likely explanations for the persistence of these gaps. One explanation is that African Americans have lower socioeconomic status than Whites and, according to Carnevale, Haghighat and Kimmel of the Educational Testing Service, family background is one of the most important predictors of test scores.

• The Census Bureau (1997) reports that 40% of African Americans and Latinos under 18 years of age live below the poverty line, compared with 15% of White children.

• Family incomes are higher for White and Asian SAT test-takers than for African American test-takers. In 1997 52% of African American SAT-takers lived in families where the annual income was below $30,000, compared with 37% of Asians and 16% of Whites.

A second explanation for the persisting differences in test scores pertains to the concentration of African American youngsters in urban, poor public schools.

• Nearly one-third of African Americans (30%) attend public elementary and secondary schools in large central cities, compared with only 5% of Whites.

• Students who attend urban schools are less likely than students who attend non-urban schools to graduate on time (Quality Counts, 1998).

• Urban school students generally lack access to the rigorous curricula, well-prepared teachers, and high expectations that make better achievement possible. Performance is worst in high-poverty urban schools, where the majority of students are poor (Quality Counts, 1998).

• In schools with greater than 50% minority student enrollment, 41% of teachers are teaching a subject that was neither their major nor minor for their bachelor's degree, compared with 33% of teachers in schools with 10% or less minority student enrollment.

Moreover, when we see gaps between African Americans and Whites we need to be asking important questions about the availability and quality of resources. For example:

• Per pupil expenditures are lower in urban school districts than suburban districts as well as in school districts with the highest minority student representation.

√ In Detroit, where minority students comprise 79% of the enrollment, the per pupil expenditure is $7,364, whereas the per pupil expenditure is $11,934 in the predominantly White suburb of Bloomfield Hills.

√ The 89% minority school district of Bridgeport, Connecticut spends $6,989 per pupil, whereas the 20% minority Greenwich school district spends $10,909 per student.

• African American children represent 16% of the school age population, but they comprise only 3% of all students nationwide who enroll in Advanced Placement Calculus, only 4% of those enrolled in Advanced Placement U.S. History, and only 2% of the students enrolled in Advanced Placement Physics. We also should be asking how many African Americans have access to Advanced Placement courses in their high school, and how many are discouraged or even prohibited from taking such courses by their guidance counselors or school psychologists.

• Over 62% of Asian and 50% of White high school students, but only about 40% of African Americans and Hispanic high school students, have taken high school physics. We should also be asking how many African Americans attend schools where physics – real physics taught by someone who knows physics and who has a college degree in physics – is even offered.

Finally, the media, policymakers, educators, and the general public need to recognize the progress that is being made.

• The educational aspirations of African American high school students are comparable to those of White high school students. More than two-thirds of African American and White high school sophomores expect at least a bachelor's degree.

• Both the number and share of African Americans who are taking the standardized tests that measure preparation for college are increasing.

• The representation of African Americans among PSAT test-takers rose from 7.4% in 1984 to 9.1% in 1995.

• The number of African Americans taking the SAT increased by 28% between 1980 and 1996, rising from 83,321 to 106,573.

Given these data, it is clear that minorities face many challenges in education and educational assessment. Each chapter of this book examines standards, principles, models and advances, practices and fairness of educational testing and assessment. In addition, there are discussions about affirmative action and equity issues minorities face as they measure up.

MEASURING UP: THE CHAPTERS

In Chapter 2, Linn takes as his starting point the nine principles adopted by the first National Symposium on Equity and Educational Testing and Assessment in 1993. Although he concedes the merits of the nine principles, he argues that many of the principles are stated at a level of generality that makes it difficult to identify practices of educational testing and assessment that violate the intent of the principles.

Linn carefully builds the context in which the principles were adopted, relating them to the six National Education Goals and particularly to the emphasis by the National Education Goals Panel on high standards for all students. He notes that subsequent legislation – Goals 2000: Educate America Act of 1994 and the Improving America's Schools Act of 1994 created additional relevance for the nine principles. In the light of the legislation Linn points to the likelihood that standards-based assessment results will be used for high-stakes decisions in areas such as promotion, graduation and school accountability. This he identifies as a major shortfall of the principles: the lack of any specific focus on the consequences of test use. In his view the principles provide no pressure toward determining whether the uses of assessment are either appropriate or inappropriate.

In Linn's critique of the principles, he frequently relates them to the obligations from the code of Fair Testing Practices in Education (1988) and pronounces the latter clearer and more specific in many areas. One concern arises in the area of accommodations and choices as educators on the one hand, produce testing results that are fundamentally not comparable. He warns that the validity of score interpretations may be compromised and result in unfair comparisons if testing results are not comparable.

In Chapter 3, Roeber begins by linking public perceptions of school failure with schools' slowness in accommodating to social change, particularly to the expectations that all students – the economically disadvantaged, minorities, and women – should achieve at a high skill level. He cites evidence from the National Assessment of Educational Progress (NAEP), and from SAT and ACT results to demonstrate how little progress has been made in student achievement levels from 1970 to 1990. Efforts to date have not had the desired payoff, leaving the question of what more can be done to raise the overall level of student performance, particularly for the three groups in question. This sets the stage for an analysis of previous and ongoing reform efforts.

In his examination of standards-based reform of education, Roeber finds more questions than answers. Issues like adequacy of resources for implementation, professional development for teachers, the overall coherence of the standards, he suggests, create major barriers to development and implementation of content standards. Nevertheless, he finds one strength of the content standards to lie in the way they encourage changes in both teaching strategies and assessment.

To the biggest challenge – "can all students learn at high levels?" – Roeber draws from a wealth of sources to answer a tentative "yes." After citing instances and circumstances of school successes, he singles out the factors that have enhanced these situations and poses them in the form of questions for consideration. He sees support for these efforts coming from two directions: assessment consortia in which state curriculum and assessment specialists, content experts and others develop frameworks and prototype exercises in various content areas; and development projects in which state officers and educators work to develop assessment standards and measures. The combination of quality programming and high expectations Roeber believes, will promote effective schools.

In Chapter 4, Badger disputes the prevailing notion that performance tests, with their emphasis on complexity and application, will ultimately produce a more rigorous and equitable education for all. She contends that this assumption has serious flaws in regard to equity because valid assessment of students cannot be achieved without two fundamental conditions. These conditions require first, that all students have the opportunity to learn the material on which they are being assessed, and second, that the assessment is seen as meaningful and valuable to students. In place of the focus on assessment, she suggests that equity might be better served by a focus on the curriculum.

Badger offers as a model for the kind of assessment that meets the two conditions a 12th grade language arts course developed by The College Board and called Voices of Modern Cultures. She describes how the course has translated into curriculum current themes of reform put forward by national bodies as well as academics and teachers. These themes at their most basic consist of the dual aspects of language: creating text and creating meaning in text. The course feeds off the assumption that student experiences and "voices" are of intrinsic value and course activities are directed toward developing student voices through the craft of language and presentation. Related skills deal with analysis and evaluation of the "texts" of others, and with self-evaluation.

While Badger cautions that data on the course's first year of implementation are limited and primarily anecdotal, she sees the results as encouraging. Students, particularly those from otherwise marginalized groups, are reported as showing greater self-confidence and improvement in their abilities to communicate and to understand the communications of others. More importantly, she says, they view the skills they are learning as relevant to their present lives and careers. From this experience, she argues that an assessment intrinsically linked to a curriculum that combines scholarship, competence and meaningfulness, is a necessary first stop toward equity.

In Chapter 5, Reckase and Welch start from the premise that new assessment tools might provide richer descriptions of student performance than do multiple-choice tests, as well as models for instructional improvement. Both describe ACT's development of the portfolio concept as a new assessment and instructional tool that will encourage positive educational outcomes. Among the criteria for development of the portfolio system were such aspects as flexibility in its application, links to instructional goals and roots in actual classroom activities. Seven schools across the country partnered with ACT in the design, development and field test of the portfolio system.

According to the authors, the design team considered the most important elements of the portfolio process to be: student involvement in the selection of entries to the portfolio; the need to develop criteria for selection and judging merit; and evidence of student self-reflection on the submissions. Initial efforts have focused on distinct portfolios in the areas of language arts, mathematics and science. Portfolios in each of these areas are generated through the use of "work sample descriptions" – general descriptions of the material that students should select to represent their capabilities in a given curriculum area. Flexibility is achieved by phrasing such work sample descriptions in generic terms so that a science description can apply to work from any science course. The authors also describe the support systems and evaluation processes that have evolved alongside the portfolio development.

In the second year of field testing, as Reckase and Welch report, the portfolio assessment system found particular favor among language arts teachers (although this did not relate to the overall portfolio score of their students). Science teachers had a more mixed reaction, citing both benefits and disadvantages, while mathematics teachers, few of whom had previous experience with portfolios, were more reluctant to change their overall grading and assessment strategies. The broader implementation in 1996-97 brought additional information about barriers to implementation through a survey of 206 participating teachers. Time was deemed the primary barrier with reference to teacher time for planning the portfolio assessments, class time for implementation and construction of the portfolios, and the lack of money to pay for release time to work on portfolio planning and implementation. The emphasis differed between urban and nonurban teachers with urban teachers more concerned by resource issues and the potential of the portfolios to interfere with mandated curriculum. Reckase and Welch suggest that this response may indicate that urban schools are less likely to embrace new curriculum movements. This study was conducted during Reckase's matriculation at ACT, Inc.

In Chapter 6, after pointing out the perceived benefits of performance assessments, Lane and Silver stress the need for empirical evidence to support the purported fairness of these assessments for various subgroups of students. Fairness, they point out, depends on validity evidence involving the appropriateness, meaningfulness, and usefulness of the inferences made from test scores for all students. They note that to date this evidence has not been forthcoming, in part they suggest, because of differences in instructional opportunities. In this regard, it is important to document the extent to which students have had similar opportunities to acquire the knowledge and skills measured by the assessment. Similarly, they express concern over differential item functioning which may bias assessment results.

To examine the operation of these factors, they probe the outcomes of the QUASAR Cognitive Assessment Instrument, which was designed to monitor the impact of innovative mathematical instructional programs in schools participating in the QUASAR project. The instrument itself consists of open-ended tasks that assess students' mathematical problem solving, reasoning and communication. Sections of the chapter describe the QUASAR project and the extent to which the instrument is sensitive to measuring changes in students' mathematical thinking and reasoning as a result of their innovative curriculum. Overall they found that the QCAI is capable of capturing performance gains for male and female middle-school students, for African American and Caucasian students, and for bilingual and English-speaking students.

Another section of the chapter examines the consequences of the assessment for schools taking part in the project. They point to a relationship between high student performance on the instrument and a high level of cognitive demands required by the instructional tasks in the classroom. Other influences included high faculty and principal turnover rate and consequent curriculum disruptions. Lane and Silver also looked at differential responses of male and female students to the tasks provided. Lane and Silver suggest that few previous studies have examined differential item functioning for performance assessments and such evidence contributes to evaluating the fairness of such assessments. While their findings were necessarily tentative, they suggest that male students may have been at a disadvantage on a few tasks because they were not as complete in showing their solution strategies or supporting their numerical answers.

In Chapter 7, Aguirre-Muñoz and Baker focus on issues of assessment validity and equity in relation to students of limited English proficiency. They point to the context of 1990s reforms demanding higher standards of performance in all areas, coupled with the requirement for inclusion of children from all backgrounds. This has created pressures for better approaches to both teaching and assessing the learning of children with limited English proficiency. Thus, the challenge arises of devising assessments in content areas other than English that are both fair and accessible for students not fully competent in English.

The authors note that little research exists on the impact of language skills on performance assessments. The paper further discusses language development issues and the kinds of accommodation strategies that have been used for these students of limited English competence.

They propose an approach that incorporates theories of knowledge representation and cognitive structure as an additional means of assessing English learners' understanding of subject matter. Such testing would include methodology such as concept mapping. Although concept mapping reduces the dependence on complex language skills, at the same time the authors point to some potential problems such as the comparability of the test administration conditions. They also suggest that the presence of ancillary or enabling skills might bias the assessments. These ancillary skills might include the students' understanding of the test's importance, their willingness to produce their best work, their understanding of the test's requirements and their mastery of communication skills necessary for measurable responses.

Nevertheless Aguirre-Muñoz and Baker maintain that it is possible to provide stimulus materials that maintain cognitive complexity and avoid bias and they are monitoring research on the application of concept mapping for English learners to determine whether valid inferences can be drawn from their scores.

Chapter 8 provides a context for examining claims that alternative assessments are fairer for all students and will narrow the achievement gaps between different groups. Here, Madaus, Raczek and Thomas explore the use of alternative assessment for a target group of seven year olds in the English school system. Their ultimate goal appears to be determining the appropriateness of such alternative assessments to high-stakes uses such as promotion or graduation that are contemplated in the United States. Their research was based on a comparison of teacher judgments of student performance and student achievement on performance-based tasks that formed part of the National Curriculum in England and Wales in 1992.

When Madaus, Raczek and Thomas compared the assessment results from teachers and from the mandated Standard Tasks, they found teacher assessments more often generated greater differences between groups. In this case the group variables consisted of gender, free meals, English as a second language, and special needs. Although there were similarities in how the two forms of assessment worked, teacher assessments in some instances widened the gap between students.

The authors end by suggesting a number of lessons for America, some salutary, and others, a caution to those Americans making equity claims for assessment technology. On the benefit side, they note the epiphany effect on teachers who were associated with the new standards and assessment reform. Less positively, they call attention to the conflict that has developed in England and Wales over the high-stakes summative uses of the assessment results, suggesting that the same outcome might be expected here.

Finally they document a retreat from authentic assessment in England, related to cost, administrative convenience and the like. Even with authentic assessment they seem to feel that significant differences will still be found between groups of students, and while factors in the English social environment mitigate group disparities, these will persist and be even more pronounced in the American context.

In Chapter 9, Gray, Nettles, Perna and Edelin first establish the background for minority education through historical and statistical data, demonstrating enrollment and credential gains since 1976. These gains are placed in the context of current challenges to affirmative action such as *Hopwood v. Texas* (1996) and California's Proposition 209, which have resulted in declines in access for African Americans. Against this background, the researchers proceed to probe and discredit the arguments that have been used by opponents of affirmative action.

Starting with the argument that women and minorities can compete without preferences, the authors cite historical data that illustrate the plight of African Americans in the White educational system. They counter the claim that one's children (obviously White) should not be penalized for something they did not do, with career data illustrating the de facto segregation that exists in many of the nation's most prestigious professions. Supporting this material is a wealth of information on school inequities and differences in educational opportunities from pre-school onward.

They challenge the argument that disputes affirmative action on the grounds that not every minority person is disadvantaged, with comparisons of poverty rates among the races and their consequent educational options. Likewise the claim that affirmative action means less qualified individuals get preference appears poorly grounded in fact. Among the nation's 120 most selective colleges and universities, three out of four African Americans are entering these institutions with scores and high school preparation similar to their Asian and White peers.

The authors also take on those who suggest that college admissions should be based on a narrow definition of merit in which standardized admissions tests and high school grades are the primary selection criteria. First they delve into the relationship between test scores and socioeconomic status; second they challenge the notion that these scores are an accurate predictor of college performance; third they point again to the differences in learning opportunities that precede the college experience. Another challenge is mounted against those who claim that affirmative action has negative effects on success and graduation rate of college students. Here the authors examine financial aid statistics and graduation rates to demonstrate some of the constraints involved.

They draw on national surveys to answer those critics of affirmative action who suggest that Blacks who benefit suffer negative psychological effects. No evidence of feelings of inferiority exist and even some positive psychological effects were found. Finally, they take on the absolutists who declare that discrimination in any form, including preferences is wrong. In response they point to the many subjective preferences, particularly in education where admissions criteria frequently include high and low socioeconomic status, athletic and other special talents, relationships to alumni or political leaders, geographic derivation, sex in fields where underrepresentation exists and national recognition for achievements or leadership. The authors conclude with recommendations for achieving equity, most of them dealing with assurance that high quality K-12 education is uniformly available.

The last chapter is an epilogue in six parts. The ephemera of academic production – the speeches, responses to speeches, "think pieces," viewpoints and the like – often are consigned to dusty files after their brief public airing. Here, a cross-section of these has been resurrected to challenge the reader to probe further, to provoke new questions and encourage renewed dialogue. The more casual tone of these offerings belies their creative roots. It is the editors' hope that readers will find the stimulation in this chapter to carry the conversation to new levels, in new directions.

In Part 1, Gray, Nettles and Millett discuss tests as barriers to access. These authors examine the impact of test scores on police department promotions, admission to law school, the distribution of limited financial resources, and admission to historically black colleges and historically white colleges (e.g., the United States & Ayers v. Fordice). Gordon, in Part 2, challenges us to think about educational standards and alternatives in educational reform. Cole, in Part 3, discusses why testing organizations and standardized testing are simultaneously the presumed culprit and the presumed solution for many of the difficult issues in college admissions and higher education. In Part 4, Baratz-Snowden argues that equity requires standards, and that standards assure a first-rate education. Stewart, in Part 5, responds to Linn's paper (Chapter 2 of this book), offering recommendations as to how assessment can best serve educational equity at all levels. And last, Nettles, Browning, and Fails-Nelson, in Part 6, grapple with readiness issues from the perspective of historical, theoretical, and related beliefs about educational practice of young children

Endnotes

For additional information and citations found in Nettles & Perna (1998) media release, please contact the Frederick D. Patterson Research Institute.

2 Validity Standards and Principles on Equity in Educational Testing and Assessment

Robert L. Linn

At the first Ford Foundation-sponsored National Symposium on Equity and Educational Testing and Assessment, held in 1993, nine principles were adopted by the leadership that were intended to make both equity and quality dominant themes in the development of new standards and assessments. Those principles are the focus of this paper. More specifically, the purpose of this paper is to review the nine principles, discuss their implications for practice, and suggest possible additions or revisions of the principles. Current conceptions of validity as articulated by measurement theorists such as Cronbach (1988; 1989), Linn (1994), Linn, Baker & Dunbar (1991); Messick (1989; 1994; 1995), Moss (1994), and Shepard (1993) will provide the framework for reviewing the principles.

The nine principles on equity adopted by the leadership at the 1993 symposium are shown in Figure 1. Although all the principles appear reasonable, they differ considerably in terms of their focus and their generality. Some of the principles clearly deal with issues normally addressed in technical and professional standards for testing and test use (e. g., the Standards for Educational and Psychological Testing, AERA, APA, & NCME; the Code of Fair Testing Practices in Education, author, 1988). Other principles fall outside that scope. Whether inside or outside the normal scope of technical and professional standards, however, most of the principles are stated at a high level of generality. The high level of generality raises questions, that I will address later, about the degree to which the principles are pointed enough to be used to identify practices of educational testing and assessments that clearly violate the intent of the principles.

The first two principles map most clearly into traditional concerns for the validity and fairness of test interpretations and uses. Indeed the rationale for the field testing of assessments with the nation's diverse population in Principle 1 is that such field testing will contribute to an evaluation of the fairness and validity of the assessment. The concern in Principle 2 that assessments accurately reflect the needed knowledge and skills is also an issue of validity. Also consonant with the second principle are

Paper presented at the second National Symposium on Equity and Educational Testing and Assessment, sponsored by the University of Michigan with support from the Ford Foundation, Washington, DC., May, 1996 traditional validity issues dealing with the adequacy with which an assessment represents the target domain (or the converse "construct under representation") and questions about the influence of skills that are ancillary or irrelevant to the intent of the measure (e.g., test taking skills or language skills not part of the content knowledge called for in standards for a content area such as mathematics or science).

Figure 1

Leadership Statement of Nine Principles on Equity in Educational Testing and Assessment[1]

---

1. "New assessments should be field tested with the nation's diverse population in order to demonstrate that they are fair and valid and that they are suitable for policymakers to use as levers to improve outcomes before they are promoted for widespread use by American Society."

2. "New standards and tests should accurately reflect and represent the skills and knowledge that are needed for the purposes for which they will be used."

3. "New content standards and assessments in different fields should involve a development process in which America's cultural and racial minorities are participants."

4. "New policies for standards and assessments should reflect the understanding that standards and assessments represent only two of many interventions required to achieve excellence and equity in American education. Equity and excellence can only be achieved if all educators dedicate themselves to their tasks and are given the resources they need."

5. "New standards and assessments should offer a variety of options in the way students are asked to demonstrate their knowledge and skills, providing a best possible opportunity for each student to perform."

6. "New standards and assessments should include guidelines for intended and appropriate use of results and a review mechanism to ensure that the guidelines are respected."

7. "New policies should list the existing standards and assessments that the new standards and assessments should replace (e.g., Chapter I standards and tests, state mandated student standards and tests) in order to avoid unnecessary and costly duplication and to avoid overburdening schools, teachers and students who already feel saturated by externally mandated tests."

8. "New policies need to reflect the understanding by policy makers of the tradeoff between the types of standards and assessments needed for monitoring the progress of school systems and the nation versus the types of standards and assessments needed by teachers to improve teaching and learning. The attention and resources devoted to the former may compete for the limited resources available for research and development for the latter."

9. "New policies to establish standards and assessments should feature teachers prominently in the development process."

Principles 3 and 9 might be classified as process rather than outcome guidelines. It seems reasonable to expect that the inclusion of perspectives brought by the nation's cultural and racial minorities in the process of assessment development (Principle 3) will increase the likelihood that the resulting assessments are valid and fair when used with students from cultural and racial minorities. It also seems reasonable to think that the involvement of teachers in development of assessments will contribute to validity. Furthermore, the process of inclusiveness may be justified in its own right. It should be recognized, however, that satisfying these process principles is not a guarantee that the interpretations and uses of assessment results will be either valid or fair.

Principles 4, 7, and 8 go beyond the normal confines of valid and fair assessment concerns. Principle 4, rightly acknowledges that standards and assessments are only two of many possible innovations that may be needed to achieve the ambitious aims of the educational reform agenda. This principle is consistent with the notion that standards and assessments cannot do the job alone, but must be part of a larger set of systemic reform measures including access to better resources and instructional materials, professional development, and more effective use of resources in order to achieve anything like the intended impact of current standards-based reform initiatives. Viewed in this light, Principle 4 raises fundamental equity issues by calling attention to the fact that it is not sufficient to set high standards of achievement and devise assessments that will validly measure their attainment. Both quality and equity demand that students be provided with adequate learning opportunities to meet those standards.

Principle 7 focuses on the testing burden and urges that new assessments not increase that burden by simply being added to existing requirements. Principle 8 recognizes an important distinction between externally mandated assessments with a heavy emphasis on accountability and assessments under the control of classroom teachers used primarily to inform day-to-day instructional decisions. It notes that these two forms of assessment are not only distinct, but may actually compete for resources. Hence, the need to attend to the possible trade-off between emphases placed on these two types of assessment.

In my view, the remaining principles, numbers 5 and 6, expand the expectations for assessments and for those who are responsible for their development and use beyond the implied requirements found in the Standards for Educational and Psychological Testing (AERA, APA, NCME, 1985) or the Code of Fair Testing Practices in Education (author, 1988). Principle 6 encourages those responsible for new standards and assessments to develop and disseminate guidelines on the "intended and appropriate uses of results." Responsible parties are also urged to establish a mechanism for reviewing actual uses of standards and assessments to "ensure that the guidelines are respected."

It is in assigning responsibility for reviewing use and ensuring that the guidelines are respected that Principle 6 pushes farther in the direction of making developers and major users of assessments such as states responsible for misuses. It is this aspect of Principle 6 that seems to go farther than the guidelines of intended uses than have normally been required by professional and technical testing standards. It brings to mind proposals of George Madaus and his colleagues (Madaus, 1992; Madaus, Haney, Newton, & Kreitzer, 1993) for the creation of an independent auditing mechanism for testing. I shall return to this idea later, but merely note at this point, that ensuring adherence to the guidelines for appropriate use of assessment results would be a major undertaking and would likely to be subject to challenge on many fronts, possibly including legal challenges.

Principle 5, though seemingly quite reasonable and hard to object to, is, perhaps, the most ambitious of all the principles. The first part of this principle is consistent with other guidelines on test use, including those from some test publishers, that warn against over-reliance on results from a single test, and call for the use of multiple sources of information. That part of Principle 5 is the "easy" part that might be met by offering multiple approaches to assessment that provide students with several ways of demonstrating what they know and can do. Even that part of the principle may raise questions of how the multiple pieces of information would be combined, but is otherwise straightforward and consistent with other professional and technical standards.

The second part of Principle 5 – "providing the best possible opportunity for each student to perform" – however, poses a more serious challenge to the assessment community. In particular, this aspect of the principle challenges the basic tenets of standardization by demanding that the assessment be individualized to maximize the opportunity that each person has for demonstrating what he or she knows and is able to do. Offering test takers choices among problems and assessment tasks is one way of individualizing assessments. Adaptations and accommodations of assessments to provide each test taker with the best opportunity to perform share a similar goal. Both the ideas of offering test takers a choice among tasks and of providing adaptations or accommodations have attracted considerable attention in the last few years and have strong adherents. As will be discussed in more detail below, however, both approaches pose substantial technical challenges and will require careful analysis of the relative gains in validity and fairness due to individualization in comparisons to potential losses in validity and fairness due to reduced standardization.

POLICY CONTEXT

Having now introduced the nine principles on equity in educational testing and assessment and stated that they seem reasonable, albeit challenging, I would now like to set a broader context before providing further analyses of the principles or suggestions for possible modifications or additions. Modern notions of validity will then be discussed and used as the primary basis for further analysis of the principles. Before I turn to a discussion of the concept of validity and its applicability to the principles, however, it is important to acknowledge the context in which the principles were developed and how that context has evolved during the three years since the principles were adopted. It is also important to comment of multiple conceptions of equity that have implications for evaluating any uses of assessment results, but particularly uses of results with high stakes and potentially long-lasting consequences for individuals.

The context is important for at least two reasons. First, the principles were explicitly targeted toward policymakers who attempt to influence education through the adoption of new standards and associated assessments. Second, validity is always a function of the inferences and actions that are based on assessment results. As Willingham (in press) has recently argued, this is also true of fairness. Thus, when we are careful, we do not conclude that a test or an assessment is valid or invalid or that it is fair or unfair. Rather, we evaluate the degree of validity and the degree of fairness of particular inferences based on assessment results (e.g., a student is proficient in mathematics) or the justification for specific uses of the results (e.g., the award of a certificate, sanctioning schools for poor performance).

THE 1993 CONTEXT

The preamble to the March 12, 1993 "Leadership Statement of Nine Principles on Equity and Educational Testing and Assessment" noted that although equity had been a focus of considerable attention in national education policy for the past three decades, important shifts in the framing of the issues occurred in the early 1990s following the 1989 Education Summit in Charlottesville, Virginia. Specifically, there was a shift of attention from compensatory education programs emphasizing basic skills for disadvantaged children to the setting of high standards of performance for all students.

The identification of national goals at the Charlottesville Summit stressed the need to ensure that all students were better prepared for the demands of internationally competitive workplaces of the 21st century. The adoption of six National Education Goals and the creation of the National Education Goals Panel focused attention on the need to set higher expectations and to assess the progress in the attainment of those goals. The Goals Panel summarized the need as follows. "Prosperity is rooted in a global context which demands different priorities and higher standards in education, work, and citizenship" (NEGP, 1992, p. xi).

The emphasis on high standards for all students was clearly articulated in the Goals Panel's second annual report which argued that educational improvement required " new, clear, and ambitious standards for the educational achievement of all students. The Goals Panel recognized early on that the absence of such standards was a critical reason for the deficient performance of our educational system" (NEGP, 1992, p. xi).

The Goals Panel's emphasis on standards was a core feature of many of the reform efforts under way in states as well as at the national level that were reinforced by the Charlottesville Summit. At the national level, both governmental (e.g., the Department of Labor's Secretary's Commission on Achieving Necessary Skills, 1991; the National Council on Education Standards and Testing, 1992; the National Assessment Governing Board, 1992) and non-governmental groups (e.g., The American College Testing Program, The College Board, The New Standards Project, the Council of Chief State School Officers) were also pressing for higher standards and associated assessments not just for an elite group of students who have traditionally competed for admission to selective colleges, but for the full range of students. A number of states (e.g.,

Kentucky, Maryland) also were advancing a standards- and assessment-based reform agenda characterized by the establishment of high standards for all students.

It was within this context of a national press for ambitious standards for all students measured by new, demanding assessments that the Nine Principles on Equity and Educational Testing and Assessment were adopted. The context has evolved during the past three years in ways that may give even greater salience to some of the principles and possibly suggest the need for some additions or revisions.

EVOLUTION OF THE REFORM EFFORTS

In the three years since the principles were adopted, the Clinton administration's education initiative was advanced through two pieces of legislation with direct relevance to the principles. These are the Goals 2000: Educate America Act of 1994 and the Improving America's Schools Act of 1994 (IASA). Goals 2000 explicates the Clinton administration's concept of standards- and assessment-based educational reform and encourages states to pursue this approach to reform on a voluntary basis by means of grants to states for the development of standards and assessments.

The conceptual approach to reform in Goals 2000 is given greater force, however, by the IASA legislation which includes the reauthorization of Title I (formerly Chapter I). IASA involves a major change in the accountability requirements for Title I programs, including the adoption of content and performance standards, the creation of assessments aligned with those standards, and the use of standards-based reporting of assessment results for the measurement of "adequate yearly progress." At the national level, the changes in Title I evaluation and accountability requirements provide, perhaps, the clearest example of the effort to shift the attention from an emphasis on basic skills for disadvantaged children to an emphasis on the same high standards for all students. The strong emphasis on equity in IASA, expressed in requirements that the same high standards apply to all students, is of particular importance because of the major impact that Title I requirements have on the amount and nature of testing throughout the nation.

Although states may use a variety of "transitional" assessments between now and the 2000-2001 school year, they are then expected to have developed or adopted standards-based assessments that have a number of specified characteristics. In particular, IASA (Section 200.4) describes State responsibilities for assessments as follows:

"(a) (1) Each State shall develop or adopt a set of high-quality yearly student assessments that measure performance in at least mathematics and reading/language arts that will be used as the primary means of determining the yearly performance of each school and LEA [Local Education Authority] served under this subpart in enabling all children participating under this subpart to meet the State's student performance standards."

"(b) Assessments under this section must meet the following requirements:

(1) Be the same assessments used to measure the performance of all children, if the State measures the performance of all children.

(2)(i) Be aligned with the State's challenging content and student performance standards; and (ii) Provide coherent information about student attainment of the State's content and student performance standards.

(3)(i)(A) Be used for purposes for which the assessments are valid and reliable, and (B) Be consistent with relevant, national, recognized professional and technical standards for those assessments."

Goals 2000 and IASA remain potentially important influences on the standards-based reform movement and the nature and uses of associated assessments in the coming years, but it should not be assumed that there are nothing but green lights and uninterrupted progress ahead. Goals 2000 generated considerable controversy from the start. Central to the controversy is the concern of opponents that it might give too much emphasis to a national (even federal, in the eyes of some) role thereby usurping state and local prerogatives. This concern was played out most clearly in two features of the Goals 2000 legislation.

First, Goals 2000 called for the creation of the National Education Standards and Improvement Council (NESIC) which was intended to be the body that would certify national content and performance standards as well as voluntarily submitted state assessment systems. Opponents quickly objected to the establishment of NESIC, characterizing it as "the Nation's School Board" and arguing that it would intrude on state rights and prerogatives in education. Because of the strong opposition, appointments of members to NESIC were not made, and, in all likelihood, they never will be.

The second focus of controversy is especially germane to a consideration of equity issues in the use of educational testing and assessment. This is the controversy over the idea of opportunity-to-learn (OTL) standards. Although referred to there as delivery standards, the concept of OTL standards was introduced in the report of the National Council on Education Standards and Testing (NCEST, 1992) in response to concerns that it would not be fair to hold students accountable for material that they had not been taught. From the beginning, however, OTL standards were resisted by those who were concerned that they would dictate local practice. The controversy was aptly characterized by Porter (1994).

"To proponents, OTL standards represent the age-old problems of equity in education. In particular, advocates of OTL standards see them as an appropriate antidote to the potentially negative effects of high stakes testing on students, who, through no fault of their own, attend schools which provide an inferior education. To opponents, OTL standards evoke all their worst fears about federal intrusion into local control of the quality and nature of education."

Because of compromises required to pass legislation that included the idea of OTL standards, the sections of Goals 2000 and of IASA dealing with OTL are clearly marked as voluntary or optional rather than mandatory. According to IASA, for example, Title I schools identified for school improvement shall:

"(i) in consultation with parents, the local educational agency, and school support team, develop or revise a school plan in ways that have the greatest likelihood of improving the performance of participating children in meeting the State's student performance standards, which may include reviewing the school's plans in the context of opportunity-to-learn standards or strategies developed by such State under Goals 2000: Educate America Act, and (ii) submit the plan or revised plan to the local education agency for approval" (P.L. 103-382, Sec. 1116, c, 2).

The emphasis on local approval and action and tentative link to OTL standards is evident.

If anything, the press for greater state autonomy, the downplaying of national emphasis on standards, and the eschewing of federal mandates have increased in the two years since IASA was signed into law. This was evident in the March, 1996 Education Summit co-sponsored by the National Governors Association, IBM, and the Education Commission of the States and attended by 40 governors and 49 leaders of major corporations. The 1996 Summit continued to press for the setting of high, "world-class" standards, but emphasized that standards need to be state- or community-based rather than national. The 1996 National Education Summit Policy Statement highlighted the emphasis on states and local school districts:

"We believe that efforts to set clear, common, state and/or community-based academic standards for students in a given school district or state are necessary to improve student performance We believe that setting clear academic standards, benchmarking these standards to the highest levels, and accurately assessing student academic performance is a state, or in some cases, local, responsibility, depending on the traditions of the state" (Text of Policy Statement Issued at National Summit, Education Week, April 3, 1996, p. 13).

The actual uses to be made of standards and assessments by states and school districts, not surprisingly, were left vague. The general tone, however, indicated that it was expected that standards-based assessment results would be used for school accountability purposes. There were also a number of indications that some of participants had in mind the use of assessment results for promotion, graduation, or certification of student performance.

President Clinton's speech at the summit highlighted the requirement of passing performance on a test for promotion at selected grades such as "from elementary to middle school, or from middle school to high school, or to have a full-meaning high school diploma" (President Clinton, quoted by Lawton, 1996, p. 15). The executives also committed to link hiring decisions more directly to student academic achievement. Specifically, the business leaders committed to "implement hiring practices within one year that will require applicants to demonstrate academic achievement through school-based records, such as academic transcripts, diplomas, portfolios, certificates of initial mastery, or others as appropriate" (Text of Policy Statement Issued at National Summit, Education Week, April 3, 1996, p. 13).

It remains to be seen how many states and districts will move ahead with high-stakes accountability systems for schools or how many will use standards-based assessments as grade-to-grade promotion requirements, to award certificates of initial mastery, or for some type of endorsed high school diploma. It seems clear, however, that the Principles on Equity and Education Testing and Assessment need to be applicable to such high-stakes uses.

Not only is there a press to increase the stakes associated with performance on educational tests and assessments, but it is occurring at a time when there are increasing attacks on affirmative action in postsecondary admissions. The rejection of affirmative action by Governor Wilson and the Regents of the University of California and the initiative to put the question of affirmative action on the ballot for a vote (Schmidt, 1996) made California one of the more visible examples. Although the Fifth Circuit Court of Appeals issued a temporary stay in the Hopwood vs. Texas case of the ruling barring the University of Texas from using race-conscious admissions (Lederman, 1996), the charge of reverse discrimination in the implementation of affirmative action in admission to law school at the University of Texas raises once again a challenge to race-conscious admissions procedures. Indeed, it is conceivable that Hopwood vs. Texas could lead to a reconsideration of the Supreme Court ruling in the Regents of the University of California vs. Bakke case that provides the foundation for considerations of diversity in admissions.

Top-down selection on the basis of test scores or admission indices based on a numerical combination of test scores and previous grades poses a threat to the intent of Principle 5. Another serious challenge to Principle 5 comes from an action in Mississippi that would require a minimum score of 16 on the ACT Assessment for student with a high school grade-point average of 2.5 for admission to historically black colleges in the state (Guernsey & Healy, 1996).

Many of the endorsers of the principles would probably consider as misuses of test results the attacks on the use of test scores within the context of affirmative action programs, the press for complete reliance on top-down selection procedures based on scores on tests or on numerical indices based on tests and previous grades, and the establishment of an absolute minimum test scores for admissions as was done in Mississippi. Given the generality of the principles, however, it is not clear, with the possible exception of Principle 5, that such policies would be obviously in violation of the principles. If one of the intents of the principles is to discourage or challenge such actions, then it may be necessary to add to or make the principles more specific with regard to such uses of the results of educational tests and assessments.

EQUITY AND QUALITY

Arguably, the standards-based reform movement is motivated by the same dual concerns of quality and equity that the principles are intended to serve. The goal of raising quality by aspiring to higher standards is obvious. The goal of increasing equity is evident, at least at the rhetorical level, by the stress on the same high standards for all students. The IASA requirement for reporting disaggregated results for segments of the student populations that have traditionally lagged behind in achievement was included specifically out of concerns for inequities in student opportunities and in student performance.

Equity is closely linked with the concept of equal opportunity. It involves concepts of social justice, impartiality, and fairness and is subject to a wide range of interpretations (Willingham, in press). Gordon (in preparation) has effectively argued that equity does not necessarily mean equality. Providing equal resources to children who come to school with enormous differences in family support and richness of experiences outside of school does not result in equity. Recognition of this distinction between equity and equality of treatment leads to the notion of compensatory education, that is, the need to provide additional resources and support for children with the greatest need.

Howe (1994) distinguishes between three competing and "highly contested" conceptions of equality of educational opportunity: formal, compensatory, and democratic. The formal conception rejects the use of "morally irrelevant" characteristics such as race/ethnicity as the basis for rewards or sanctions but would accept "morally relevant" ones such as performance on a test or assessment (as long as it is shown or presumed to be unbiased).

The compensatory conception of equal educational opportunity goes a step farther and seeks to provide a level playing field by providing additional assistance to those who, through no fault of their own, come to school with an educational disadvantage. The press for opportunity-to-learn standards is consistent with the compensatory notion of equal opportunity in that it would require that there be some demonstration that children had had an "adequate opportunity to learn well" the material specified in the content standards before using the assessment results and performance standards to assign rewards or sanctions.

Howe equates such a compensatory view with a utilitarian perspective, and argues that it falls short of an egalitarian conception as articulated by Rawls (1971) who rejected both utilitarian and meritocratic principles on the grounds that

> "individuals come by their talents in ways that are largely beyond their control For Rawls, this renders natural talents 'arbitrary from a moral point of view', which is to say that individuals deserve neither credit nor blame for the natural talents they possess or fail to possess, for the social circumstances into which they are born, or for what flows from either o[f] these" (Howe, 1994, p. 29).

Thus, the egalitarian perspective would add the redistribution of tangible goods and resources as well as opportunities. Howe's democratic conception of equal opportunity goes one step farther and includes groups who have been excluded in the past in the determination of what is to count in the distribution of educational goods. The same content standards, performance standards, and assessments for all would surely conflict with Howe's description of a democratic conception of equal opportunity.

No matter how valid the assessments, standards-based reforms that assign rewards and sanctions to students based on performance will not satisfy either Rawls' egalitarian concept or Howe's democratic concept of equity. Adding requirements for demonstrating that students are provided an "adequate opportunity to learn" the material specified by the content standards will not change this general conclusion.

I present this argument, not to reject or belittle efforts to seek greater equity within a framework of assessment uses in a standards-based system, but to point out that social justice arguments about equity cannot be resolved within such a framework. Moreover, questions of equity and fairness are likely to remain contentious as long as the current "savage inequalities" (Kozol, 1991) in distribution of resources continue to exist in our society.

Despite this bleak conclusion, I believe that efforts to achieve greater equity within either the meritocratic or utilitarian perspectives on equal educational opportunity are worthwhile. All to often the perfect can become the enemy of the good. I believe that it would be an example of this principle to reject a system that relies on measured performance to reward student achievement because it falls short of a utopian notion of equity in either the sense of Rawls' egalitarian or Howe's democratic conception of equality of opportunity. My pragmatic perspective would require a demonstration, not that the system was perfectly fair in such a utopian sense, but that it was fairer than the current system or obvious alternatives. I believe this requires attention to fundamental questions of validity and fairness of the assessment system.

VALIDITY: A FRAMEWORK FOR THE PRINCIPLES ON EQUITY

The requirements such as those illustrated above in IASA that the assessments be valid and reliable for the purposes for which they are used and that they be consistent with professional and technical standards are not unusual in legislation dealing with testing and assessment. States frequently include similar language in legislation mandating assessment programs. In addition to requiring that the assessments are "valid and reliable," legislation often requires that they are "fair" or "unbiased." Although it may be important to add the admonition that tests or assessments are fair to highlight the importance of attending to issues of fairness and equity, they are issues that fit naturally within a comprehensive validity framework. Analyses of the degree to which an assessment is fair to diverse groups of test takers and the degree to which test use enhances or diminishes equity contribute to an overall evaluation of validity. Thus, if taken seriously, the validity requirement is quite demanding, especially if validity is interpreted in the sense of modern theorists such as the late Sam Messick.

Consistent with common-sense notions, early discussions of validity emphasized two validity perspectives. Put simply, these aspects are concerned with "truth" and "worth." Cronbach (1988) provided the following description of these perspectives.

"In the very earliest discussions of test validity, some writers said that a test is valid if it measures 'what it purports to measure.' That raised, in primitive form, a question about truth. Other early writers, saying that a test is valid if it serves the purpose for which it is used, raised a question about worth" (p. 5).

Cronbach characterized the view stressing the degree to which a test serves the intended purpose as the functionalist perspective. As he argued, the functionalist perspective is more concerned with worth than truth. Even measures that may rank high on the truthfulness aspects of validity, may face serious validity challenges due to the consequences of inferences or actions that are based on assessment results.

The concerns for truth and worth have continued to be important as validity theory has evolved during the past several decades. The early concerns about truth have evolved into an elaborated theory of construct validity. The emphasis on worth has evolved from a simple notion of achieving certain aims to a coherent discussion of the "consequential basis of validity" (Messick, 1989). According to Messick (1989),

"Validity is an integrated evaluative judgment of the degree to which empirical evidence and theoretical rationales support the adequacy and appropriateness of inferences and actions based on test scores or other modes of assessment" (p. 13, emphasis in original).

Messick used a 2 by 2 table to highlight critical aspects of the validation process. The columns of the table distinguish between interpretation and use of test results while the rows distinguish between the bases for evaluating the adequacy and appropriateness of the interpretations and uses – referred to as the "evidential-basis" and the "consequential-basis" of validity. The consequential basis of validity has been made prominent by Messick (1989; 1994; 1996) and Cronbach (1988) and has been ascribed to and elaborated by a number of other authors (e.g., Linn, Baker, & Dunbar, 1991; Moss, 1992; Shepard, 1993).

There are two key ideas that direct the search for evidence relevant to an evaluation of the validity of the interpretations and uses of an assessment. Messick refers to these ideas as construct-underrepresentation and construct-irrelevant variance. Although the nature of the evidence relevant to these two ideas may be multifaceted and quite complex, the basic ideas are relatively straightforward and intuitively reasonable. Content underrepresentation occurs to the degree that the assessment excludes or gives inadequate attention to aspects of the intended domain of measurement (e.g., ignores hard-to-measure skills and understandings specified in the content standards). Construct-irrelevant variance refers to the degree to which scores are dependent on ancillary skills that are irrelevant to the intent of the measure (Haertel & Linn, 1996).

Evidence about construct-irrelevant variance is especially important to an evaluation of the fairness of an assessment because groups may differ in a wide variety of attitudes, experiences, and capabilities that are not explicitly a part of the intended focus of measurement. The assessment would have reduced validity and be less fair to the degree that those ancillary skills and characteristics affect performance on the assessment. It should be noted that skills that are considered ancillary or sources of construct-irrelevant variance for one interpretation or use of assessment results may be relevant for part of the intent of measurement for another interpretation.

Principle 2 states that "standards and tests should accurately reflect and represent the skills and knowledge that are needed for the purposes for which they will be used." This principle is quite consonant with validation work designed to identify and minimize both construct-underrepresentation and construct-irrelevant sources of variance in scores. Skills not needed for the purposes for which assessments will be interpreted or used are ancillary for those purposes and therefore represent construct-irrelevant sources of variability. One of the most obvious threats to validity and fairness of new forms of assessment in some content areas is their dependence on reading and writing. An assessment in mathematics, for example, which has substantial reading and writing demands, is likely to put language-minority students or, for that matter, many other students who have difficulty in reading or writing, at a disadvantage in demonstrating their understanding and skills in mathematics.

Principle 1, which calls for field testing assessments on the nation's diverse population, can also be viewed as relevant to the need to obtain evidence about the construct validity of the assessment. There is a big difference, however, between collecting the data on performance for diverse groups and using those results either to draw conclusions about validity and fairness or to make changes that improve those characteristics. Group differences in average performance on an assessment do not, by themselves, imply invalidity or unfairness in the assessment. They do indicate that certain uses of assessment results will result in adverse impact (e.g., higher failure rates for a lower scoring group, disproportionate representation in admissions rates to selective colleges or honors programs).

Group differences in performance demand additional analysis, in part, because they signal the likelihood of adverse impact, but also because they raise the questions that the score differences may be due, partially or wholly, to differences on skills, attitudes, or other characteristics that are irrelevant to the intent of the assessment. There are a variety of statistical techniques such as differential item functioning analyses, comparative factor analyses, and differential prediction analyses that have been used in an effort to identify irrelevant sources of variance or "bias" in tests. There are also a variety of logical analyses and expert judgment review procedures (e.g., sensitivity reviews) that are usually employed. The urging in Principle 3 that cultural and racial minorities participate in the development process is consistent with such procedures.

Unfortunately, none of the techniques provides a fail-safe procedure for identifying and eliminating unfair construct-irrelevant sources of variance that might be thought of as bias. Such procedures are nonetheless desirable because they decrease the likelihood that materials might unintentionally put one group of test takers at an unfair disadvantage due to experiential differences that are irrelevant to the construct that the assessment is intended to measure. Increasing sensitivity to cultural and racial differences in experiences and perspectives through involvement of minorities in development and review process also reduces the likelihood of inadvertently including material that is offensive to members of a minority group.

The following two obligations stated in the *Code of Fair Testing Practices in Education* (1988) relate to Principle 1.

> • "Indicate the nature of the evidence obtained concerning the appropriateness of each test for groups of different racial, ethnic, or linguistic backgrounds who are likely to be tested" (Code, 1988, guideline A.7).

> • "Investigate the performance of test takers of different races, gender, and ethnic backgrounds when samples of sufficient size are available. Enact procedures that help ensure that differences in performance are related primarily to the skills under assessment rather than to irrelevant factors (Code, 1988, guideline C.15).

These guidelines from the *Code* share a common goal with Principle 1 but they are more specific and therefore provide a clearer basis for determining whether specific practices satisfy the guidelines. They also are somewhat less ambitious, and maybe more realistic. Certainly, it would be desirable "to demonstrate that they are fair and valid and that they are suitable for policymakers to use as levers to improve outcomes" (Principle 1). A more realistic goal than "demonstrating" that assessments are valid and fair is to provide evidence that enables an evaluation of the degree to which the interpretations and uses of assessments results are valid and fair. Judgments of suitability for use as levers requires much more than field testing. At a minimum, it requires analyses of evidence of the consequences, both intended and unintended, of such uses.

CONSEQUENCES

Although leading theorists (e.g., Messick, 1989) have emphasized the need to include considerations of consequences of the uses and interpretations of assessment results in an evaluation of validity for some time, practice has lagged behind. This gap is hardly surprising given the difficulty of evaluating consequences. The need to give greater attention to consequences, while not new, is exacerbated by the fact, discussed above, that a key part of the rationale for the new standards and assessments depends on their presumed impact on instruction and learning. Thus, as I have argued elsewhere (Linn, 1994; Linn, Baker, and Dunbar, 1991), there is a need to give greater priority to investigations of assessment consequences.

The expectations of new standards and assessments are high. Assessments are expected to be cognitively demanding, engaging, authentic, and closely aligned with content standards. They are expected to provide a valid and fair way of determining whether students have met rigorous performance standards. They are also expected to contribute to reforms in education that will result in improved student learning (i.e., serve as levers for policymaker to use to improve outcomes). Each of these expectations corresponds to a validity claim. A comprehensive program of validation research is needed to evaluate these and other expectations. In Messick's terminology, these expectations demand attention to the consequential-basis of the validity of specific interpretations and uses of assessment results.

To begin with, there is a need to evaluate the degree to which intended consequences (e.g., increased student performance) are realized. As experience with test-based reforms of the past has demonstrated, increases in test scores do not necessarily mean that student understanding and achievement in the domain the test is intended to measure have increased to the same degree. Such an evaluation requires more than simply monitoring changes in assessment results from year to year. Alternative explanations such as increased familiarity with the test, teaching to the test, or other, more blatant, forms of inappropriate test preparation that were shown to contribute to the Lake Wobegon effect need to be evaluated (see, for example, Linn, Graue, & Sanders, 1990). A comprehensive validation also requires evidence regarding plausible unintended consequences of particular uses of assessment results (e.g., increased student dropout when assessments are used to determine grade-to-grade promotion, certificates of initial mastery, or high school diplomas).

I have argued that group differences in average scores on assessments do not necessarily mean that the assessment is invalid or unfair. Such differences may be valid reflections of the results of years of inequities in opportunity. An evaluation of particular score uses, however, needs to go beyond evidence that the differences are valid reflections of the developed abilities and achievements of students at a given point and not the result of construct-irrelevant sources of variance. The consequences, such as adverse impact, of particular uses need to be included in the overall evaluation of the appropriateness of that use. Adverse impact that would result from top-down selection of college applicants, for example, needs to be compared to alternative approaches, such as affirmative action college admissions procedures, as part of the evaluation of alternative uses of results.

Evidence of the consequences of alternative uses of test results in an admissions context obviously will not resolve the current heated battle over affirmative action. That is the proper role for social and political institutions, not for validators or assessment developers. But, as Cronbach (1988) has said, "validators have an obligation to review whether a practice has appropriate consequences for individuals and institutions, and especially guard against adverse consequences" (p. 6), and, I would add, they have an obligation to present the results of their evaluation of consequences to policymakers and to the broader public. The principles on equity need to reinforce these obligations explicitly.

In my view, the biggest gap in the principles on equity is the absence of any specific principle focusing on the consequences of test use. The discussion of a policy lever in Principle 1 certainly invites attention to consequences, but the requirement of field testing does not call attention to the need to evaluate intended and unintended consequences. The call for guidelines for appropriate use and review of compliance with those guidelines in Principle 6 also suggests that developers need to distinguish positive from potentially negative uses of assessment results, but Principle 6 does not require the development of a consequential basis to evaluate the validity of the uses that are judged to be either appropriate or inappropriate in the guidelines. Thus, I would urge the addition of one or more principles that expressly address the consequential basis underlying the validity of recommended interpretations and uses of assessment results.

Such an addition with regard to intended consequences would be consistent with the *Code of Fair Testing Practices in Education* (1988) which states that test users should:

> • "Obtain evidence to help show that the test is meeting its intended purpose(s)" (*Code*, guideline B.13).

It would be desirable to push a step beyond this position in the *Code* to add the requirement to evaluate plausible unintended consequences. This does not mean that users should be responsible for obtaining evidence on all possible consequences. That would hardly be feasible. Nor can developers be expected to evaluate consequences prior to putting in place high-stakes uses of results. It is obviously impossible to evaluate effects of such policies without actually putting them into effect. With most high stakes uses, however, there are some unintended consequences that are highly plausible and sometimes even reasonably predictable based on experience with previous testing requirements. For example, there is substantial evidence regarding the effects, many of which have found to be negative, of grade retention (e.g., Shepard & Smith, 1989). Thus, if a new standards and assessment program that involves the use of performance standards for grade-to-grade promotion is implemented, it should be required to accumulate evidence regarding the effects on student achievement, on the probability of dropping out of school, and similar outcomes suggested by previous grade retention research. Obviously, such information cannot be obtained prior to implementation, but it should be built into the validation work in the early years of the program. I believe the principles need to make explicit the requirement to accumulate and evaluate systematically such evidence of impact.

COMPARABILITY

An approach that has long been relied upon to enhance validity of tests by removing construct-irrelevant sources of variance is standardization. Although the term "standardized test" is often interpreted to imply a multiple-choice, norm-referenced test, the much more important meaning of "standardized" concerns the whole range of procedures that are used to make the administration of an assessment as nearly constant from one situation to another as possible. Standard instructions, a fixed set of items or assessment tasks, uniform administration conditions, and a constant amount of time to complete the assessment are examples of steps that are usually involved in standardization.

The immediate goal of standardization is to make the resulting scores as comparable as possible from one test taker to another. Comparability is important for enhancing fairness and validity by eliminating or reducing the influence of irrelevant sources of variability in scores that may give one person or one group a relative advantage. The priority given to standardization as a means of achieving comparability has been challenged on at least two fronts by some of the recent calls for new standards and assessments.

First, some of the content standards encourage that greater priority be given to depth of study of a few topics selected by teachers and/or students, generally at the expense of breadth of coverage. Projects and portfolios of student work clearly involve elements of choice and a willingness to give up many of the characteristics of standardization. Presenting students with several possible tasks and allowing them to choose the task or subset of tasks is another example of an approach that may allow students to demonstrate their depth of understanding of a topic for which they have special expertise or familiarity. But the cost is the loss of some degree of comparability of results.

Second, the desire to include all, or nearly all, students in the assessment has increased the need to be able to find appropriate adaptations or accommodations to allow students to participate in the assessment who would not otherwise be able to do so. The sort of adaptation that allows students with limited English proficiency to demonstrate what they know and are able to do in content areas other than English is one obvious example. Extended time for students with learning disabilities, oral presentations of tasks for students with reading difficulties, and large print or Braille versions of an assessment for students with visual impairments, are a few of the possible accommodations that may be needed for students with handicapping conditions.

It is clear that there is an increasing demand for various forms of adaptations and accommodations for new assessments in order to more nearly achieve the goal of including all students. Section 200.4 (b)(7) of IASA, for example, stipulates that assessments used to meet the IASA requirements must provide for:

> "(i) Participation in the assessment of all students in the grades being assessed;
>
> (ii) Reasonable adaptations and accommodations for students with diverse learning needs necessary to measure the achievement of those students relative to the State's standards, and
>
> (iii)(A) Inclusion of limited-English proficient students who shall be assessed, to the extent practicable, in the language and form most likely to yield accurate and reliable information on what those students know and do to determine the students' mastery of skills in subjects other than English."

Although the motivation for enhancing choice and providing needed accommodations is clear, so too, is the challenge. The fundamental challenge of accommodations and of choice is that we lack "the technical wherewithal to make their scores comparable and therefore fair for administrative decision-making" (Willingham, in press, p. 34 of typescript). Thus, efforts to make an assessment fairer to individuals by tailoring the tasks to the student or accommodating them to the student's special needs may actually reduce fairness of comparisons of performances among individuals who respond to different tasks or to a given task under different conditions. That is, there is a tension between standardization and individualization of assessments that involves a trade-off between enhancing fairness for some individuals or groups at the expense of others.

Although Principle 5 ("New standards and assessments should offer a variety of options in the way students are asked to demonstrate their knowledge and skills, providing a best possible opportunity for each student to perform.") does not explicitly mention choice of tasks, adaptations, or accommodations it might be interpreted to call for any or all of them. I support the goal of inclusion, but believe some caution is called for because the validity of score interpretations and uses may be compromised and result in unfair comparisons based on results that are fundamentally non-comparable.

I believe the position taken in the *Code of Fair Testing Practices in Education* (1988) represents such a reasonable compromise. According to the code, test developers should

> • "When feasible, make appropriately modified forms of tests or administration procedures available for test takers with handicapping conditions. Warn test users of potential problems in using standard norms with modified tests or administration procedures that result in non-comparable scores" (*Code*, 1988, guideline, C.16).
> Developer Responsibilities

Before closing, I want to return briefly to Principle 6: "New standards and assessments should include guidelines for intended and appropriate use of results and a review mechanism to ensure that the guidelines are respected." The first part of this principle is consistent with aspects of three of the guidelines in the Code of Fair Testing Practices in Education. Specifically, guidelines A.1, A.2, and B.11 state that test developers should:

> • "Define what each test measures and what the test should be used for. Describe the population(s) for which the test is appropriate" (*Code*, 1988, guideline A.1).

> • "Accurately represent the characteristics, usefulness, and limitations of tests for their intended purposes" (*Code*, 1988, guideline A.2).

> • "Warn users to avoid specific, reasonably anticipated misuses of test scores" (*Code*, 1988, guideline B.11).

The above statements in the Code are obviously a bit more detailed and provide more guidance than the first part of Principle 6, but there is a general compatibility. The big difference has to do with the admonition to review use and ensure compliance. Although ensuring compliance is a laudable goal, it may place unreasonable demands on developers. Thus, I would suggest a slight modification in the last part of Principle 6 that required developers to adhere to the just quoted guideline B.11 from the Code. In addition, developers could be required to notify users when they know of specific misuses of assessment results. That would still fall short of "ensuring that the guidelines [on test use provided by the developer] were respected."

CONCLUSION

Doing a better job of translating the fundamental principles of validity and fairness into practice is one of the major challenges for the measurement profession. The principles on equity in educational testing and assessment provide useful guidance to developers and users of new standards and assessments that should contribute to greater validity and fairness. As is evident from a comparison of the principles to the Standards for Educational and Psychological Testing (AERA, APA, NCME, 1985) or the Code of Fair Testing Practices in Education (1988), many other principles could be stated. Principles 1, 2, 3, 5 and 6, however, highlight some of the central concern. As was suggested, some modifications may be useful in Principles 1, 5, and 6, but the basic intent of these 5 principles is sound and they all have the potential to enhance equity by increasing validity.

Standards 4, 7, 8, and 9, while potentially useful, address concerns that seem to go beyond the primary focus on equity. The one substantial addition I suggested concerns explicit treatment of the issue of consequences of the uses that are made of assessment results. Both the intended consequences (e.g., increased student learning), and plausible unintended consequences (e.g., narrowing of curriculum coverage, increasing the proportion of students who drop out of school) should be encouraged through a principle focusing on consequences. The addition of one or more principles focusing on the consequences of the uses of assessment results would add to the value of the principles.

Finally, there is a need to consider whether the principles are at such a high level of generality that they cannot be used to unambiguously identify particular practices, whether they be misinterpretations of scores or unjustified actions taken on the basis of assessment results, that are in clear violation of the principles. The currently salient case in point involves the ongoing attacks on affirmative action that press for selection "by the numbers" in a strictly top-down fashion based on test scores or indices combining test scores and previous grades.

References

American Educational Research Association, American Psychological Association, and the National Council on Measurement in Education. (1985). *Standards for Educational and Psychological Testing.* Washington, DC: American Psychological Association.

Code of Fair Testing Practices in Education. (1988). Washington, DC: Joint Committee on Testing Practices. American Psychological Association.

Cronbach, L. J. (1988). Five perspectives on validation argument. In H. Wainer, & H. Braun (Eds.), *Test validity* (pp. 3-17). Hillsdale, NJ: Lawrence Erlbaum.

Cronbach, L. J. (1989). Construct validation after thirty years. In R. L. Linn (Ed.), *Intelligence: Measurement theory and public policy.* Proceedings of a symposium in honor of Lloyd G. Humphreys (pp. 147-171). Urbana, IL: University of Illinois Press.

Gordon, E. W. (in preparation). *Human diversity and educational assessment. A monograph of the implications of human diversity and cultural pluralism for an equitable system of educational assessment.* Review and discussion draft. New York: City University of New York.

Guernsey, L. & Healy, P. (1996). Federal court orders Mississippi's historically black colleges to raise their admissions standards. *The Chronicle of Higher Education, 42,* No. 29, A48.

Haertel, E. H. & Linn, R. L. (1996). Comparability. In G. W. Phillips (Ed.), *Technical issues in performance assessment.* Washington, DC: National Center for Education Statistics.

Howe, K. R. (1994). Standards, assessment, and equality of educational opportunity. *Educational Researcher, 23*(8), 27-33.

Kozol, J. (1991). *Savage inequalities.* New York: Crowne Publishers.

Lawton, M. (1996). Summit accord calls for focus on standards. *Education Week,* April 3, pp. 1, 14-15.

Lederman, D. (1996). Appeals court stays its order barring use of race in admissions. *The Chronicle of Higher Education, 42,* No. 34, A26.

Linn, R. L. (1994). Performance assessment: Policy promises and technical measurement standards. *Educational Researcher, 23* (5), 4-14.

Linn, R. L., Baker, E. L., & Dunbar, S. B. (1991). Complex, performance-based assessment: Expectations and validation criteria. Educational Researcher, 20 (8), 15-21.

Linn, R. L., Graue, M. E., & Sanders, N. M. (1990). Comparing state and district test results to national norms: The validity of claims that "everyone is above average." *Educational Measurement: Issues and Practice, 9*(3), 5-14.

Madaus, G. F. (1992). An independent auditing mechanism for testing. *Educational Measurement: Issues and Practice, 11*(1), 26-31.

Madaus, G. F., Haney, W., Newton, K. B., & Kreitzer, A. E. (1993). *A proposal for a monitoring body for test used in public policy.* Report submitted to the Ford Foundation and the Carnegie Corporation. Newton, MA: Boston College.

Messick, S. (1989). Validity. In R. L. Linn (Ed.), *Educational Measurement,* 3rd ed. (pp. 13-103). New York: Macmillan.

Messick, S. (1994). The interplay of evidence and consequences in the validation of performance assessments. *Educational Researcher, 23*(2), 13-23.

Messick, S. (1996). Validity of performance assessments. In G. W. Phillips (Ed.), *Technical issues in performance assessment.* Washington, DC: National Center for Education Statistics.

Moss, P. A. (1992). Shifting conceptions of validity in educational measurement: Implications for performance assessment. *Review of Educational Research, 62,* 229-258.

National Council on Education Standards and Testing. (1992). *Raising standards for American education.* Washington, DC: Author.

National Education Goals Panel. (1992). *The national education goals report: Building a nation of learners.* Washington, DC: Author.

Rawls, J. (1971). *A theory of justice.* Cambridge, MA: Belknap Press.

Secretary's Commission on Achieving Necessary Skills. (1991). *What work requires of schools: A SCANS report for America 2000.* Washington, DC: U.S. Department of Labor.

Schmidt, P. (1996). Californians likely to vote on ending racial preferences. *The Chronicle of Higher Education, 42,* No 25, A34.

Shepard, L. A. (1993). Evaluating test validity. *Review of Research in Education, 19,* 405-450.

Shepard, L. A. & Smith, M. L. (Eds.). (1989). *Flunking grades: Research and policies on retention.* London, Falmer Press.

Willingham, W. W. (in press). *A systemic view of test fairness.* In S. Messick (Ed.), Hillsdale, NJ: Erlbaum.

Endnotes

[1] Adopted at the First National Symposium on Equity and Educational Testing and Assessment, Washington, DC, March 12, 1993.

3 The Implications of Content Standards and Assessments for the Economically Disadvantaged, Minorities and Women

Edward D. Roeber

INTRODUCTION

The American public has become increasingly focused on the achievement of the students in our nation's public schools in recent years as one report after another purports to document how our schools are failing to educate our nation's children and youth. Perhaps the report that began this public dialogue over the quality of our schools was *A Nation at Risk: The Imperative for Educational Reform*. The most famous quote from this report charges that "the educational foundations of our society are presently being eroded by a rising tide of mediocrity that threatens our very future as a nation and a people" (National Commission on Excellence, 1983, page 5). After this report was published, other reports followed and began what has been a concerted effort to improve the educational system through new policies and practices, such as new testing requirements, new graduation requirements, and other changes.

Other authors, however, have suggested that student achievement is as good as it has ever been, perhaps better, and that widespread concern about student achievement declines is unwarranted. They argue that achievement levels have not dropped, but have been maintained or increased. There is certainly some evidence to support this point of view. Yet, the annual Phi Delta Kappa polls about education continue to indicate that the American public feels that while their own schools (the ones in their neighborhood and to which they send their children) are relatively effective, schools in general are not doing a good job. For example, in a poll taken by *U.S. News & World Report* just prior to the Governors' Summit in March, 1996, 44% of the respondents called their local schools good or excellent and 45% called local education fair, poor or very poor, while only 31% said that public education in the nation was good or excellent and 62% indicated the nation's education system was fair, poor, or very poor. Higher educational standards were supported by 75% of the respondents, but they were split as to whether these standards should be set at the national, state, or local levels. In addition, relatively few respondents (5%) indicated that low standards are the most serious problem facing public education (*Lansing State Journal*, March 24, 1996).

As has been argued elsewhere (Roeber, 1995), some of the concern raised about the level of educational achievement may reflect a lack of public understanding of the change in the educational system and the broader society. Could it be that student achievement is better than it has ever been, but not yet satisfactory? For example, one study indicated that although students are not at-risk, they are not work ready. This report indicates that for at-risk populations, the mismatch between workplace needs and workplace skills is even greater (National Alliance for Business, 1987). Substantial changes have occurred in the mix of students attending our schools. The percentage of minority students, the percentage of English-language learners, and the percentage of students living in poverty have all increased in the past 20 years. These are all students whose educational needs have historically been greater and whose past educational accomplishments have been lower, indicating the presence of greater educational needs. When we make longitudinal comparisons of educational achievement, these demographic changes are usually ignored.

Two decades ago, many students could receive a basic education, and, with a high school diploma, could find lifetime employment in a manufacturing or other job that required little skill, yet which paid decent or better wages and benefits. The American educational system operated as a screen among youth to allocate some to high paying positions based on extended post-secondary education, while many youth entered the workforce in jobs that did not require high skill levels (nor post-secondary education or training). Testing served as one vehicle to screen, sort, and select youth into work or college tracks, assigning life chances to students based on their test scores and academic performance. "Winners" went to college and got good jobs; "losers" went to work at jobs requiring much lower skills, but still paying relatively well. Unfortunately, some youth, such as the economically disadvantaged, minorities, non-English speakers, and special education students, didn't get much of a chance to even compete.

However, during the past decade, substantial change has occurred in the nature of the skills needed for successful employment. Low skill-high pay positions are much rarer today. The educational levels needed for high-paying jobs have substantially increased (and even the skill levels of entry-level positions have increased), many moderate skills jobs have disappeared (leaving a gulf between low skill/low wage and high skill/high wage jobs), and economic competition between U.S. and international businesses has increased (serving to focus more attention on efficient, low-cost production).

When we look to the future, the fastest growing occupations require employees to have much higher mathematics, language, and reasoning capabilities than do current occupations (Hudson Institute, 1987). Gone are the days when a high level of education could be provided to a small segment of the student population without harming the life aspirations of many students. Work, if not society in general, requires a higher level of literacy than has been demanded in the past, and workers without this level of literacy are often left behind economically and socially.

The implications of these changes for the American educational system are profound. We have had some successes with females and minorities, many more of whom graduate from high school and go on to some form of post-secondary education or training. However, this is not enough. While constant or slowly rising achievement levels may be viewed as "success" by some, this does not mean that students are achieving at satisfactory levels of performance as measured against the requirements of higher education or the workplace.

It could be argued that our schools are not keeping pace with the overall changes in our society because we have not substantially raised the expectations for all students, particularly the economically disadvantaged, minorities, and women, all of whom have historically achieved at lower levels. The unfulfilled aspirations of students and the unmet needs of business are not a failure of our schools (since the level of student performance has not dropped), but a failure of our schools to keep pace with changes in our society. A system that has served as an efficient sorter of students must shift its focus to producing high skill level for all students. It is clear that our schools need to educate all students to much higher levels of literacy and identify ways to meet the needs of the students with the most to gain.

WHAT IS THE LEVEL OF STUDENT PERFORMANCE?

Much of the debate about student performance is based on the "conventional wisdom" that students aren't learning as much today as they used to; at least, they don't know what they need to know. However, what is the evidence about student learning? In particular, what is the evidence concerning the students of concern in this paper: minorities, the economically disadvantaged, and women?

The evidence that is available comes mostly from the National Assessment of Educational Progress (NAEP), which has been assessing students annually or biannually in areas such as mathematics, reading, science, and writing since the late 1960s. Since NAEP has been carefully designed to provide long-term trend information regarding the performance of students in sub-groups, it can show whether performance has improved, remained stable or declined over nearly three decades.

In a report published in 1990 which summarized the longitudinal results from NAEP from 1970 to 1988, the authors indicated the following regarding overall levels of student performance:

> "Taken in total, the results of The Nation's Report Card [NAEP] provide evidence that we have a daunting challenge before us if we are to reach our national student achievement goal by the 21st century.

> "Students' current achievement levels are far below those that might indicate competency in challenging subject matter in English, mathematics, science, history, and geography...Students can read at a surface level, getting the gist of material, but they do not read analytically or perform well on challenging reading assignments.

"Small proportions of students write well enough to accomplish the purposes of different writing tasks; most do not communicate effectively.

"Students' grasp of the four basic arithmetic operations and beginning problem-solving is far from universal in elementary and junior high school; by the time that students near the end of high-school graduation, half cannot handle moderately challenging material.

"Only small proportions of students appear to develop specialized knowledge needed to address science-based problems, and the pattern of falling behind begins in elementary school

"Trends across the past 20 years suggest that, although some ground lost in the 1970s may have been regained in the 1980s, overall achievement levels are little different entering the 1990s than they were two decades earlier

"Despite progress in narrowing gaps, the differences in performance between White students and their minority counterparts remain unacceptably large. Little progress has been made in reducing gender gaps favoring males in mathematics and science and females in writing.

"Large proportions of students, even including those in academic high-school programs, are not enrolled in challenging mathematics and science coursework

"Across the past 20 years, little seems to have changed in how students are taught. Despite much research suggesting better alternatives, classrooms still appear to be dominated by textbooks, teacher lectures, and short-answer activities" (ETS, 1990, pages 9-10).

Other evidence can be found in the performance of high school students on the college entrance tests. This information is less comprehensive in nature because these tests are voluntary at the student level. However, long-term trends on both the American College Testing Program (ACT) and the College Board Scholastic Achievement Test (SAT) have demonstrated that the performance of students has remained relatively flat, showing slight increases in some years, and slight declines in others, following modest declines in performance during the 1960s. On both tests, there have been large increases in the numbers of students taking the exams, and increased participation of minorities. Perhaps, stable performance is relatively good news.

Additional evidence on the level of student learning, particularly for the economically disadvantaged, can be found in the national evaluations of the compensatory education programs that have been in place since the Elementary and Secondary Education Act (ESEA) was adopted in 1965. Recent evaluations of the impact of Chapter I (now Title I) have not been very encouraging (supporting, in part, calls for dramatic change in the nature and types of programs used to close the gaps between the students served in the programs and other students). In the new plan for the National Assessment of Title I, past student achievement is summarized as follows:

> "NAEP student score trends show a narrowing of the gap in achievement between students in disadvantaged urban communities and those in more advantaged communities during the 1970s and most of the 1980s. However, as the National Assessment of Chapter I noted, recent information indicates a lack of progress in closing the gap. The latest NAEP data show that between 1990 and 1992, the gap in mathematics performance widened in the lower grades between racial/ethnic minority students and white students. The 1994 reading results show that the disparities in reading performance between minority and white students did not diminish between 1992 and 1994. While results by racial/ethnic group are an imperfect proxy for assessing the performance of students at risk of school failure, these data raise concerns because minority students are disproportionately found in high-poverty schools.

> "An unpublished reanalysis of NAEP trends in reading suggests that students in high-poverty schools (those with at least 75% of students eligible for subsidized lunch) lost ground relative to students in other schools between assessments in 1984 and 1992. For 9-year-old students in 1984, the gap between high- and low-poverty schools was 20 points. By the time this cohort of students reached age 17 in 1992, the gap had widened in 34 points" (U.S. Department of Education, 1996, pages 11-12).

The evidence is clear: our students are not learning what they need to know, there are gaps in performance, and although there have been some improvements in performance, student achievement is not at a satisfactory level for many students. Much time and effort have been put into educational reform, but these efforts have not had the desired payoff. This leaves us with the important question of: how do we help raise the overall level of student performance, and in the process, how do we help the economically disadvantaged, minorities, and women reduce the gap in performance and achieve at the same high levels? Can this be done?

PAST EDUCATIONAL REFORM EFFORTS

The response to these reports of low student achievement in the past has been various efforts at reform of the educational system. Indeed, the recent history of American education is filled with efforts to reform and to change learning, teaching, and assessment, one element at a time. *A Nation at Risk* prompted just such piecemeal approaches to school reform. Legislatures, governors, chief state school officers, and state boards of education grappled with what to do about the situation of students not learning. One fad followed another as policy makers, educators, and others wrestled with the task of improving student achievement. Some reforms took the carrot approach, giving students, teachers, or others rewards (financial or otherwise) for improved performance. Other reforms applied sanctions when performance failed to improve. Some reforms were addressed to teachers, some to administrators, some to students, some to parents, and others at the educational infrastructure. Instructional improvement efforts were directed at developing "teacher-proof" materials; one-shot staff development training sessions were initiated; minimum competency tests became a requirement for high school graduation in about twenty states; technology was touted as the answer, and so forth. Unfortunately, failures resulted from most attempts to "fix" the educational system that took into into account only one or two variables and attempted to make changes in these.

Increasingly, however, we have come to realize that such efforts are unlikely to succeed. Even the public has grown weary of the constant reform and change of the educational system. Although each reform is praised in glowing terms as the answer to what ails the system, it rarely is followed by improvement in student performance, at least improvements that outlast the reform.

The current educational enterprise is a system of interlocking responsibilities at the national, state, and local levels. At each level, there are key programs which often interact. For change to be effective, it must occur across the programs at any one level (e.g., the state level), as well as interact with programs at higher or lower levels. Change needs to occur systemically, with multiple elements being changed or aligned simultaneously. The very idea of systemic reform involves multiple programs at multiple levels, all changing to accommodate a new goal (e.g., higher performance standards for students in mathematics). Obviously, it is difficult for several programs at one level to change together in the same direction; it is even more difficult for the components at different levels to be in sync and move together. Different programs moving in different directions for differing purposes are the norm in the nation's systems of public education.

Several factors mitigate against such systemic reform. These include a diffuse governance structure, which itself is under constant change (witness the regular turnover among local school superintendents and chief state school officers), the pressure from different citizen groups, each with its own ideas on how to reform the schools, and the independent nature of education at the local levels: individual teachers can have incredible power to determine what gets taught and how it gets taught. These and other factors mitigate against reform occurring in a manner that will allow sustained reform and improvement to occur. Indeed, one of the major factors that reduces the likelihood of systemic reform taking place derives from the classroom. Often the skills or outcomes being addressed by teachers are resident in the instructional materials and the tests used by the teachers, and do not represent a decision made consciously by the educators. Hence, if the learning of students is to be improved, then what students are taught, how they are taught it, and how their learning is assessed must be affected. It is this idea that has given rise to "standards-based" reform.

STANDARDS-BASED REFORM OF EDUCATION

Given the educational needs that student assessment has continued to demonstrate, calls for change and improvement have become commonplace. The persistent educational needs cited earlier, and the failed attempts at reform, have left the American public and educators with "a sense of urgency that the educational system needed to be stronger, and that in addition to what states and districts and individual schools were doing, we needed a stronger presence at the national level We recognized that we didn't need a national curriculum, so national goals and voluntary national standards came to be seen as a good mechanism for providing a focus" (Selden, in O'Neil, 1995, page 12).

While *A Nation at Risk* served to alert the nation to the potential problems in American education, it was the Education Summit held by President Bush and the nation's governors in 1989 that served to focus the nation's attention on the educational systems of our nation. By stating six national education goals for the country, the Summit made academic achievement a national priority. In particular, Goals 3 and 4 focused attention on how well students were performing in academic areas such as mathematics, science, English, history, and geography (later expanded to areas such as the arts).

Soon after the Summit, the U.S. Department of Education embarked on a course of action to fund various efforts to define the content standards in all of the content areas, modeled after the work pioneered by the National Council of Teachers of Mathematics (NCTM). At the time, NCTM was completing the development of curriculum, assessment, and instructional standards for their area through a professionally controlled consensus process. As a result, content standards have been developed nationally for all areas in the national educational goals, plus other areas not explicitly mentioned, such as health education and physical education. Oftentimes federally and/or privately funded, these efforts have served to define what it is that students should know and be able to do at critical times during their schooling. At the current time, content standards have been developed in the arts, civics, English language arts, foreign languages, geography, health education, U.S. and world history, mathematics, physical education, science, and social studies.

Each set of standards has described not only content standards, but also performance standards (how well should students perform at various levels in the educational system). Several of these sets of standards have also served to define the types of learning opportunities that students should have, and the manner in which their learning should be measured. As a result of the standards movement, new vocabulary is being used (although not always consistently): content standards, performance standards, and opportunity-to-learn standards.

Collectively, the content standards that have been developed and published define a vision for American education. Some of the standards have been well received; others have served as points of controversy (some of which continues today). There are two key assumptions contained within each of them, however: 1) *all* students need to achieve at much higher levels than they currently achieve; and 2) *all students are capable of achieving standards such as those laid out in the standards documents.*

Never in our nation's history have we made the bold statement that *all students* are capable of learning at the high levels described in the standards documents. Indeed, one of the debates regarding the viability and utility of the standards is whether students not now learning at high levels will be capable of learning at the much higher levels described in the various standards documents, and if some do not, is this the fault of the student, the environment in which the student lives, or the educational system.

Although the educators from various subject areas have enthusiastically embraced the idea of national standards, there are certainly those that believe that national standards will not help to improve American schools. As a fledgling effort to define important learning on a national basis, the movement to develop content standards has been fraught with questions and criticisms. Among these are the following:

Adequacy of Resources for Implementation?

While the content standards may lay out a visionary plan for student learning, have the resources needed to implement these visionary plans been provided? Typically, resources for education are being held constant or reduced, particularly at the federal and state levels. Will the necessary resources be made available to implement the changes?

Will Teachers Know What to Do?

The content standards, both individually and collectively, define quite different learning opportunities for students. How prepared are teachers to implement these new ways of teaching, and the new types of content standards? Will the necessary professional development opportunities be made available?

Evidence of Universal Learning?

Is there any evidence that in fact all students can learn at high levels? If not, won't the content standards just prove to be another barrier separating "haves" and "have-nots"?

Coherence?

Do the standards as a set provide a coherent view of learning and teaching? Particularly at the elementary level, do the standards fit well together and will teachers be able to integrate the different sets of standards? Is there overlap and redundancy among them? Are there gaps between them?

Reasonableness?

Collectively, the various content standards documents lay out a considerable volume of material for teachers. Is it possible, particularly at the elementary level, for teachers to actually teach the collective sets of standards in the number of school days and hours typically available in our country? As a set of materials, the volume is just overwhelming.

Respect for Traditional Learning?

When subject matter experts define what is important to know and be able to do in a subject area, are they respecting the traditional core content that the American public expects to be taught to students? The controversy surrounding the traditional Western civilization examples used within the history content standards is a good example of the debate between the experts and the public over core content.

National Curriculum or National Reform?

One of the most heated debates is whether the content standards set a national direction for reform discussions and efforts at the state and local levels, or whether the publication of content standards at the national level is really just the first step in the implementation of a common curriculum for all states and school districts. Although the nationally developed content standards have already had a considerable impact on state and local district standards, curriculum and assessment frameworks, it is not always popular to acknowledge such influences. Citizen groups in a number of states have mounted efforts to stop the development or implementation of national and state standards in states and local school systems.

Some cynics have indicated their belief that the content standards movement is just another fad, this year's version of the "quick fix" that will not and can not work. For example, in a speech, Musick (1996) has questioned the extent to which state content standards, and the assessments that measure them, have actually served to raise standards, or whether the level of these standards is at a more minimal level, which may not serve to help all students learn at high levels. He backs his supposition with the presentation of NAEP data at the state level, along with percentages of students passing the state's assessment tests. In each of three cases presented, the NAEP results are substantially lower than those presented by the state on its assessment program.

To many, however, the newer content standards being developed at the national and state levels represent a real opportunity to define what students should know and be able to do, and could serve to focus the energy, resources, and attention on helping all students achieve the really important ideas and concepts needed for later success in and out of school. They can provide the clear focus to guide subsequent reform efforts.

STANDARDS-BASED EDUCATION AND THE IMPROVEMENT OF STUDENT ACHIEVEMENT

In spite of the controversies surrounding the development and intended uses of the standards, the content standards do serve as the vision for the reform of learning and teaching. They provide an alternative to the current mode of instruction which suggests a passive approach to learning on the part of students, a model in which textbooks and tests emphasize memorization of information. The content standards documents also suggest changes in the manner in which students are assessed. Several of the national standards documents suggest an increased emphasis on performance assessment, including both the use of hands-on assessment measures and the increased use of open-ended written responses. Change in both teaching strategies and assessment is suggested by the content standards.

One implication of the need to change both learning and teaching strategies, as well as the methods of assessment, suggests that considerable professional development will be needed for teachers now in schools, as well as in teacher education programs to better prepare teachers for the future. It does little good to simply change the expectations of students, or the measures of these expectations, without changing the manner in which instruction is organized in classrooms. Yet, such decisions are often made in schools or classrooms with little reference to district, state, or national efforts at reform.

To what extent, however, have the national content standards documents had an impact on state-level standards? Have states been developing comparable standards for use at the local level? What is the status of implementation? Some of the answers to questions such as these may come from a recent study of the extent of development and implementation of content standards at the state level (American Federation of Teachers, 1995). This report, which is based on a survey of all 50 states, points out that many states are just at the beginning stages in the development and implementation of standards-based reform efforts. The research project was directed at answering five questions:

1. Does the state have standards or curriculum frameworks in the core academic subjects?

2. Are the standards clear and specific enough to form the basis for a core curriculum?

3. Does the state have student assessments aligned with the standards?

4. Are there stakes for students attached to the standards? More precisely, are students expected to meet these standards in order to graduate?

5. Are these standards benchmarked to world class levels? (American Federation of Teachers, 1995)

The AFT report goes on to report the following findings:

"1. States are strongly committed to standards-based reform Every state except Iowa is developing academic standards for its students

"2. Only 13 states have standards that are strong enough to carry the weight of the reforms being built upon them The standards we reviewed looked very different from state to state. Some states have short pamphlets that barely cover each core subject, others have large volumes with hundreds of pages and standards – and the quantity may or may not go hand in hand with clarity

> "As to the question of whether states will be basing their student as-
> sessments on the standards they are developing, there is good news
> and bad news. The good news is that a majority of states (31) recog-
> nize the importance of clearly connecting their assessments with the
> standards. The bad news is that over half of those states (18) will be
> basing their assessments on standards that aren't strong enough…"

"3. Most states will not hold students accountable for meeting rigorous standards. One of the most disturbing findings has to do with how few states will be creating incentives and consequences for students to work hard and strive for the standards Only seven states report that students will be required to meet their 10th, 11th, or 12th grade standards in order to graduate.

"4. Most states don't have "world class" standards... No state has done a thorough job of international benchmarking. And only seven states have taken any significant steps in this direction" (American Federation of Teachers, 1995, pages, 13-16).

As presented in the AFT report, the picture among the states appears to be relatively bleak. Not surprisingly, however, several states have challenged the information contained in the state-by-state analysis section of the AFT report. For example, Iowa has indicated that the state has or is developing content standards at the state level. Additional commentary or disagreements were received from Alabama, Indiana, Kentucky, and others.

CAN ALL STUDENTS LEARN AT HIGH LEVELS?

Inherent in the development of content standards at the national level and the emerging development of such standards at the state level is the assumption that clear, concise statements of student expectations can lead to higher achievement for all students. Is this feasible? Is it realistic to expect that it will occur on a wide-scale basis? In other words, will effective standards-based reform help all students, including those traditionally under-served, learn not only at higher levels, but at levels needed by such students for success in school, work, and the broader society? Is there evidence of such success?

Unfortunately, given the newness of the national content standards, as well as the apparent "under construction" status at the state level, there is not an abundant number of examples of successful implementation of standards-based reform. This is not to say that such examples do not exist, for they do. What is less certain is whether these examples are merely freak occurrences which are not replicable in other circumstances, or whether they can realistically serve as lighthouses to others striving to help students at risk achieve at much higher levels. At least such examples do exist, and something is known about the conditions correlated with their success. To begin to answer the questions about replicability will require others to strive to implement such ideas in new settings that have been less than successful to date.

The first line of evidence comes from research carried out in Michigan and elsewhere during the 1970s on effective schools. Researchers such as Wilbur Brookover, the late Ron Edmonds, and Larry Lezotte carefully partitioned the state assessment results for schools serving high proportions of the economically disadvantaged and minorities. Unlike conventional wisdom that says that all such schools will have low performance on tests such as those used in the state assessment program, these researchers found that there were a significant number of highly effective schools. These were schools that defied conventional wisdom.

The researchers began a several-year effort to determine why one set of schools, serving identical types of students as the other set of schools, could turn out such high performing students. Setting aside the issue of inappropriate test preparation or administration procedures (which, too often, is given as an excuse by low performing schools and the public why a few schools are quite successful, apparently from a belief that such schools can not be successful), the researchers examined the factors in successful versus unsuccessful schools. The researchers found factors most related to success in high achieving schools were: clear definition of instructional goals, assessment information related to these goals, high levels of teacher, student and parental expectations, higher levels of time on task, good discipline, and the appropriate use of praise (for substantial achievement, not trivial accomplishments). In other words, there are factors under the control of educators and others (albeit not easy to alter) that are related to the success of economically disadvantaged and minority students. If this is the case, why do we act as if we do not know how to help such students learn?

Another instance of evidence that schools serving minority and poor students can be effective is described in a paper written by Cindy Brown:

> "I hope you have a chance to visit some high poverty schools experiencing dramatic student achievement improvements. Drop in on any "Success for All" school working with Bob Slavin and his colleagues at Johns Hopkins University. Or stop by many of the schools following the tenets of James Comer or the Accelerated Schools model developed by Hank Levin, or any of several innovative schools operating under the sponsorship of the New American Schools Development Corporation (NASDC).

> "One caveat though – you must not pick schools that are only partially implementing these models or following them in name only. The way to be sure, or better yet, to find home-grown successes, is to match local and state achievement scores with school poverty rates – preferably over time so you can see progress. Every district usually has some high performing, high poverty schools, and it's always enlightening to pay them a visit.

> " There are too few high poverty schools on a timely path to academic success with all their current students" (Brown, 1996, pages 2-2).

Our ability to locate successful schools that serve the economically disadvantaged, minorities, and women demonstrates that schools can be successful serving students such as these. These effective schools demonstrate that it is possible to help all students achieve at high levels, even in instances where initial levels of students' needs are high and the level of resources may be less than adequate.

The question that remains then is: can we help all schools serving the economically disadvantaged, minorities, and women be equally successful? Can all students learn the high level, rigorous content standards that we expect of the more advantaged students? Can we reduce the gaps in achievement between the economically disadvantaged, minorities, and women and other students? These are profound questions that cut to the heart of whether the American public school system can and will be effective, or whether alternatives to it are needed.

Several factors affect our responses to these questions:

Do we expect to be successful?

As simple as it may sound, do the educators, the parents, and the students expect success in academic learning? If we lack high expectations, the initial stumbling in learning that the economically disadvantaged, minorities, and women experience may confirm our low expectations and cause us to give up lest we "frustrate" the students. Learning at high levels is hard work, but we need to expect and strive for success, so that initial lack of learning simply motivates us (and students) to try harder, not bail out with our fears confirmed.

Does the school have the resources to provide quality instruction?

While it is true that simply raising funding levels for schools will not guarantee higher student performance (since the majority of funds expended go for salaries, not instructional resources), there are instances in which the resource levels are simply not adequate. Current textbooks, other instructional materials, a well stocked library, computers, calculators, access to on-line resources, clean and safe classrooms are some of the resources which money can buy that will have a positive impact on learning. Schools need the resources to adequately teach students.

Do we give students opportunities to learn?

A major question that schools serving the economically disadvantaged, minorities, and women will have to ask is whether we provide the course and instructional opportunities for these students. For example, is mathematics and science offered to all students? If science is not taught in the elementary school, how can students take advantage of middle school and high school science courses? Without an adequate background, advanced courses are beyond the reach of women and minorities. Yet, too many schools serving the economically disadvantaged, minorities, and women concentrate on only reading, writing, and mathematics. Schools need to teach all important content standards.

Do we encourage students to take advantage of the opportunities provided?

It does little good for the school to offer courses that provide rich, challenging learning opportunities to students if the students are not encouraged to enroll in the courses, and to maintain their interest in learning. For example, fewer women and minorities enroll in college-preparatory and advanced placement high school mathematics and science courses, so they tend to score lower on college entrance tests in these areas. Yet, when type of high school course of study is controlled for, these achievement differences virtually disappear. Is the high school counseling program adequate? Are parents and students adequately engaged in the counseling program?

Do teachers have the skills needed?

The content standards developed at the national level, and under development in many states, imply significant changes in what students need to know and be able to do, as well as the manner in which they will learn these important outcomes. Do teachers have a current knowledge about these outcomes and the most effective means of providing them to students? Without good knowledge on the part of the teachers, the content standards will remain an unrealized dream in the lives of the economically disadvantaged, minorities, and women.

Do teachers know how to assess students?

Relatively few teachers have learned much about how to assess student knowledge and skills. Few teacher training programs include formal instruction in either traditional or alternative assessment strategies. This leaves many teachers ill-prepared to assess student learning on a day-to-day basis. Is the teacher proficient in the use of extended-response, hands-on performance assessment, or portfolio assessment procedures? Is the teacher able to construct adequate multiple-choice or short-answer questions? Does the teacher know when to use the more traditional measures and when to use the alternative procedures? Since assessment can affect learning, it is important that teachers be proficient in classroom assessment methods.

Do teachers and other education decision-makers have the data they need to monitor student progress and make adjustments to student learning experiences?

Waiting for end-of-year assessment results or student grades implies that adjustments can be made only at the beginning of the school year. Current record-keeping systems do not make it easy for teachers to access needed data about students, and teachers are not encouraged to work with others in the school system to plan ways to meet the needs of individual students. If teachers know how to collect better data on student progress and they can merge this information with data from teachers and others within the school system, then strategies can be developed to assist students before they are too far behind.

HOW ORGANIZATIONS SUCH AS CCSSO HELP EDUCATORS ADDRESS THE PERTINENT ISSUES

The Council of Chief State School Officers (CCSSO) has several ways to assist states in their standards-based reform efforts. First, the Curriculum and Instructional Improvement Program (CIIP) works with states, local school districts, and professional organizations to develop, review and to implement content and performance standards that are rigorous and high quality. A portion of this effort has been devoted to the development of criteria and review procedures for the review of state content standards, as well as models for the roll-out or implementation of standards at the state and local levels. Each of these is extremely useful in helping states and others to determine that content standards under development can serve as the basis for standards-based reform within the states.

The State Education Improvement Partnership (SEIP), which is a consortium of state-level policy groups, including the National Governors Association, the National Association of State Boards of Education, the National Conference of State Legislatures, the Education Commission of the States, and CCSSO, works on standards-based reform from the policy and policy-implementation perspective. This helps to ensure that the needed conditions and resources for standards-based reform efforts to take root and to grow are available as standards and assessments are being developed and implemented.

The Council's Resource Center works directly with program staff of state agencies, local school districts, and others to help develop models and strategies for implementing standards-based reform at state and local levels. Such efforts may be directed at changing compensatory education programs, helping improve programs for English language learners, or other efforts to improve educational programs for students.

Finally, the State Collaborative on Assessment and Student Standards (SCASS), a program within the State Education Assessment Center of the Council, is designed to assist states develop needed student standards and assessments working with other states with similar needs. The purpose of SCASS is to improve the quality of the student assessments that states are developing and using, to speed the time that it takes for innovations in assessment to be adopted on a wide-scale basis, and to reduce the costs required to develop these assessments.

Two types of activity are taking place. The first is assessment consortia in which state curriculum and assessment specialists, content experts, and others develop state consensus frameworks and prototype exercises in various content areas. Assessment consortia have been established in the areas of literacy (reading and writing), the arts, technical guidelines for performance assessment, assessing special education students, assessing limited-English proficient students, comprehensive assessment systems for IASA Title I/Goals 2000, and workplace readiness. Consortia meet several times per year to discuss these and other topics. Some consortia generate assessment prototypes, while others are more issues-oriented and provide information and models for states' consideration.

The second type of activity involves development projects in which states work together to develop needed assessment standards and measures. States are invited to join one or more of the projects which will develop standards and student assessments through pooled resources and effort. These projects will be linked to the emerging national standards in the area, as well as to new ideas about appropriate assessment methods. Several projects are currently under way in the areas of science education, primary-level assessment system, health education, limited-English proficiency assessment, social studies, and the arts.

Over 40 states are participating in one or more of the projects. In each project, states initially plan the development work and then will work together to carry it out. States may join the initial effort to plan the project and then later decide whether to participate in the development phase. Funding for SCASS activities is being provided by participating states, as well as foundations and other sources. By working together, states and local districts can learn from one another, can develop resources more quickly, can share in the expense of such development, and can accomplish more at higher quality, than they could do alone. It is one way in a time of shrinking resources for accomplishing more with less.

THE DREAM OF HIGH PERFORMANCE FOR ALL

As this paper has described, the level of current achievement is not adequate for many students, particularly the economically disadvantaged, minorities, and women. Whether due to demographic changes in our society or the changing nature of work, schools are not adequately preparing many students for their future. One result has been the delineation of content standards for each content area to spell out what students should know and be able to do in each content area.

The content standards that have been developed could be used to impact what students learn and how they will learn. Indeed, they are beginning to be used to affect the types and content of the student assessment programs being implemented at the national, state, and local levels. The content standards in most areas are too new, however, to have had much of an impact yet on student learning. However, after exposure to such standards for schools and students, the American public will expect performance to improve in the near future.

The content standards will have an impact on the economically disadvantaged, minorities, and women, particularly if local educators respond to the challenge of the higher standards by implementing programs to help all students learn. Schools can be effective, particularly if we believe they can be effective. It is time, however, for us to activate our high expectations by implementing quality programs to address the needs of the economically disadvantaged, minorities, and women, and helping these students learn at high levels.

References

American Federation of Teachers. (1995). *Making standards matter: A fifty-state report on efforts to raise academic standards.* Washington, D.C.: American Federation of Teachers.

Brown, C.G. (1996). *Supporting significantly improved student achievement in high poverty schools.* Washington, D.C.: Council of Chief State School Officers.

Hudson Institute. (1987). *Workforce 2000: Work and workers for the 21st century.* Indianapolis, IN: Hudson Institute.

Marzano, R.J., and Kendall, J.S.. (1996). *The fall and rise of standards-based education.* Denver, CO: Mid-continent Regional Educational Laboratory.

Mullis, I.V.S., Owen, E.W., and Phillips, G.. (1990). *Accelerating academic achievement.* Princeton, NJ: Educational Testing Service.

Musick, M. (1996). *You can't catch up in education by setting low standards.* Manuscript.

National Alliance of Business. (1987). *The fourth R: Workforce readiness.* New York, NY: National Alliance of Business.

National Commission on Excellence in Education. (1983). *A nation At risk: The imperative for educational reform.* Washington, DC: U.S. Department of Education.

O'Neil, J. (1995). On using standards: A conversation with Ramsay Selden. *Educational Leadership, 52* (6), pages 12-14, 1995.

Public divided on school goals, poll shows. (1996, March 24). *Lansing State Journal.*

Roeber, E. D. (1995). Using new forms of assessment to assist in achieving student equity. In Nettles, Michael T. and Arie L. Nettles (Eds.) *Equity and excellence in educational testing and assessment.* Boston: Kluwer Academic Publishers.

U.S. Department of Education. (1996). *Mapping out the national assessment of Title I: The interim report* Washington, D.C.: U.S. Department of Education.

4 Finding One's Voice: A Model for More Equitable Assessment

Elizabeth Badger

CHALLENGES TO PERFORMANCE ASSESSMENT

In the early nineties, when educational reformers rejected multiple-choice tests, their most potent arguments were made in the name of validity. It was argued that highly structured tasks, requiring a single response, could not form valid measures of the complex thinking and application of skills that are valued as the goals of education. Nor could they measure the constructive approach to knowledge that is seen as the key to learning. In the words of Frederickson and Collins (1989), multiple-choice tests lacked "systemic validity." They did not reflect the processes and outcomes of education, as we would wish them to be. In contrast, performance tests, with their emphasis on complexity and application, were seen to have the capability of measuring what the educational system should be striving to achieve: critical and creative thinking applied to the kinds of problems that challenge us in everyday life. In addition, performance tests were thought to be inherently more equitable through their link to educational standards. If standards are based on educational goals which are directly linked to the experience of the classroom, then all students are potentially capable of achieving them.

In the few years since then, as authorities begin to develop and use performance tests in large scale assessments, questions of validity have become paramount in the discussions that surround their use. Although sources of measurement error (e.g., the generalizability of results, the reliability of judgments and classifications, the strong effects of task situations) have challenged and sometimes puzzled measurement experts and policy makers, the argument has remained strong that performance tests are justified on the grounds of their consequential validity: that is, that they will result in an improvement of teaching and learning, particularly when such testing is mandated. In the oft repeated slogan of the movement, teachers will teach what is tested.

It may be too early to judge the actual effectiveness of performance testing in reforming classroom instruction, particularly when many state curriculum standards are only now being put into place. However, their stated link to curriculum has led to a renewed interest in the curriculum itself and to some very interesting and revealing discussions, particularly in regard to equity. One stems from the fact that performance tests have provided strong evidence for differences in the instruction that is delivered to the wealthy and to the poor. It should come as no surprise that teachers of relatively disadvantaged students have been shown to be staunch advocates of the status quo: rote learning, drill and practice, and the accumulation of facts. In response to questions about their students' preparedness to answer different open-ended test questions, the salient item characteristic that accounted for differences between teachers in wealthy and poor schools was the extent to which the tasks relied upon judgment, inference, and reasoning in unfamiliar contexts. "Teachers of students in Low Advantaged schools generally did not believe that their students were prepared for this type of thinking" (Badger, 1995, p.302). On the other hand, there is by no means a general consensus that the curricular model embraced by the mainly affluent schools is necessarily the ideal. Ogbu, Banks and others have pointed to the inadequacies of that curriculum in involving and addressing the concerns of minorities and others. They have attacked the relevance of this curriculum to students who live outside the purported mainstream culture and have asked, "How can we make the content and processes of schooling more relevant to these students?" Some have questioned the validity of the standards themselves, asking whether they are not merely further entrenching the existing bias in our educational system (Howe, 1994, Martin, 1994).

In the following paper, we will attempt to address such concerns in the context of assessment. We will take as our primary premise Messick's contention that "such basic assessment issues as validity, reliability, comparability and fairness… are not just measurement principles, they are social values that have meaning and force outside of measurement wherever evaluative judgments and decisions are made" (Messick, 1994). Using this premise, we will explore a model that attempts to resolve the tension between the standards of competence that are valued by the mainstream society and the relevance of those standards to groups who may be marginalized from that society. We will begin by reviewing the basis for valid assessment and then describe a model for the use of performance tests as valid measures of students' achievement. Finally, we will examine evidence for the effectiveness of that model in promoting equity for poor and minority children.

PERFORMANCE TESTING AS A BASIS FOR REFORM

The logic for the use of performance tests as a basis for reform rests on its relationship to standards and curriculum – what is valued and what is taught. Given the requirement of consequential validity which has been used so effectively in support of performance testing, we argue that when teachers, districts or states use performance tests to judge their students' achievement, there must be an alignment of standards, curriculum and assessment. That is, for an assessment to be valid it must contain a set of tasks that adequately reflects what is taught in the curriculum. This curriculum must, in turn, reflect the larger values that are reflected in a set of publicly accepted standards. See Figure 1.

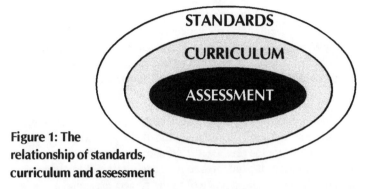

Figure 1: The relationship of standards, curriculum and assessment

Let us examine each in turn. **Standards** form the foundation for curriculum and assessment, codifying the educational values of society. Although educators and academicians with special knowledge of a discipline have usually assumed responsibility for this task, it does not necessarily follow that codification in itself is sufficient for standards to be accepted (e.g., the World History Standards). To form a valid basis for the curriculum and assessment, standards must be generally accepted by the public as a set of worthwhile goals for education. As a result, the standards that have been put forth by professional organizations and by state governments usually entail the participation of many constituencies and are not limited to lists of knowledge. Instead, they include the processes of thinking and acting that are considered necessary to function wisely in the community.

Curriculum is the translation of the standards into classroom instruction. Given the premise that all students have the potential of attaining the behaviors described in the standards, curriculum represents the best efforts of the educational community to ensure this. Whereas the standards themselves articulate goals, or end points, the curriculum delineates how students will achieve these goals. Like the standards, curriculum does not focus only on content, but deals with the application of knowledge and skills to the real world. It also includes specific ways of bringing about this behavior, and is developed with an underlying educational philosophy about learning and teaching.

Assessment consists of using a representative sample of tasks that are aligned with the curriculum in order to make inferences about the extent to which students have attained the valued behaviors that constitute the standards. These tasks are designed to measure what is relevant and to exclude, as much as possible, what is irrelevant to the construct which describes the behavior. In order to claim that these tasks are valid indicators of these constructs, various technical criteria have been established. However, underlying all the technical criteria is the requirement that the measures be fair and that the tasks reflect the taught curriculum. In other words, there is a fundamental assumption that the performance tasks, representing valued behavior in society (i.e., reflecting the standards), also represent behaviors that students have been given the opportunity to learn.

In this paper we propose that Pacesetter, a program developed by The College Board, is an appropriate illustration of this model. It satisfies the technical criteria for the validity in terms of content coverage and relevance. In addition, it satisfies a fundamental criterion of fairness – not only because of its alignment with standards and curriculum, but because it elicits students' genuine involvement in the assessment tasks, thus providing a more valid indicator of their competencies than those tasks which lack personal meaning.

Pacesetter was developed by the College Board with the intent of exposing all students to an instructional environment that includes the intellectual stimulation and challenges that are often reserved for the privileged. (See above.) The program includes a theory of pedagogy that is based on students' active construction of knowledge, a curricular approach that is based on standards within the subject area, and a teacher professional development program that prepares teachers for continuous evaluation of their students. Presently, three Pacesetter courses are being implemented in the schools: **Precalculus Through Modeling, Nos Conocemos? (Do We Know Each Other? Do We Know Ourselves?)** and **Voices of Modern Culture**. All were developed with the assistance of professional organizations, academicians, and teachers, representing the most current thinking in their respective subject areas. None of the courses is easy, nor are they meant to be: all demand a personal engagement in the serious pursuit of knowledge. For the purposes of this paper, we will limit our discussion to the content and assessment components of the language arts course, **Voices of Modern Cultures**, although similar analyses could be made of the others.

NEW PERSPECTIVES ON LITERATURE AND LANGUAGE ARTS

As in the case of other subject areas, we have seen a major change in the way language arts and literature are viewed. New ideas include:

- an extension of the notion of "text " beyond traditional print material;

- a recognition of the social and cultural context in which text is created;

- a privileging of personal versus "accepted" interpretation of text.

Beyond this view of the literature, there is also a pragmatic theme: the need to communicate ideas and information in a clear, effective, and powerful voice. Thus, communication has replaced moral edification as the overriding value in literature and language arts. This move has had major consequences, among which is the demystification of literature. No longer the province of the cognoscenti, literary interpretation is seen to involve an understanding of how expressed ideas reflect the values of the writer and how these ideas are connected to those of the reader. Similarly, the notion of what should be regarded as text has been broadened, as it becomes increasingly apparent that "literacy" must include the ability to read text as it is presented in films, videos, graphics, and spoken language, in addition to the printed word. In a sense, the literary arts have been democratized.

The National Council for Teachers of English and the International Reading Association clearly delineate these ideas in their recently published Standards for Language Arts (NCTE and IRA, 1996). Although such ideas have been influencing teaching and literary criticism for many years, their effect on the classroom curriculum has been less obvious than, for example, the effect of the "mathematics revolution," as documented in the Mathematics Curriculum and Evaluation Standards (1989). This is because the ideas expressed in the English Standards represent a change in the perception of the nature of language arts and literature rather than a change in the content itself. For example, unlike the mathematics standards, which challenged the hegemony of arithmetic as the major content of elementary schooling, these standards do not do battle with the traditional canon as such. Rather, they argue in broader terms for relevance and inclusion – in regard to media, genre, content, and audience.

On the other hand, outside the confines of the published standards, issues of content have not been ignored. The broadening of the concept of literature has led to challenges in regard to the canon, that set of literary works that reflect the (often implicit) values and value judgments about particular writers and texts and the criteria on which they should be chosen (Purvis 1993). One of the more important challenges has been in the form of multiculturalism which, in its simplest form, advocates the replacement of some or all of these traditional works, primarily representing an historically dominant white male culture (Applebee, 1990), with works that are more reflective of the culturally diverse world that actually exists in the United States.

THE PACESETTER CURRICULUM

How well does Pacesetter's English curriculum reflect both the publicized standards of the NCTE and IRA, as well as individual state standards, and the unofficial but strong debate about the adequacy of the canon for all students?

The Task Force which was responsible for the development of the course was representative of those educators and academicians who have been translating the new concepts of language arts into the realities of the classroom. They also represented a diverse group of school constituencies. As a result of their debates, it was decided that the over-riding goal of Pacesetter is students' attainment of "textual power." This complex notion refers, not only to the power that results from expressing one's own thoughts and feelings, but that which comes from understanding the communications of others, both on the surface and "between the lines." It presupposes a knowledge of the techniques of language and how genre and media contribute to its effect. It means that students are able to analyze language, to evaluate it, and to understand how it is related to the world around them. To quote Robert Scholes (1995), one of the major developers of the course:

> "Every text offers its audience a certain role to play. Textual power involves the ability to play many roles – and to know that one is playing them – as well as the ability to generate new texts, to make something that did not exist before somebody made it. That – all that –is what this course is about" (p. 5).

As its title proclaims, **Voices of Modern Cultures** is also about making connections across cultures. Recognizing that we all speak from a particular social and historical context, the course is intended to help students discover their own voices, to recognize the voices of others who may seem like them or very foreign, and to find connections that are sometimes unexpected. This means learning to think about a literary text as a conversational piece, written by someone from a particular time and place. It means trying to understand the context in which it was written, while at the same time discovering the universal or specific threads that connect it to one's own life or feelings. This is not an easy task. It requires an openness and a sense of empathy that is not explicitly called for in more traditional literature classes. Some students have found it initially difficult; more have been able to overcome the difficulty.

The course is also extremely practical, introducing students to the concept of language as a tool by which they can express their own thoughts and feelings appropriately and effectively to different audiences. Here, the metaphor "voice" is used to convey how situations influence the semantics, syntax and the tone of our communication with others. Students begin the course by examining the different voices they use at home, at work, at play, in different roles, and to different people. Recognizing that the often-muted "school voice" is seldom the most authentic one, they begin to explore, share, and gain confidence in their ability to use their other, possibly more powerful, voices. At the same time, they learn to recognize the diversity afforded by other voices and, by analyzing the techniques of the craft of language as practiced by others – in written narrative, spoken presentation, films, visual material – they learn how to amplify their own voices through different media.

Finally, the course is about critical analysis, the ability to analyze one's own work, as well as the work of others. To achieve this, students are introduced to criteria that define excellence and to models that demonstrate that excellence. Sometimes the models are those who we would all know and accept as masters of their craft; sometimes the models are the work of other students. The message is that both can be analyzed and learned from.

These goals are worked out in a course of six units, each organized around a major issue of language use in contemporary cultures, with each centering around a network of a single type of text. For example, students "read" poetry and essays, short stories, a novel, a play, films and the news media in order to understand what is said, but also to understand the techniques that account for its power. Although each of the units is described with reference to certain texts, which illustrate how the goals of the course are actualized, these texts are given as illustrations only. Teachers are encouraged to select other texts that may be more relevant and understandable to their students, provided that these texts satisfy a set of "key features" which characterize the intent of the unit. In this way, the "canon" is reconceptualized in terms of the characteristics of different texts rather than in terms of content, author, or some more amorphous criteria. For example, instead of "the fourth year Shakespeare play," the criteria for choice of drama requires that the play deal with an encounter between a character who is an outsider and a specific community and that it be produced widely. Thus, *Othello* (the illustrative text for the unit on drama) can be replaced by *The Elephant Man, Hyacinth Halvey, A Doll's House* or *Pygmalion*, depending on the needs and interests of their students.

To illustrate this inter-weaving of different perspectives (what text is communicating and how text is communicating, or "creation" versus "evaluation"), it may be useful to examine how Unit 2 is realized within the course. Entitled *The Stranger in the Village: Encountering the Other, Being the Other*, the intent of the unit is to look at the way culture and language work to include or exclude individuals. The genres that form the language focus of the unit are essays and short stories. Students analyze a set of essays that describe their authors' personal experiences of being an outsider in a situation; they reflect upon similar experiences in their own lives; they analyze the literary techniques that the authors use to portray their thoughts. Then, using the essays that they have read as models, students write their own essays describing similar experiences that they have encountered.

These essays go through a series of critical reviews by peers, by the teacher and, of course, by the individual student. They are presented orally or collected in written form as part of the student's portfolio. This process is more or less repeated with a set of short stories, supplemented by other texts including films, works of art, letters or drama as a prelude to creating a fictional piece for the same or a similar experience. This allows students to participate in the diverse range of experiences and forms of communication that tend to exist in the world outside the classroom walls.

PACESETTER ASSESSMENT

The assessment model that we propose is sensitive to the objectives of the local school or district, while yielding important information to the classroom teacher and to the individual student. It provides a multitude of assessment opportunities, administered at different times and through different types of tasks. Most important, perhaps, it is directly linked to what is being taught, providing a valid indication of what students have learned.

The goals of **Voices of Modern Cultures** are translated into learning dimensions that fall under two broad headings that refer to students' responses to the texts of others (Making Meaning from Text) and to their own ability to create text (Creating and Presenting Text). These two dimensions cut across different media and different genre, different degrees of formality and informality, and different modes of expression. Furthermore, a number of more discrete skills contribute to each of the dimensions. (See Table 1.)

PACESETTER ENGLISH
Table 1: Voices of Modern Cultures
Aspects of performance assessed in portfolios: making meaning from texts.

Students understand written, oral and visual texts from a variety of times and cultures in a variety of media and genres.

Aspects	Key Ideas
Respond to texts: Students respond to texts in terms of their own cultural backgrounds and personal experiences. They present their own impressions of texts - of the ideas, views, emotions and stories. They make predictions and speculations, and express personal opinions about textual elements such as characters, events and ideas.	• links to own background and experiences • personal impressions, predictions, speculations and opinions
Analyze texts: Students analyze the effect of the voices and points of view in texts. They also explain how a variety of techniques - such as form, organization, imagery, word choice, details, examples, and use of music or visual text - influence the overall meaning of texts. They use criteria to evaluate the effectiveness of others' texts and presentations.	• effect of voices and points of view • influence of various techniques on meaning • effectiveness of texts & presentations
Put texts in context: Students examine cultural and historical influences on authors and their texts. They explain the significance of the historical period portrayed in the text to the overall meaning. They make connections between the text and other texts, fictional characters, real people, current events and cultures. They discuss ways in which texts are related to recurring themes.	• cultural and historical influences on settings of texts • connections to texts, people, events, cultures and themes
Reflect on and evaluate processes for making meaning: Students reflect on and evaluate processes they have used to explore and develop their own ideas about and understandings of texts. They set goals for improving how they make meaning from texts.	• reflection on and evaluation of own processes • goals for improving processes

PACESETTER ENGLISH
Table 2: Voices of Modern Cultures
Aspects of performance assessed in portfolios: creating and presenting texts.

Students communicate ideas through oral, visual and written texts, in both informal and formal modes of presentation.

Aspects	Key Ideas
Use their own voices: Students communicate in a variety of their own voices, reflecting both their own culture(s) and their unique points of view, as they develop their own style(s) in relation to various audiences and purposes.	• variety of a student's voices • student culture(s) and points of view • personal style(s)
Develop and present texts: Students communicate in a variety of genre, media and forms. They develop texts using a variety of strategies such as use of anecdotes, examples, reasons, quotations and questions. They create focused and coherent texts. They integrate information from various types of resources and credit information accurately in written and oral presentations. They use effective language and appropriate presentation for various audiences and purposes.	• variety of genre, media and forms • variety of development strategies • focus and coherence • varied resources that are credited • effective language use and appropriateness for audience and purpose
Demonstrate technical command: Students use oral and written language effectively and precisely. Their texts employ grammatical usage, sentence and paragraph structure, spelling and punctuation that are appropriate for the intended audience. Some texts are polished to meet the standards and expectations of academic and public audiences.	• effective and precise language • appropriate usage, structures and conventions • some polished texts
Reflect on and evaluate how own texts are created and presented: Students reflect on and evaluate how they develop oral, visual and written texts and the effectiveness of their communications. They set goals to improve both the texts they present and the processes they use to create them.	• reflection on and evaluation of own processes and products • goals for improvement

With reference to the measurement of achievement, these dimensions are broken down in terms of five levels of proficiency. Although originally constructed with the help of practicing teachers in order to evaluate portfolios, these descriptions are being recognized for their instructional value and are increasingly being used, not only by teachers to judge the work of students, but by students to judge their own work. An example of one description is below.

Dimension:	Creating and Presenting Texts.
Ability:	Use their own voices to create and present.
Components of Ability:	A variety of student's voices; student culture (s) and points of view; personal style

LEVEL	DESCRIPTION
Beginning	The same impersonal voice that does not reflect the student's own culture or unique points of view is always used.
Developing	The same voice is usually used with infrequent and limited use of another voice.
Promising	Some individual voices that are usually appropriate to the audience and purpose are used.
Accomplished	A range of voices employs a personal style that represents the student's own cultures and points of view
Exemplary	A range of distinctive voices in a personal style incorporates the student's cultures and points of view and is aesthetically pleasing or convincing.

Assessment on these dimensions takes a number of different forms: continuous evaluation of student work by teachers, students, and their peers; portfolios, which consist of common tasks for each unit, as well as other material that the student wishes to include; and a timed assessment administered under standardized procedures. We will discuss each briefly.

Continuous evaluation

Occasions for both teacher evaluation of students, student evaluation of each other, and student evaluation of their own work are built throughout the course. The class and group discussions which propel the course also provide a milieu for teacher observations. In addition, the cycle of critical analysis and revision is a fundamental component. Such occasions put teachers in the role of mentor, helping students recognize ways in which they can evaluate their performance and shape it more effectively.

Again using Unit Two: **Stranger in the Village** as an example, the James Baldwin essay, which is used as the illustrative example, is accompanied by a student piece which describes and reflects on a similar experience of alienation. That this essay is given equal precedence with the Baldwin piece sets a level of expectation for student work: it is not necessary to be an experienced writer in order to produce a moving piece of literature. In addition, it acts as an example of exemplary performance, without the didactics that usually accompany this type of message.

Finally, most of the formal evaluative tasks are preceded by preparatory activities. For example, in Unit Two where one of the formal assessment tasks consists of writing a fictional piece, preparatory activities include: a brief stream of consciousness or interior monologue from the point of view of one of the characters from one of the designated short stories ; a monologue from a character that the student creates; journal entries; a fiction piece in the form of an exchange of letters; a descriptive paragraph modeled on a short passage chosen from one of the short stories. The instructional purpose of this array of activities is to help students generate the material that they will use for their final work. However, it also gives students the opportunity to try out material on their classmates and teachers in a non-judgmental environment in order to receive the kind of feedback that will help them shape their final product.

Common tasks

Two formal assessment tasks are provided within each unit. The purpose of these common tasks is to ensure that the course is anchored in the cognitive framework on which instruction is based, to provide evidence of student achievement for the portfolios, and to lend greater reliability to portfolio scoring. These tasks are described in the booklets which students receive at the beginning of the course. Accompanied by a set of specific questions, these tasks form the basis for the evaluation criteria. In other words, the evaluative tasks and the criteria are an integral part of the instruction. Again, we will use example from Unit Two.

Under the general theme, Stranger in the Village, students work with two genre: essays and short stories, supplemented by films, works of art, and other media that may help students to understand and empathize with the meaning of the texts. For each of the main genre, they are required to create a piece of their own, presented in either written or oral form. In the case of the essay, they are reminded of the essay structure and provided with a list of specific questions about content, organization, tone, and significance. They use these questions to evaluate and revise their work. Only after this is done, do they present their work to a larger audience for formal evaluation. In this case, students may substitute an oral presentation for a written essay. However, whatever the format chosen, the criteria for proficiency are essentially the same.

The two assessment tasks that are included in this unit will be collected into a working portfolio; however, the decision of whether or not they will appear in the final, summative portfolio is a decision for the student. Near the end of the course, students are asked to choose their "best" works, with an accompanying rationale, for final submission to their teacher. These portfolios are judged by a set of criteria that has been refined during the past year by a group of teachers who have participated in the course.

The Culminating Assessment

The final, standardized assessment provides an occasion for students to perform a task under the pressures that they may soon meet in the workplace or college. However, unlike more traditional testing and more consonant with workplace requirements, students are given a chance to "enter into the situation" before they are asked to produce an original work. Also similar to workplace situations, they are asked to use work that they have already completed in a different context.

Specifically, the "culminating assessment" consists of two parts. One part asks students to reflect upon their portfolio of previous work to answer a question. Given the fact that students' portfolios will contain some, if not all, of the common tasks, this allows for a certain uniformity in the material used to respond. Furthermore, it allows students the experience of using their portfolio as a resource rather than only as a collection of evidence.

The second part of the assessment is designed for students to show their ability to understand how language works within a particular kind of medium. The timed portion of this task is composed of a series of short responses, which provide a measure of students' knowledge and understanding of the more technical features of language. This is preceded by an introductory activity, discussed in a group setting, which functions in much the same way as the preparatory activities that precede the common assessments: that is, it allows students to start thinking about the general topic, to share understanding, and to ease anxiety.

In summary, the features of Pacesetter that contribute to its validity as a measure of achievement are:

• The goals of the course and the criteria for achieving those goals are clearly articulated both for teacher and students.
• Assessment tasks are explicitly related to the goals of the course so that students can recognize how their work contributes to the end results.
• Assessment tasks are varied, placed in different contexts and demand the diverse range of skills that is needed in life and articulated in local and national standards.
• Portfolios are used as a continuous form of assessment and to document students' growth, to promote reflection on the part of students, and to provide a medium for teacher/student consultation.
• Evaluation is viewed as a necessary component of the course. Students are expected to evaluate the texts which they read, but they are also expected to apply those same critical skills to their own work and the work of their classmates.

PACESETTER AND ITS RELEVANCE TO EQUITY

Voices of Modern Culture is now in its first year of full implementation in the schools. Consequently, data are limited and results must be looked upon with appropriate caution. Nevertheless, trends are encouraging. One set of findings comes from a formative evaluation which was conducted in seven pilot schools during the 1994-95 school year. The other consists of anecdotal reports from Dade County, where the program has been administered on a district-wide scale for two years. The reports cited here refer to the 1995-96 school year.

Evidence from the Formative Evaluation

Overall, results from a comparison of pre-post course questionnaires show a positive change in the attitudes of the students from all racial/ethnic groups toward the Pacesetter English course. Among these changes cited by Hispanic students were:

- more students (64% vs 54%) indicated that they enjoyed reading books;
- more students (55% vs 46%) felt confidence in speaking in front of groups;
- fewer (37% vs 44%) believed that they had a hard time expressing their thoughts to others;
- more (51% vs 42%) believed that English can be a lot of fun.

The effect on African-American students was on different aspects of English:

- more (50% vs 37%) agreed that they feel confident to write a lot in their future work;
- fewer (19% vs 26%) considered that they had a hard time expressing their thoughts to others;
- fewer (33% vs 41%) found it difficult to understand what authors are trying to say in the books read in school.
- more (69% vs 58%) practiced skills of editing and evaluating their work before handing it in.

Levels of agreements with the following statements among different groups of students are as follows:

"My portfolio really helped me see the progress I made throughout the year."

African American	Asian	Hispanic	White
52%	58%	68%	41%

"Reflecting on my work was useful in understanding my strengths and weaknesses."

African American	Asian	Hispanic	White
78%	52%	68%	52%

"Overall I thought Pacesetter English was a valuable experience."

African American	Asian	Hispanic	White
76%	52%	61%	57%

Interviews with the teachers in these pilot sites give some indication of the characteristics of the course that accounted for these attitudes.

On the diversity of cultures reflected in the reading material:

There was an awareness. We had discussions of racial issues. Dealing with the language was central. None of the kids complained about it. They felt they should be doing this. It gave the opportunity for students to discuss. There was no animosity.

On honoring personal experiences and viewpoints:

I could see the benefits especially in the kids that had personal background which they hadn't previously brought up. Some kids became very open about family and grandparents; the literature lent itself to it.

On respecting students as young adults:

It provided the feeling that the students have a lot of power and responsibility in class. The material and the way it's taught have more to do with real life.

Students are willing to take risks and see peers as support. From the teachers' perspective, you have to acknowledge and honor students as part of it.

On the usefulness of different pathways to showing achievement:

The medium to low achiever had stronger benefits because many different things counted. More students had the chance to be a leader and to feel they've been successful. I heard, 'I haven't made Bs in English before.'

The writing is better. It's more personal, it's livelier. I can see personalities come through, it's more focused.

Anecdotal Reports from Dade County

A senior administrator, who is responsible for the Pacesetter program in Dade County, provided us with the following information:

• High School A reports that at the third grading period failure notices sent to English Pacesetter students were 50% of the failure notices sent to non-Pacesetter students in Grade 12.

• High Schools B, C, and D report attendance is significantly higher among Pacesetter students than among non-Pacesetter students.

• At High School E, which caters to students who have a significant drop-out history, the third nine-week completion rate is precipitously higher among students in Pacesetter classes than in non-Pacesetter classes, thereby significantly affecting the number of students who are likely to finish the school year. In the words of the school official, this is "profoundly amazing."

Again, we interviewed teachers who are responsible for implementation in order to better understand the mechanisms that produced such results. One teacher, whose classes are primarily of Hispanic students with some African Americans, described the various reasons that students in her class chose Pacesetter. Some are students who are taking Advanced Placement courses in other subjects but wished to take a less traditional English course. Some are students who have just been moved from transitional bilingual programs who will be helped by the group support that Pacesetter offers. Some are students in an On-the-Job training program who value the experience in speaking and presentation that Pacesetter affords. And others are "in the middle." What do they find in Pacesetter that is different from other courses?

> *Pacesetter talks to them from the first assignment when it begins with their own voices. Nobody had ever asked them what they think or has given them the opportunity to say who they are.*

> *When they get to literature, there is something more contemporary than what they are used to. "This is fun." They have a chance to articulate what they know. They perform their work for the class. The usual routine moves from self-reflection, to cooperation with others, then back to self for revision, then presentation to the whole group.*

> *There are lots of opportunities for success. They always finds something that they can do well, that can be honored.*

> *They believe that the program has a value beyond the high school. College students have come back and said that everything we did prepared them for college.*

CONCLUSION

In response to this evidence, one might object: "But this is about curriculum, not measurement. What evidence do you have that the program promotes equity through measurement?"

In this paper we have argued that that a valid assessment presupposes that students are instructed in the kinds of knowledge and skills that are valued by society. In addition, however, we would add another criterion: that the assessment (and we would argue, the curriculum) must hold value to students, that it be seen as a useful pursuit that will have positive effects on their lives. If the student lacks an underlying intent to succeed in the assessment task, the instrument is effectively worthless. Unlike physical phenomenon, the measurement of competency needs the willing cooperation of the person whose competency is being measured.

Kenneth Howe, Jane Rowlands Martin, Nel Noddings, Henry Gates, among others, have argued that the current curriculum that is taught in schools has little to do with the lives, aspirations, and views of many groups in our society.

> "It is difficult to see the present clarion call for more precise and rigorous educational standards and assessments as doing anything other than simply articulating and further entrenching the educational status quo. And, as noted previously, the status quo has not been particularly congenial to marginalized groups. Assessing all students in terms of it is thus liable to the charge of a form of bias implicit in the very standards that are to serve as the anchor of assessment. " (Howe, 1994, p.30)

We would argue that Pacesetter avoids that bias. It does this by acknowledging that each student brings a unique set of voices to the classroom conversation and that the role of education must be to help amplify those voices and make them more effective. This process begins with very personal experiences that involve the students' own world and cultures. However, as their own voices receive affirmation, they are encouraged to recognize the underlying message of voices that appeared to be unlike theirs, spoken in different times and cultures. As one student remarked with some astonishment after studying Othello, "Shakespeare really knew a lot about people!" As teachers agreed, Pacesetter English is about gaining power and making connections. It is also about offering students the opportunity to perform, not just in the traditional written formats that have dominated the school culture, but in a variety of ways that allows for the display of diverse talents. This is equitable assessment.

Perhaps the last word in this argument should come, not from the world of measurement but from an administrator who has been responsible for implementing the course in one large school district:

Pacesetter is a fundamentally conservative course, dealing with skills, achievement, a product. The difference is that it invites students into the conversation. It uses the power of the richness of tradition to give students power. It is one thing to give general comments about access. After you say "excellence for all," what do you do next? The difference with Pacesetter is that it answers that question first. It shows teachers a way, demonstrating what to do. Only, at the end, does it give the message: "excellence for all"

– Jenny Krugman, District Supervisor
for Secondary Advanced Academic Programs, Dade County

NOTES

Acknowledgments are extended to Michael Johanek for his thoughtful suggestions for expanding the discussion of diversity in the Pacesetter curriculum and to Harriet Fether for allowing us to quote from her observations of Pacesetter in the classroom.

REFERENCES

Appleby, A. (1990). Book-length works taught in high school English courses. *ERIC Digest.*

Badger, E. (1995). The effect of expectations in achieving equity in state-wide testing: lessons from Massachusetts. In M. Nettles and A. Nettles (Eds.), *Equity and Excellence in Educational Testing and Assessment* (pp. 289-308). Boston: Kluwer

Frederiksen, J. R., and Collins, A. (1989). A systems approach to educational testing. *Educational Researcher, 18*(9), 27-32.

Howe, K. (1994) . Standards, assessment, and equality of educational opportunity. *Educational Researcher, 23* (8), 27-33.

Krugman, J. *Personal communication.* 1996.

Messick, S. (1994). The interplay of evidence and consequences in the validation of performance assessments. *Educational Researcher, 23* (2), pp. 12-23.

Morris, L., Leung, S., and Tannenbaum, R.(1995) *Pacesetter English Evaluation Report.* Unpublished paper.

National Council of Teachers of English and International Reading Association. (1996). *Standards for the English Language Arts.*

Purvis, A. (1993). Setting standards in the language arts and literature classroom and the implications for portfolio assessment. *Educational Assessment, 1*(3), 175-199.

Resnick, L. and Resnick, D. (1992). Assessing the thinking curriculum. New Tools for educational reform. In B.R. Gifford and M. C. O'Connor (Eds.), *Changing assessments: Alternative views of aptitude, achievement and instruction* (pp. 37-75). Boston: Kluwer.

Scholes, R. (1995). Pacesetter English overview: "Voices of Modern Cultures". In *College Entrance Examination Board and Educational Testing Services. Pacesetter English* (pp. 5-14).

5 Advances in Portfolio Assessment with Applications to Urban School Populations

Mark D. Reckase*
Catherine Welch

Over the last few years, there has been increasing interest in using the assessment process to directly support classroom instruction. For example, the National Commission on Testing and Public Policy recommended that "Testing policies and practices must be reoriented to promote the development of all human talent" (1990). This recommendation was based on a belief that testing was obstructing the educational process rather than supporting it.

A second common belief that has led to a call for reorienting the educational assessment process is the idea that the use of multiple-choice tests is harmful. This belief is clearly stated by Ruth Mitchell in her book entitled *Testing for Learning* (1992). "No matter how sophisticated the techniques, however, multiple-choice tests corrupt the teaching and learning process " This is an extreme view, but many in the educational community echo these types of reactions to multiple-choice tests.

While there are numerous negative comments about the use of multiple-choice tests, most of them are not substantiated by actual examples from high quality standardized tests. Poetry is not disparaged as a literary form because there are many bad poems. Rather poetry is valued because of a relatively few great works. Similarly, the multiple-choice form is not the demon that is destroying education. While there are poorly constructed tests, there are also tests that accurately measure important educational outcomes. For example, ACT has identified the higher-order thinking skills that are assessed by its multiple-choice tests produced for use at Grades 8, 10, and 12 (ACT, 1992). High quality tests are much more sophisticated than is commonly believed. The tests serve their purposes well, continuing to be widely used despite frequent criticism.

If quality multiple-choice assessments work well, is there a need for other assessment techniques that use other formats? That question can be answered from both an assessment perspective and an instructional perspective. If the goal is to actively support the instructional process, multiple-choice tests are not the vehicle of choice. They have

* This study was conducted during Mark Reckase's matriculation at ACT, Inc.

seldom been proposed as anything other than measurement tools. Measurements are useful to guide instruction, but they do not specify the type of instruction that is needed nor do they provide rich examples of students' performance. Stating that the temperature is 80 degrees Fahrenheit does not provide the same message as being on a beach with palm trees when the temperature is 80 degrees. Measurements are summaries rather than rich descriptions.

New assessment tools could provide richer descriptions of student performance than do multiple-choice tests and may assess characteristics that are not addressed by existing tests. Motivation, ability to work on extended projects, creativity, time management, and self discipline might be assessed. Because of the difficulties in assessing these characteristics, these new assessments will not likely be as efficient in either cost or time as multiple-choice tests, but the added information might well be worth the price.

New assessment tools might also provide models for high quality student class work. If the models are directly tied to national curriculum standards, they might also directly facilitate quality instruction. Of course, instructional improvement is only likely to be the result if teachers and students attend to the models presented by the assessments. Assessments can only provide information and structure. Assessment is not a substitute for dedicated teachers, quality instruction, and strong support for education.

Within the context of criticisms of multiple-choice tests, the desire to support instruction through assessment, and the need for models of high quality student work, ACT began a developmental project in 1993 to create a new assessment tool. This tool would directly support instruction, would assess skills that were not already included in other ACT tests, and would meet the statistical and psychometric requirements for reporting at the level of the individual student. The goal of this project was to use the concept of a portfolio of student work to form a new assessment and instructional tool that would directly support positive educational outcomes.

The selection of the portfolio concept was based on work such as LeMahieu, Gitomer, and Eresh (1995) who argue that portfolio assessment supports instructional practice through the use of comprehensive and consistent tasks, providing detailed evidence of student thinking and encouraging students to become more active in their learning. Further, portfolios may help teachers and administrators to focus on meaningful outcomes.

Freedman (1993) describes the necessary links that need to be in place between large-scale testing and classroom assessment in order for large-scale portfolios to contribute in this situation. Portfolios do fit naturally with good instruction and are a potential tool for thoughtful classroom assessment and portfolios can be used for large-scale testing. The challenge is to make the links (p. 47). The hope for linking the two entities is directly tied to gaining a better understanding of the measurement issues associated with portfolio assessment and with the classroom issues associated with the successful implementation of portfolios. ACT, in the development of the ACT Portfolio

System, has attempted to address many of these issues while attempting to produce an equitable, technically sound assessment system.

THE ACT PORTFOLIO PROJECT

The use of portfolios of student work for assessment is not a new idea. Twelve years ago, Elbow and Belanoff (1986) suggested that portfolios of students' work be used in place of proficiency tests. Unfortunately, actually implementing portfolios for assessment has had somewhat mixed success. While portfolios are widely used for classroom assessment, implementation for large-scale, formal use has been difficult. For example, the reliability of evaluations of portfolios obtained from students in Vermont was determined to be too low for use at any level of detail beyond a general state-level report (Koretz, McCaffrey, Klein, Bell, & Stecher, 1993). Thus, the development of a portfolio system for use nationwide that would support instruction and provide accurate student-level information was considered as a tremendously challenging undertaking.

To focus the project, a set of formal goals were defined. These were to:

• Produce a system that could be used at high schools throughout the United States;

• Produce a system that would directly support the instructional process;

• Develop a reporting mechanism that would provide information for individual students; and

• Summarize the information from the portfolios in a way that would facilitate use beyond the classroom.

As the project evolved, several assumptions were made to help guide the developmental efforts. These assumptions evolved directly from the goals for the project.

• The portfolio system should be flexible and customizable so that it would fit within the curriculum and instructional systems of high schools across the country.
Recognizing that the curricula for secondary schools vary considerably across the country, there was a concern that an ACT-designed portfolio would be limited in its usefulness for some schools. Therefore, flexibility was a key component in the design.

• The portfolio system should provide evidence of the acquisition of important national educational outcomes.
This assumption was included to provide structure to the components of the portfolios. If the use of portfolios was to support instruction, instructional goals needed to be an integral part of the design of the system.

• The development of the portfolios should be embedded within regular instructional activities. Portfolios should contain examples of actual student class work in response to assignments rather than materials produced specially for the portfolios.
There was a concern that the use of portfolios for assessment would be too time consuming to be practical. There was also a desire to avoid artificial tasks. The idealistic

goal became to produce a portfolio system so embedded in the instructional process that the boundary between instruction and assessment would become indistinct.

THE DEVELOPMENT PROCESS

A direct outcome of the development of goals and assumptions was a realization that the only way that the constraints could be met was to directly involve teachers and high school staff in the design of the portfolio system. To bring about this direct involvement in the design, ACT asked representatives of various national educational organizations (e.g., NASSP, CCSSO, NCTE, AFT) to nominate high schools to participate in the design, development, and field test of a national portfolio assessment system. The nominated schools were sent an invitation letter and were asked to submit a formal application to be a member of the project design team. High schools were asked to commit to working on the project for three years. They also were asked to agree to appoint a teacher from the school to the design team.

From the high schools that formally applied to be part of the project, seven were selected. The criteria for selection included representing the diversity of types of schools from across the country, and being dedicated to the support of teachers in the improvement of instruction. The seven schools that were invited to participate in the project are listed in Table 1.

Table 1

Design Partner High Schools
Du Sable High School Chicago, Illinois
Cherry Creek High School Englewood, Colorado
Branford High School Branford, Connecticut
Libertyville High School Libertyville, Illinois
Culver City High School Culver City, California
Mountlake Terrace High School Mountlake Terrace, Washington
Tupelo High School Tupelo, Mississippi

Teachers from the seven schools, ACT staff, and three consultants with experience in the use of portfolios met for the first time during the summer of 1994. The remainder of this chapter is a report of the progress that has been made by the design team toward the goal of developing a national portfolio system.

Subsequent sections of the chapter are organized around three topics. The first topic is a description of the portfolio assessment system that has been developed by the design team. In this section, the portfolio concept is defined and the details of the process for implementing the system are presented. The second topic is a description of the pilot and field tests that are being conducted to gain information about the functioning of the system. This information is being used to further refine the design. A particular focus of the second section is the use of the portfolio system in high schools in an urban setting.

The third topic is a discussion of the portfolio system design relative to the nine principles governing assessment and equity given in Nettles and Bernstein (1995). The goal of this final section is to place the portfolio assessment system within a wider context of national assessment policy.

THE ACT PORTFOLIO SYSTEM

The first step in the design process for the ACT Portfolio System was to come to agreement on a definition of portfolio that would be acceptable to all individuals involved. After reviewing the definitions that could be found in the literature on portfolio assessment, the following definition (Meyer, Schuman & Angello, 1990) was accepted as the one that best represented the beliefs and needs of the design partner schools.

> A portfolio is a purposeful collection of student work that tells the
> story of the student's efforts, progress, or achievement in given areas.
> This collection must include:
>
> • student participation in selection of portfolio contents;
> • the guidelines for selection;
> • the criteria for judging merit;
> • and evidence for student self-reflection.

The design team considered the requirements that students be involved in the selection of entries to the portfolio, the need for criteria for selection and judging merit, and the evidence of self-reflection to be particularly important components of this definition. These features of the definition had a major impact on the subsequent design of the system.

Early in the design process, the design team decided to limit initial efforts to the areas of language arts, mathematics, and science. This decision was made so that the project would be manageable in scope rather than on grounds of relative importance of subject matter. Three distinct portfolios are part of the system, one for each of these content areas. Depending on decisions at the school level, students might be asked to develop a portfolio in one or more of the three areas.

Another early decision was to develop a portfolio system that spanned Grades 9 through 12. That is, each year students would be asked to develop new portfolios in the three target curriculum areas using materials from that year's courses. The eventual goal would be to document the improvement that results from each student's program of study. The decision to span more than one year was important because the decision required that the structure of the portfolio be applicable to different levels of courses and different academic programs of study.

SYSTEM DESIGN

The current design for the portfolio system, which is still evolving in response to input from the schools, was driven by the need for a flexible system, one that is related to the national curriculum standards, and one that is as embedded in the instructional system as possible. The result of the design efforts is a loose structure for defining a portfolio of student work at the course level that is supported by teacher training, rigorous evaluation procedures, and a collaborative network of teachers and schools. The key concept in the design is a general description of the work to be placed in the portfolio called a "work sample description."

Work Sample Descriptions

A Work Sample Description is a fairly general description of the material that a student should select to represent his or her capabilities in a given curriculum area. For example, one of the Work Sample Descriptions for science is:

> *To respond to this Work Sample Description, please provide a sample of your work that demonstrates your ability to review and evaluate scientific literature on a specific topic.*

The Work Sample Description is written in a general way so that it can apply to work from any science course. If a student is currently taking biology, they can select scientific literature from biology as the focus of his or her work. If the student is in a physics course, physics material can be selected.

Each curriculum area has an extended menu of Work Sample Descriptions that are used to design a custom portfolio at the school. For science, there are 10 Work Sample Descriptions on the menu. Mathematics and language arts have similar menus with 12 and 13 Work Sample Descriptions, respectively. The current set of science Work Sample Descriptions is summarized in Table 2.

The ACT Science portfolio Work Sample Descriptions are specifically designed to cut across a broad range of skills that are of value in the secondary science classroom. A variety of approaches are presented to the teacher and student that allow for the identification and selection of student work that matches classroom activities. The science work sample descriptions may include literature review and evaluation, integrating sci-

Table 2
The current set of science Work Sample Descriptions

Science Work Sample Descriptions
Literature Review and Evaluation This work sample requires you to review and evaluate scientific literature on a specific topic.
Integrating Sciences This work sample requires you to explain how something works or why something happens by integrating scientific concepts or principles from two or more fields of science.
Applications This work sample requires you to show how scientific concepts or principles can be used to explain every day events or processes.
Societal Context of Science This work sample requires you to describe how science affects people's lives.
Historical Perspective This work sample requires you to describe how a scientific theory or model has changed over time.
Evaluating Scientific Claims This work sample requires you to evaluate the credibility of a scientific claim.
Laboratory Observation This work sample requires you to perform a laboratory investigation to improve your understanding of a scientific concept or principle.
Laboratory Experiment This work sample requires you to perform a laboratory experiment to test an hypothesis or resolve a problem.
Design a Study This work sample requires you to design a study to test an hypothesis or solve a problem.
Design and Perform a Study This work sample requires you to design and carry out a scientific investigation.

ences, societal context, historical perspectives, evaluating scientific claims, laboratory observations, laboratory experiments, design studies, and performing studies. Each of these work sample descriptions is evaluated using criteria that is relevant to the task being performed. These criteria include such features as communicating the depth of scientific understanding, specifying the appropriate purpose and hypotheses, developing and following an appropriate design, presenting procedures and results in an organized and appropriate format, analyzing and evaluating information and drawing conclusions and citing sources of information.

The Language Arts portfolio Work Sample Descriptions follow the same format as the science and mathematics in that they provide for a broad range of activities. The language arts Work Sample Descriptions may include analysis and evaluation, business and technical writing, explanatory writing, imaginative writing, persuasive writing, relating a personal experience, research writing, responding to a literary text, writing a review of visual or performing arts and writing about out-of-class reading. Criteria used for evaluation include completeness, development, clarity, audience awareness, voice and mechanics.

The Mathematics portfolio Work Sample Descriptions provide the opportunity to analyze data, solve word problems, collect and analyze data, compare notions, demonstrate the use of a technological tool, make logical arguments and show connections between branches of mathematics. Criteria for evaluation may include understanding the methodology being used, the correctness of interpretation of data and conclusions, and clarity of explanation.

The Work Sample Descriptions are not prompts or specified class activities. Rather, they are general guidelines for selecting material that is already produced in response to class assignments. Teachers can devise unlimited numbers of classroom activities that will result in work that can match the criteria given in the Work Sample Descriptions.

Along with the basic statement of the Work Sample Description are specific criteria for including material, a number of sample class assignments, and criteria for evaluating the material that is submitted. Teachers' guides also include actual examples of work submitted by students in response to the Work Sample Description.

As curriculum areas are modified, the Work Sample Description list will change to reflect new curriculum standards. Teachers are also challenged to produce additional Work Sample Descriptions to match class activities that they consider to be important, but that are not covered by the current list.

Portfolio Structure

The actual portfolio to be produced for a specific curriculum area at a specific grade level is guided by the selection of five Work Sample Descriptions from the menu plus the requirement that students write a letter to the persons who will be reading the portfolio describing the reasons the materials were selected. The five Work Sample Descriptions are selected by the school staff in any way that is determined to be appropriate. Some schools have the teachers in a curriculum area select a common set of five Work Sample Descriptions that all students will use to structure the portfolios. Other schools allow each teacher to select the Work Sample Descriptions that best match the goals of the courses they teach. It is also possible to involve parents and students in the process of selection of Work Sample Descriptions.

Once the five Work Sample Descriptions are selected, a detailed example of each is given to the students in a Student Handbook. This handbook includes criteria for selecting materials to match the Work Sample Descriptions, evaluation criteria, and information about requirements for the letter to the reader of the portfolio. The teachers are also encouraged to identify class activities that will produce materials that fit the requirements of the Work Sample Descriptions. Students are informed of the match of these class activities to the requirements of the portfolio structure at appropriate points in the instructional process.

During a course, students temporarily store materials in a folder for possible use in their portfolio. At the end of the course, these materials are reviewed and those that provide the best information about student capabilities related to the Work Sample Descriptions are selected for inclusion in the formal portfolio. After the materials have been selected, each student is asked to write the letter to the reader that explains why the materials were selected and what they tell about the student's capabilities. The goal of this letter is to help students learn to evaluate their own work and to provide additional information about the context of the portfolio production to the reader. Engaging the self-reflective steps needed to write the letter benefits the student in at least two ways: it makes visible to the student and to the teachers the student's strengths, values and goals; and it enhances the thoughtfulness and quality of the final letter that is included in the portfolio. The self-reflective letter allows students to describe their work and to explain what they believe they have accomplished.

Every piece of work that is included in the portfolio is the result of a class assignment that is a standard part of the instructional process. Students are directed to include only material that is graded by the teacher as a usual part of class assessment activities. Nothing should appear in the portfolio that was produced solely for the portfolio and was not part of the class lesson plan. Ultimately, it is hoped that the portfolio development process will become a usual part of the classroom instructional approach. However, inserting the system into the instructional procedures takes some organizational efforts. The typical pattern of activities is:

1. Prior to the beginning of the school year, select the five Work Sample Descriptions for each of language arts, mathematics, and science using procedures determined by the school.

2. Identify class activities that generate materials related to the selected Work Sample Descriptions.

3. Inform students about the portfolio system and the contents for the portfolio (the Work Sample Descriptions and the letter).

4. Have students collect potential materials.

5. Students select entries for portfolio to match Work Sample Descriptions.

6. Students write letters to readers.

7. Portfolios are submitted for evaluation.

Support Systems

Critical to the proper functioning of the portfolio system is an in-depth understanding of the Work Sample Descriptions and their relationship to instructional activities. To ensure that teachers are well informed about the workings of the system and the relationship to their lesson plans, two workshops are built into the system.

The first workshop is designed to help teachers facilitate the implementation of the system at their school. Each school that uses the system is required to have a local expert, called a facilitator, who is resident at the school. The facilitator is a teacher that is well versed in all aspects of the system and who is willing to serve as a resource to other teachers who will be implementing the system. Each summer, facilitators' workshops are provided to inform teachers about the working of the system, the nuances of the Work Sample Descriptions, and how to communicate the system to other teachers.

The second workshop focuses on the process used to evaluate the portfolios. A teacher from each of the three curriculum areas from each school is invited to participate in the scoring process workshop. During this workshop, teachers review student work and compare their own evaluations to those developed by special evaluation panels. The scoring process is refined during the workshop and methods for communicating results to students and other interested parties are developed. Along with the workshops, materials are provided for communicating the operational components of the system to teachers and students. These materials include portfolio folders and dividers, and handbooks with descriptive materials.

Evaluation

The final component of the portfolio system is the process for evaluating student work. Each Work Sample Description has a six-point rubric that is used for evaluating and reporting student performance. In addition, there is a four-point holistic rubric for evaluating the portfolio as a complete document. The holistic portfolio evaluation and the evaluations of each work sample are reported back to the student and teachers. For the pilot and field tests of the system, ACT is evaluating all of the portfolios. As the number of users increases, subsamples of portfolios from participating schools will continue to be evaluated. Options exist for evaluating every student's portfolio.

Scoring Rubrics

A specific scoring rubric is designed for each Work Sample Description. Student responses from the pilot test administration were selected to illustrate each score point of the rubric. The process of selecting responses included all participating schools, taking into account the various representations and approaches to the particular Work Sample Descriptions across the schools. This selection process ensures that the various cultural backgrounds and course offerings and opportunities are taken into account.

Based on this process, the Work Sample Descriptions are refined to be as broad as possible while still maintaining the ability to be evaluated in a consistent manner. Evaluators note particular difficulties associated with Work Sample Descriptions during the scoring process. This information is used to further refine the Work Sample Descriptions. Work Sample Descriptions that proved to be too difficult or were misinterpreted in their intent were revised and reviewed prior to the next pilot test administration. As with the development and design of the Work Sample Descriptions, a variety of classroom teachers, multicultural educators, content specialists and measurement specialists work to develop the scoring rubrics.

Summary

Explaining the portfolio system is more difficult than actually implementing it. While the system is complex and requires support to function properly, it also provides a process that can be merged into usual class activities. A number of schools have successfully implemented the system, but others have found barriers to implementation. The next section of this chapter will describe some of the practical information about the system that has been gained through the field test process.

IMPLICATIONS FOR USE IN URBAN SCHOOLS

The previous sections of this chapter have summarized the goals and assumptions that guided the development of the ACT Portfolio System and have described the basic components of the system. This section provides some information about how the design supports the three foundational concepts that underlay the goals. These concepts are: (1) to support instructional improvement; (2) to provide sound assessment information; and (3) to provide staff development opportunities for teachers. Directly following from these concepts are ways that portfolio use can support the educational process at urban schools. Support activities are intended:

1. To assist schools with the task of developing a portfolio assessment culture. *ACT works directly with the teachers within a school to establish a structure that will be effective within a particular school environment. For example, facilitators that are selected for participation in an implementation workshop are trained to return to their particular school and work with the other participating teachers to establish a system that is specific to their instructional and curricular needs. The best possible facilitator for the successful implementation of such a system is a faculty member that is familiar with the particular needs of a school.*

2. To provide a portfolio system flexible enough to be useful to teachers across a variety of school contexts. *The system was designed by classroom teachers, school administrators, content experts, multicultural educators and measurement specialists, helping to ensure that the resulting product blends considerations of content and curriculum as well as important equity and psychometric issues. The successful implementation of the system rests with the facilitators and participating teachers at a particular school. The system is able to accommodate wide variations in curriculum and student populations to be useful to all types of schools.*

3. To facilitate good instructional practice. *Students will benefit from improved instruction. Improved instruction is a result of focusing on important educational outcomes, including teachers in the selection of work sample descriptions and associated classroom activities, including teachers as facilitators within a school, and including teachers as part of the workshop designed to explain the scoring criteria.*

4. To provide a portfolio system able to meet the diverse educational needs of students, teachers, parents, and school administrators. *The system has been designed to take into account the broad range of activities and classroom practices that are currently in place. The system's success does not depend on certain classroom resources. Rather, it is adaptable to a host of classroom experiences.*

5. To provide administrative and management systems that will help teachers use portfolios in their classrooms. *The system provides a simple management system that is designed to be the responsibility of the student. The administration system provides an opportunity for increased collaboration between teachers within a particular school. Teachers work together to select work sample descriptions, identify activities that are consistent with the work sample descriptions and to explain to the students the scoring criteria that are being used.*

6. To promote the beneficial student-teacher and teacher-teacher interactions that can be realized through portfolio implementation and lead to improved instruction. *Schools participating in the first two years of the ACT Portfolio System recognized the value of the student participation in the process. For those schools that found the system most successful, students actively selected their work and wrote self-reflective pieces to accompany their selections. These self-reflections provided a new avenue for the teacher to become involved in the student's work. It provided a new source of information about the student and his/her thinking process.*

EQUITY ISSUES

Resources

The Work Sample Descriptions that are presented to the teachers and students offer a number of task formats and allow a variety of representations and strategies to be used to produce a response. This variation helps to ensure that the resources available to the student within the classroom are not a barrier to the successful completion of a particular work sample description. Figure 1, for example, provides two examples of student work that was rated as being at the same level during the scoring process. The examples were submitted to meet the requirements of "Laboratory Observation" Work Sample Description given in Table 2.

Figure 1

Two Submissions to the "Laboratory Observation"
Work Sample Description with Equal Ratings

The Effects of Temperature Change
on the Heart Rate of *Daphnia magna*

In this hands-on activity, the student observed how ambient temperature affects the heart rate (an indicator of metabolic rate) of *Daphnia* (an animal that does not generate its own body heat). The student presented data tables, equations, and graphs along with text describing the procedures, results, and conclusions. Equipment needed includes the following:

- Living culture of *Daphnia* (small tube of broth with the microorganisms, which can be ordered from most biological supply companies)
- Glass chamber with magnifying glass or low power microscope (to hold *Daphnia* for observation in water of a given temperature)
- Thermometer
- Stop watch
- Water of various temperatures (from tap)
- Paper and pencil (to record results)

Cardiovascular Fitness

In this hands-on activity, the student monitored the heart rates of her classmates before and after exercise. In addition, she recorded body weight of her classmates and noted whether or not each person smoked. The student presented data tables and graphs to show the following: 1) the relationship between resting heart rate and body weight, 2) the effect of exercise on heart rate for smokers and non-smokers. The student discussed the implications of her results. Equipment needed includes the following:

1. Clock with a second hand
2. Bathroom scale
3. paper and pencil (to record results)

One of the goals of the project is to develop Work Sample Descriptions and scoring procedures that focus on the quality of student work, rather than the resources that the student has available. Note that the "Cardiovascular Fitness" work sample required minimal equipment while the "Daphnia" work sample required a culture and laboratory equipment. Despite the differences in facilities required, the work samples received the same evaluation.

In addition to the Work Sample Descriptions that are submitted as part of the portfolio, students provide some context about the instructional task that was assigned as part of this activity. This contextual information helps the evaluator to further understand the classroom activities and the directions that are provided to the student.

Range of tasks

The Work Sample Descriptions offer students a variety of options from which to select representations of their best work. In addition to the Work Sample Descriptions, students and teachers are provided with numerous descriptions of classroom activities that may fulfill a requirement for a particular Work Sample Description. Figure 2 presents two examples of the types of tasks that can be completed in response to a Work Sample Description that deals with Evaluating Scientific Claims. One task requires reading and researching existing documents. The second requires the completion of a laboratory experiment. Both tasks provide an equal opportunity to supply high quality work for this particular work sample description.

Figure 2
Examples of "Evaluating Scientific Claims"

Work Sample Description

Your work sample should demonstrate your ability to evaluate the credibility of a scientific claim. To complete this entry, you should do the following:

•   Identify a Scientific claim in some form of persuasive communication. Be sure that the claim is scientific and can be evaluated with concrete scientific evidence.

•   Collect scientific information to evaluate the scientific credibility of the claim. For example, you may review published scientific literature and/or may collect data of you own (i.e., laboratory investigation).

•   Present your report in an informative format (e.g., a magazine article, report, speech, editorial, etc.). Analyze and evaluate the relevant scientific information or evidence in terms of its impact on the scientific claim. Include examples, figures, graphs, and tables as appropriate. Cite the sources of your information.

•   Prepare a bibliography of your sources.

Examples of Classroom Activities

Assignments similar to these could provide the basis for appropriate work samples:

• Several years ago, a team of scientists proposed that a giant asteroid caused the extinction of dinosaurs on Earth. Review the literature for evidence supporting and/or refuting this idea. Discuss other possible factors/events that may have caused or contributed to the extinction of the dinosaurs. Focus on scientific evidence rather than popular opinion.

• A certain company claims that their antacid is "most effective" for reducing stomach acidity. Perform a laboratory investigation to evaluate the credibility of this claim.

Throughout the development and review stages, classroom teachers were featured as the primary developers of the portfolio system. In addition, the development and review of the Work Sample Descriptions involved content specialists, multicultural educators and measurement specialists. The initial Work Sample Descriptions were pilot tested on a sample of schools that represented a range of school types, geographic locations and student populations. These schools were selected to be as representative as possible of the nation's diverse geography and population. After the initial pilot administration, the Work Sample Descriptions and accompanying scoring rubrics were reviewed and revised and prepared for a larger field test. Following the field test, educators will again refine the descriptions and the rubrics to make the system as accessible as possible. The field test was broader in scope than the pilot administration and allowed for the selection of a more representative sample of schools.

EVIDENCE FROM PILOT AND FIELD TESTS

Pilot Test

As described in Reckase (1996), the ACT Portfolio Project is in its third year of development and its second year of field testing. The project was originally pilot tested on seven design partner schools during the 1994-1995 academic year. Teachers from these seven schools contributed to the overall design and development of the content and management of the system. During the first pilot year, teachers from the partner schools were asked to use the ACT Portfolio System in at least one classroom. Representatives from three content areas – language arts, mathematics, science – were included at each school. These participants piloted the system for six months.

Following the first year of the ACT Portfolio Pilot Project, 35 teachers who participated in the pilot implementation of the system during the 1994-1995 academic year were surveyed concerning their level of involvement in the project, their experiences, and the match of the project to their expectations. The teachers also provided information about their prior experience with portfolios, their students' response to the portfolio project, their assessment of the ACT Portfolio System, the impact of the system on conference and preparation time, what they perceived as concerns and barriers to portfolio use both inside and outside their particular school system. The reactions from the teachers were codified and compared across content areas.

Participating teachers responded to a total of 23 questions as part of the pilot year one survey. As part of these analyses, 11 questions were selected and their responses compared to the performance of classrooms for the particular teachers. All questions were open-ended and encouraged teachers to provide as much detail as possible. The survey results were received from six of the seven pilot schools. These schools are described in Table 3. Two of the six schools were urban schools. A total of 11 teachers from these two schools responded to the survey.

Table 3

Description of Pilot Schools - Year One

Pilot school	Region	Type	Language Arts Teachers	Science Teachers	Math Teachers
1	midwest	urban	4	1	1
2	midwest	suburban	5	3	2
3	south	rural	1	3	2
4	NE	suburban	4	2	2
5	West	suburban	1	3	1
6	West	urban	0	1	2

Language Arts Results

Language arts teachers had considerable experience with portfolio assessment prior to becoming involved in ACT's project. This is consistent with responses that indicated few negative reactions to the use of portfolios. However, the level of experience did not appear to relate to the overall portfolio score of their students.

Language arts teachers also indicated the best match between the work sample descriptions and their curriculum. Again, there did not appear to be any relationship with performance. Most language arts teachers indicated that they use student portfolios to guide and improve their future instruction. Many of the language arts teachers indicated that the use of portfolios did not affect the manner in which they assessed students. Many indicated that they never use standardized tests in their classrooms and that the use of portfolios is consistent with the types of assessments that they currently use. Most language arts teachers also indicated that they have not changed their grading procedure as a function of the portfolio project. For those that indicated a change in procedure, it was primarily due to the increased involvement of students in the evaluation process. Most teachers indicated a desire to incorporate an assessment of student's whole portfolio into the grading scheme. The response to this question produced the strongest relationship between overall portfolio score and response to the question. Students of teachers that did not plan to incorporate an assessment of the whole portfolio tended to score higher than students of teachers that did intend to incorporate the overall portfolio score. Most language arts teachers also planned to use or were currently using the portfolio to assess or monitor student learning and growth.

Finally, when asked about the barriers and hurdles to implementation that they had encountered, they reported that there was not an obvious relationship between the type of barrier and the performance of the students within a classroom. The barriers most often cited as interfering with implementing the portfolio process included student and teacher resistance, student attendance, time and adequate space to store materials. Some teachers indicated that portfolios are often viewed as additional paperwork with little or no value in the final assessment of student progress.

Science Results

Most science teachers that participated in the pilot study had little or no prior experience with portfolios in their classroom. Most science teachers indicated mixed reactions from their students about the use of portfolios. The amount of writing required as part of the ACT portfolio was cited as a negative in the science classrooms.

Most participating science teachers indicated that there was a good match between their curriculum and the work sample descriptions provided as part of the portfolio. They also indicated that they use or plan to use student portfolios to guide and improve their future instructions. The use of self-reflection strategies was cited as a way to use portfolio results to prepare for future classes. As with language arts, the science teachers did not indicate that the use of portfolios had affected the manner in which they assessed students. Science teachers indicated the need for continued chapter exams and the need to assess facts and relationships among the facts are important. Those that did indicate a change cited less of a reliance on the use of multiple-choice tests and the addition of more variety in their assessing techniques (activities and presentations). Consistent with their testing procedures, most science teachers have not or do not plan to change their grading procedures as a result of the use of portfolios. Most teachers in science do not plan to incorporate an assessment of the student's whole portfolio into their grading procedures and will continue to assess on separate pieces of student work that have already been graded. Many teachers indicated using the portfolio to assess or monitor student learning and growth. They saw portfolios as an avenue for students to examine their own growth and improvement.

As with language arts, when asked about the barriers to implementation and use, science teachers indicated time was their primary barrier to successful implementation. Other barriers included the lack of space for storage and the amount of paper work necessary to maintaining such a system. The teachers' identification with a lack of time was consistent with their responses when they were asked to estimate the amount of time that they spend conferencing with each student on a monthly basis. Several teachers indicated that there was not adequate time available to provide such conferencing time to the individual student.

Mathematics Results

Few participating mathematics teachers indicated any prior significant experience with portfolios. Rather, of those responding, only three had any experience at all. Consistent with this lack of experience was the teachers' responses when asked about the reactions of their students to the portfolio process. Most indicated either a negative reaction or a student contribution only because it was required in the classroom.

The match between Work Sample Descriptions and classroom curriculum was less strong in mathematics than it was in either science or language arts. Although there was consistency among responses from teachers from the same school, there was an inconsistent pattern between schools, indicating that there were some differences in mathematics curricula between schools.

The respondents were split between using the student portfolios to guide and improve instruction versus not using them in this way. One potential use of the portfolio in the mathematics classroom was to examine the written reflection to gain further knowledge of a student's understanding of the problem. Most teachers indicated that portfolios had little or no effect on the manner in which they assessed students. Those not affected indicated that they continue to use teacher-made tests to assess on a regular basis. Consistent with that finding was a mixed response to the effect on grading procedures. Those indicating a change cited additional student involvement in evaluation and multiple evaluations throughout the grading cycle as positive changes in grading procedures. Surprisingly, seven of the ten responding teachers indicated that they plan to incorporate an assessment of the student's whole portfolio into their grading scheme. This response pattern seemed to be somewhat inconsistent with their reluctance to change their overall grading and assessment strategies.

As with language arts and science, when asked about the barriers to implementation and use, mathematics teachers indicated time was their primary barrier to successful implementation. Consistent with their lack of exposure to portfolios in the classroom, mathematics teachers also indicated that student involvement posed a barrier. This involvement may include students not completing assignments, students not remembering to contribute to their portfolios, students being negative about the use of portfolios or students not interested in writing in a mathematics classroom.

Field Test

During the field test, 20 schools were asked to participate. These included the seven schools from the first year plus an additional 13 new schools. The purpose of the field test was to evaluate the materials contained in the ACT Portfolio System and revise them prior to operational use during the 1996-1997 academic year. Schools participating in the second year were asked to have at least nine teachers use the ACT Portfolio System in their classrooms (three teachers per content area) for the entire 1995-1996 academic year.

The implementation survey was completed by 206 participating teachers. Many of the questions on the survey were specific to the implementation of ACT's system, however a few were framed as more broadly defined questions. For example, when asked about their primary motivation for using portfolios in the classroom, 46% indicated instructional improvement as their primary motivator. Others cited professional development (22%), student interest (16%), personal interest (16%) and a school mandate (10%). When teachers were asked for what purpose portfolios were being used in their classrooms, student reflection received the greatest number of respondents (31%), followed by grading (21%), program evaluation (16%), student conferences (13%), and parent-teacher conferences (10%).

In addition to the implementation survey, teachers were asked to complete a survey that elicited their views about the seriousness of potential barriers to the implementation of portfolio assessment. One goal of portfolio assessment is to give students, teachers, and policy makers authentic roles in the assessment of students at all levels of a system and to provide results that are appropriate and useful. However, involved teachers, students and administrators often identify potential barriers to the successful implementation of portfolios within a classroom or school. The adoption of any new system requires a shift in the focus of curriculum and instruction. And, as with any type of educational reform numerous potential barriers exist that may prevent teachers from adopting portfolio assessment in their classrooms (Wolfe and Miller, 1996). Aschbacher (1992, November) describes the barriers identified in the implementation of performance assessments in mathematics and social studies classrooms. The study identified seven categories of barriers including: emphasizing instructional activities, specifying criteria for judging student work, assessment anxiety, lack of time, lack of training and support, lack of a long-range implementation plan and reluctance to change by teachers.

Surveys were completed by 198 of the participants. Forty-five percent of the teachers were language arts, 35% mathematics and 20% science. Of the 198 respondents, 36 teachers were from five urban schools. Each potential barrier was stated so that it could be coupled with one of four descriptions of the severity of that barrier. *Unlikely problems* received a score of 0 and were described as likely to have no impact on the use of portfolios. *Minor problems* received a score of 1 and were described as causing the teacher to use portfolios differently than he or she would like. *Difficult problems* received a score of 2 and were described as causing the teacher to reconsider the use of portfolios and *serious problems* received a score of 3 and were described as causing the teacher not to use portfolios at all. A summary of the barrier survey results for urban-school teachers and nonurban-school teachers is provided in Table 4.

Table 4

Responses to Barriers Survey — Field Test

Question	Urban Mean	Urban SD	Nonurban Mean	Nonurban SD	Difference
A lack of available information	.53	.65	.73	.84	-.20
A lack of training	.97	.77	1.16	.91	-.19
A lack of an implementation plan	.91	.98	1.08	.90	-.17
A lack of personal motivations	.42	.69	.52	.77	-.10
A lack of a support group	.56	.61	.53	.66	.03
A lack of perceived benefits gained	.89	.95	.94	.93	-.05
Amount of teacher time required	1.46	.92	1.48	.81	-.02
Amount of class time required	1.31	.92	1.29	.82	.02
Amount of class time for tions	1.33	.99	1.30	.79	.03 construc-
A lack of special materials	1.19	1.09	.72	.72	.47
A lack of storage facilities	.97	1.08	.80	.83	.17
A lack of money for release time	1.63	.94	1.12	1.01	.51
A lack of money for staff development opportunities	1.31	.99	.99	.91	.32
Resistance from students	1.06	.84	.90	.71	.16
Objections from parents	.46	.66	.68	.78	-.22
Resistance from teachers	.71	.93	.74	.79	-.03
Resistance from school administrators	.50	.86	.27	.64	.23
Resistance from curriculum coordinators	.49	.82	.28	.63	.21
Difficulty of communicating scoring criteria to students	1.40	.91	1.17	.85	.23
Difficulty of communicating scoring criteria to parents	1.14	.91	1.19	.94	-.05
Concern about use of portfolios outside the classroom	1.20	1.02	.94	.91	.26

Question	Urban Mean	Urban SD	Nonurban Mean	Nonurban SD	Difference
Difficulty of preparing portfolios	1.12	.91	1.12	.82	.00
Extent portfolio use will require changes in curriculum	.89	.87	.96	.82	.07
Extent portfolio use will require changes in instruction	1.03	.86	.92	.83	.11
Difficulty in creating scoring rubrics	1.20	.96	1.17	.82	.03
Difficulty in creating cover letters	.71	.79	.69	.72	.10
Difficulty of using portfolios to guide instruction	.94	.80	1.03	.83	.11
Difficulty of using portfolios to assign grades	.91	.92	1.17	.88	-.26
Difficulty of scoring portfolios	1.14	.81	1.27	.82	-.13
Interfering with state or district-mandated curriculum	.97	1.10	.69	.82	.28

Consistent with the pilot one year results, teachers from all types of schools identified time as their primary barrier. Time referred to:

• The amount of teacher time required for planning to use portfolio assessments

• The amount of class time required for implementing portfolio assessments

• The amount of class time needed to construct finished portfolios

• A lack of money to pay for release time for portfolio planning and implementation.

However, teachers from the urban schools were more likely to identify a lack of money to pay for release time for planning and implementing portfolios. Urban school teachers also were more likely to see a lack of materials for constructing portfolios and a lack of money for education opportunities to learn more about portfolio assessment (e.g., workshops, conferences, books, etc.) as problems. These teachers also were more likely to see the portfolio's interference with state- or district-mandated curriculum as a problem. They had more concerns about the ways that portfolios may be used outside of the classroom. Finally, they were more likely to see the use of portfolios as a way to assign grades as a benefit to the use of portfolios.

As expected, teachers did not identify any barriers with respect to the influence of others, such as administrator resistance, curriculum coordinators, parents or teachers. There was a slight resistance identified with students creating portfolios, however not significant. Also, because the philosophy of portfolio assessment is so closely tied to classroom instruction, it was not surprising that teachers did not identify the influence of curriculum and instruction as major barriers to the implementation of portfolios.

Summary

It is clear that a major concern of the teachers that were involved with the project was the amount of time that was required to implement the portfolio system in their classroom. Part of their concern is due to the fact that the project is new – the details of some of the procedures need to be worked out. Another factor is that any time a new procedure is put in place, it takes time to integrate it with existing procedures. Regardless of the cause for the concern about the time needed to implement the portfolio system, the issue needs to be addressed. A goal of the project is to make portfolio use so second nature that teachers and students do not consider it as something extra that needs to be done.

It is interesting, but not surprising, that language arts teachers have the most experience with portfolios. What is more surprising is that science teachers have more experience and are more receptive to portfolios than mathematics teachers. The practical implication of this result is that mathematics teachers will need the most support if they are expected to implement portfolios in their classes.

The major result in the comparison of the responses of urban and nonurban teachers is that most items showed no significant differences in ratings of severity. It was also notable that most responses indicated that not many barriers to implementation were present. The largest differences were related to available resources and to clashes with the required curriculum. Resource issues are a continuing problem in urban schools and it is unlikely that the use of portfolios will solve that problem. The mismatch with the required curriculum is more troubling because the portfolio system was designed with the national curriculum standards as the basis. The response to the curriculum item may indicate that urban schools are less likely to quickly embrace the new curriculum movements.

NINE PRINCIPLES GOVERNING EQUITY IN ASSESSMENTS

Given the purpose of this symposium, it seemed appropriate to evaluate the development effort relative to the nine principles (Nettles & Bernstein, 1995) presented in the book published as a result of the first National Symposium on Equity and Assessment. Each of the Nine Principles is listed below along with a statement about the match of the Portfolio System design process to the principle. While this is not a formal evaluation process, it should provide stimulus for further discussion.

1. New assessments should be field-tested with the nation's diverse population in order to demonstrate that they are fair and valid and that they are suitable for policymakers to use as levers to improve outcomes they are promoting for widespread use by American society.

    For both the seven-school pilot test and the 22-school field test of the portfolio system, schools were recruited to represent the full range of school settings in the country. The schools range from inner-city 100% minority schools to small rural schools. Both parochial and public schools are participating. We believe the requirements of this principle have been met.

2. New standards and tests should accurately reflect and represent the skills and knowledge that are needed for the purposes that they will be used.

    The skills assessed by the portfolio system were selected from an analysis of national curriculum standards and state curriculum frameworks. Since the portfolio system is designed to assess student achievement so as to improve instruction, these skills and knowledge seem appropriate.

3. New content standards and assessments in different fields should involve a development process in which America's cultural and racial minorities are participants.

    Through the selection of the design partner schools, teachers that represent the diversity of the population of the United States have been involved in the design process.

4. New policies for standards and assessments should reflect the understanding that standards and assessments represent only two of many interventions required to achieve excellence and equity in American education. Equity and excellence can only be achieved if all educators dedicate themselves to their tasks and are given the resources that they need.

    The portfolio system is designed to be more than an assessment tool. The system also focuses on in-service programs for teachers and instructional improvement goals. Further, the system provides a support network for educational improvement activities.

5. New standards and assessments should offer a variety of options in the way students are asked to demonstrate their knowledge and skills, providing a best possible opportunity for each student to perform.

The portfolio system is both one of a variety of options and also provides a variety of ways for students to show what they can do within the system. The system is designed to augment other assessments by providing measures of student characteristics that are not covered in other assessments. Through the menu options for defining the portfolios, the assessments can be customized to each educational setting. Finally, the student selects the work that will represent his or her skills. Numerous options are available throughout the process.

6. New standards and assessments should include guidelines for intended and appropriate use of the results and a review mechanism to ensure that the guidelines are respected.

Since the portfolio system is a new assessment tool, the full documentation for the system is not yet available. However, all ACT programs provide guidelines for appropriate use. There is every expectation that the portfolio system will contain such guidelines as well.

7. New policies and assessment should be accompanied by a list of existing standards and assessments that they intend to replace.

As a service that schools must purchase from ACT, there is no means to require that the portfolio system replace any other system. Implementation of this principle is a local choice.

8. New policies need to reflect the understanding by policymakers of the tradeoff between the types of standards and assessments needed for monitoring the progress of school systems and the nation versus the types of standards and assessments needed by teachers to improve teaching and learning. The attention and resources devoted to the former may compete for the limited resources available for research and development of the latter.

Since this principle refers to policymakers, it is unclear whether it applies to the portfolio system. However, every attempt has been made to produce a system that provides both sound assessment information and that supports improvement in instruction. To the extent that the system is successful in achieving the goals stated for it, the portfolio system should make decisions about tradeoffs easier. Perhaps it is possible to support both instructional efforts and assessment in a single program.

9. New policies to establish standards and assessments should feature teachers prominently in the development process.

At every step in the development of the ACT Portfolio System, teachers from the design partner schools have been active participants in the design and review process.

Our review of the match of the developmental process for the ACT Portfolio System and the Nine Principles seems to indicate that the principles have been followed very closely. As the developmental efforts progress, we will continue to follow the spirit of the principles.

References

ACT (1992). *Thinking Skills Measured in ACT's Assessment Programs.* Iowa City, IA: ACT.

Aschbacher, P.R. (1992, November). *Issues in innovative assessment for classroom practice: Barriers and facilitators.* Los Angeles, CA: Center for the Study of Evaluation (ERIC Document Reproduction Service No. ED 355 280)

Elbow, P., & Belanoff, P. (1986). Portfolios as a substitute for proficiency examinations. College *Composition and Communication, 37,* 336-339.

Freedman, S.W. (1993). Linking large-scale testing and classroom portfolio assessments of student writing. *Educational Assessment, 1,* 27-52.

Koretz, D., McCaffrey, D., Klein, S., Bell, R. & Stecher, B. (1993). *The reliability of scores from the Vermont Portfolio Assessment Program* (CSE Technical Report 355). Los Angeles: CRESST.

LeMahieu, P., Gitomer, D. & Eresh, J. (1995). *Portfolios beyond the classroom: Data quality and qualities.* Princeton, NJ: Center for Performance Assessment, Educational Testing Service.

Meyer, C., Schuman, S., & Angello, N. (1990, September). Northwest Evaluation Association white paper on aggregating portfolio data. Portland, OR: Northwest Regional Educational Laboratory.

Mitchell, R. (1992). *Testing for Learning: How new Approaches to Evaluation Can Improve American Schools.* New York: The Free Press.

The National Commission on Testing and Public Policy. (1990). *From Gatekeeper to Gateway: Transforming Testing in America.* Chestnut Hill, MA: Author.

Nettles, M. T. & Bernstein, A. (1995). Introduction: The pursuit of equity in educational testing and assessment. In M. T. Nettles & A. L. Nettles (Eds.) *Equity and Excellence in Educational Testing and Assessment.* Boston: Kluwer.

Reckase, M. (1996, April). *The design and field test of the ACT Portfolio System.* Paper presented at the Annual Meeting of the National Council of Measurement in Education, New York, NY.

6 Fairness and Equity in Measuring Student Learning Using a Mathematics Performance Assessment: Results from the Quasar Project

Suzanne Lane
Edward A. Silver

Performance assessments that have the capability of measuring a broad range of reasoning and thinking skills are considered to be fundamental tools in the educational reform movement (Linn, 1993). They are being used to document the need for educational reform as well as to monitor the impact of reform at the national, state, and local levels. Many advocates of performance assessments are optimistic that these assessments will be sensitive to measuring the impact of educational reform and that the differences in performance on these assessments among ethnic, linguistic, and gender subgroups will be narrower than those observed on multiple-choice tests. Thus, performance assessments are considered by many to be fairer and more equitable assessments of achievement for various subgroups than multiple-choice tests. It is important, however, to ensure that empirical evidence is obtained to support the fairness of the assessment for various subgroups of students.

The fairness of an assessment is closely connected with all sources of validity evidence and therefore, can be conceptualized in various ways. In general, if the inferences that are made from test scores are less valid for some examinees than others, then the fairness of the assessment for some examinees is questionable. Accordingly, ensuring a fair assessment requires evidence to support the appropriateness, meaningfulness, and usefulness of the inferences made from test scores for all students. The collection of evidence to support the fairness of an assessment is not a simple and straightforward endeavor in that the fairness of an assessment can be examined from various perspectives.

Evidence for fairness and equity of performance assessments as defined by narrower subgroup differences has not been forthcoming, despite the optimism of advocates of performance assessments purporting that differences in performance on these tasks among ethnic and linguistic subgroups would be narrower than those observed on multiple-choice tests. Some evidence suggests that the performance differences are about the same regardless of item type (Baker, O'Neil, & Linn, 1991; Bond, 1995; Dunbar, 1987; Dunbar, Koretz, & Hoover, 1991; Feinberg, 1990; Linn, Baker, & Dunbar, 1991) or that they may even be greater for some constructed-response questions (Dossey, Mullis, & Jones, 1993). For example, Linn et al. (1991) indicated that score differences for African-American and Caucasian students on written essays on the NAEP were about the same sizes as those found on multiple-choice reading tests.

These results are not surprising since performance differences on tests are considered by many to be largely a consequence of differences in instructional opportunities (Baker & O'Neil, 1994; Barr & Dreeben, 1983; College Entrance Examination Board, 1985; Darling-Hammond & Snyder, 1991; Oakes, 1990; Resnick, 1990). Accordingly, it cannot be expected that the form of assessment will have a major impact on the quality of performance unless the quality of instruction improves for all students. As Linn (1993) has indicated, performance assessments are not immune to problems of adverse impact. For that reason there is an inherent flaw with this conceptualization of the fairness of an assessment in that the various subgroups may truly differ with respect to what the assessment is measuring because of inequitable access to quality curriculum and instruction. However, if different subgroups of students have access to the same curriculum and instruction, one type of evidence in support of the fairness of the assessment may be similar achievement gains for the different subgroups of students even when the groups' initial performances may differ.

Therefore, in examining the fairness of the assessment, it is important to document the extent to which students have had similar opportunities to acquire the knowledge and skills measured by the assessment. If students have had differential access to the content and skills being assessed as well as differential familiarity with the nature and format of the assessment, differences in performance gains may not be a result of an unfair assessment, but may be a result of differential access to quality instruction and differential familiarity with the nature and format of the assessment.

Another source of evidence for the fairness of an assessment is the extent to which the assessment is free of statistical bias. Bias refers to differential meaning of test scores for any definable, relevant subgroups of examinees due to the test measuring one or more irrelevant components. One procedure for examining statistical bias is differential item functioning (DIF). Differential item functioning refers to items that do not function the same after groups have been matched with respect to the construct being measured (Holland & Thayer, 1986). Differential item functioning is a statistical finding and may not necessarily warrant removal of items that are flagged as DIF when the content quality of the assessment may be jeopardized (Angoff, 1993; Doolittle & Cleary, 1987), but rather items that exhibit DIF may have implications for curriculum and instructional changes (Harris & Carlton, 1993).

PURPOSE OF THE CHAPTER

The purpose of this chapter is to examine the extent to which a mathematics performance is sensitive and fair in measuring students' thinking and reasoning skills regardless of their gender, ethnic, and linguistic backgrounds. This is accomplished by examining the fairness of the assessment from multiple perspectives. The performance gains of various subgroups of students are examined in light of the learning opportunities afforded to these student subgroups. Further, the extent to which students have had similar opportunities to become familiar with the nature and format of the assessment is addressed since the familiarity with the assessment can affect performance. Differential item functioning is also examined to provide statistical evidence for the fairness of the assessment. The examination of the fairness of the assessment from multiple views, rather than a single view, provides a more comprehensive evaluation of the assessment.

The assessment of interest is the QUASAR Cognitive Assessment Instrument (QCAI; Lane, 1993; Silver & Lane, 1993) which was designed to monitor the impact of innovative mathematical instructional programs in schools participating in the QUA-SAR project. The QCAI consists of open-ended tasks that assess students' mathematical problem solving, reasoning, and communication. It was administered in the QUASAR schools since the project began in 1990.

The first section of the chapter provides a brief description of the QUASAR project and the QCAI. The next section examines the extent to which the QCAI is sensitive to measuring changes in students' mathematical thinking and reasoning as a result of the innovative instructional programs that have been implemented at the QUASAR schools. The examination of overall performance gains was considered important in that the students attending the schools are from various ethnic and linguistic backgrounds and such an analyses would provide evidence for the capability of the assessment for measuring change for a diverse group of students. More importantly, this section compares student performance gains on the QCAI for various gender, ethnic, and linguistic subgroups. For the ethnic and linguistic subgroup analyses, comparisons among students are made within a school to ensure that the subgroups compared have had the same access to instruction.

The third section of the chapter examines the differential consequences of the assessment for the schools participating in the project. This was deemed important to study because if the consequences of the assessment differ across schools, students may have had differential exposure to the types of performance tasks on the assessment and as a result, may show differential performance gains. Lastly, the extent to which male and female students differentially respond to the tasks is provided. There is an abundance of studies that have examined gender-related DIF for multiple-choice tests, but few studies have examined it with respect to performance assessments and such evidence would contribute to evaluating the fairness of such assessments.

THE CONTEXT: THE QUASAR PROJECT

The data for this chapter are from the middle schools that participated in the QUASAR (Quantitative Understanding: Amplifying Student Achievement and Reasoning) Project. QUASAR is a national reform project aimed at assisting schools in economically disadvantaged communities to develop instructional programs that emphasize thinking, reasoning, and problem solving in mathematics. QUASAR is based on the premise that prior low levels of participation and achievement for poor urban students were not due primarily to a lack of ability but rather to a set of educational practices that failed to provide them with high-quality mathematics learning opportunities (Silver & Stein, 1996). QUASAR was undertaken to demonstrate the feasibility and responsibility of designing and implementing meaning-oriented, high-level instructional programs in schools that serve such students, students who otherwise would have been exposed to non challenging, procedurally based instruction.

Four middle schools in various geographical locations throughout the country were selected to participate in the QUASAR project in the spring of 1990 and began implementation in the fall of 1990. Two other schools began working with the project in 1991. Two of these six QUASAR schools serve a student population that is predominately African American, two serve primarily a Hispanic student population, and the other two schools serve ethnically diverse student populations. In the two schools that serve primarily a Hispanic student population, the majority of students speak English as their second language.

The mathematics faculty at each school works collaboratively with a resource partner – typically a mathematics educator from a local university—to provide students with instructional practices that promote student engagement with challenging mathematical tasks, student discourse about mathematical ideas, and student involvement in collaborative mathematical activity. The specific programs that have been developed at each school are unique in that they meet local needs and build on their strengths and resources.

QUASAR COGNITIVE ASSESSMENT INSTRUMENT

The QUASAR Cognitive Assessment Instrument (QCAI) is designed to measure student outcomes and growth in mathematics, and to help evaluate attainment of the goals of the mathematics instructional programs at the QUASAR schools (Lane, 1993). The QCAI consists of a set of open-ended tasks that assess students' mathematical problem solving, reasoning, and communication. Throughout the development process, steps were taken to ensure that the QCAI assesses students' knowledge of a broad range of mathematical content, understanding of mathematical concepts and their interrelationships, and capacity to use high-level thinking and reasoning processes to solve complex mathematical tasks (NCTM, 1989). Figure 1 provides an example of a public-released QCAI task.

Figure 1: QCAI Graph Interpretation Task

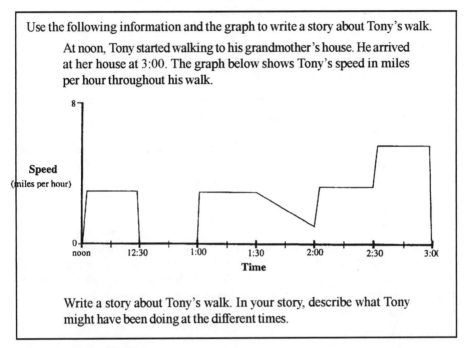

Use the following information and the graph to write a story about Tony's walk.

At noon, Tony started walking to his grandmother's house. He arrived at her house at 3:00. The graph below shows Tony's speed in miles per hour throughout his walk.

Write a story about Tony's walk. In your story, describe what Tony might have been doing at the different times.

Design of the QCAI

The specification of the QCAI includes four major components: mathematical content, cognitive process, mode of representation, and task context. The content areas that were specified are number and operation, estimation, patterns, pre-algebra, geometry, measurement, probability, and statistics. These content areas are crossed by cognitive processes including understanding and representing mathematical problems; discerning mathematical relationships; organizing information; using strategies, procedures, and heuristic processes; formulating conjectures; evaluating the reasonableness of answers; generalizing results; justifying answers or procedures; and communicating mathematical ideas. The types of representations include text, pictorial, graphic, and arithmetic and algebraic expressions. Lastly, some of the tasks are embedded in "real world" contexts, while others are not. The components and categories within the components are interrelated; therefore, the framework allows for an individual task to assess topics in more than one content area and to assess a variety of processes. Lane (1993) provides a more comprehensive discussion of the conceptual framework for the QCAI.

There are two versions of the QCAI: one appropriate for the 6th and 7th grade levels and another appropriate for the 8th grade level. Each version of the QCAI consists of 36 open-ended tasks, which are distributed into four forms, each containing nine tasks (Lane, Stone, Ankenmann, & Liu, 1994). The 8th grade version of the QCAI consists of approximately half the tasks that are in the 6th/7th grade version, and the remaining tasks are unique to the 8th grade version. This allows for longitudinal analyses across 6th, 7th, and 8th grade students. Although the forms in each of the two versions are not considered to be parallel, the tasks were distributed systematically across the forms to help ensure that the forms were as similar as possible with regard to content, processes, modes of representation, context, and difficulty.

Because two of the schools serve predominantly Hispanic or Latino students, a Spanish bilingual version of the QCAI was developed. The Spanish bilingual version of the QCAI presents the English and Spanish version of the task on adjacent pages so that students have the option to read the task in Spanish and/or English and to respond in either language. Lane and Silver (1995) provide more details with regard to the design and administration of the bilingual version of the QCAI.

Administration of the QCAI

The QCAI is administered within one class period (i.e., approximately 40-45 minutes). The data for these studies were from the administration of the QCAI to students in the fall and spring between 1990 and 1995[1]. The sample consisted of approximately equal numbers of male and female students with the following ethnic characteristics: 45% African-American, 31% Latino, 18% Caucasian, and 6% other (e.g., Asian-American, Native-American).

Scoring Student Responses

A focused holistic scoring method was used for scoring the student responses to each task. This was accomplished by first developing a general scoring rubric that reflected the conceptual framework used for constructing the assessment tasks (Lane, 1993). The general scoring rubric incorporates three interrelated components: mathematical conceptual and procedural knowledge, strategic knowledge, and communication. In developing the general scoring rubric, criteria representing the three interrelated components were specified for each of five score levels (0-4).

Based on the specified criteria at each score level a specific rubric was developed for each task. The emphasis on each component for a specific rubric is dependent on the cognitive demands of the task. The criteria specified at each score level for each specific rubric is guided by theoretical views on the acquisition of mathematical knowledge and processes assessed by the task and the examination of the actual student responses to the task.

Student responses were rated by middle school mathematics teachers. The raters scored the student responses after they were formally trained. First, the general rubric was presented and discussed. Then, the specific rubric for a task and pre-scored student responses were presented and discussed. Next, raters practiced scoring student responses individually, and their scores were discussed in relation to scores previously assigned by the QUASAR assessment team. After the formal training session, raters scored the actual student responses. Each response was scored independently by two raters. If the raters disagreed by more than one level, the assessment team rated the student response and it was this score that was used in subsequent analyses.

In addition to scoring the student responses as described above, the responses to some of the tasks were scored using an analytic procedure. This analysis provided information on the types and appropriateness of the strategies used by students, the quality of student explanations and justifications, and the types of misconceptions displayed in student responses.

Validity Evidence for the QCAI

Both logical and empirical validity evidence for the QCAI has been obtained through a number of studies. The construct domain of mathematics, the task specifications, and the scoring rubric specifications were explicitly delineated to ensure that the tasks and scoring rubric reflect the construct domain (Lane, 1993).

Evidence was obtained to support the validity of inferences or generalizations based on the sample of tasks on the QCAI to the more broadly defined domain (Lane, Liu, Ankenmann, & Stone, 1996). The generalizability of the derived QCAI scores was assessed through the use of generalizability theory (Cronbach, Gleser, Nanda, & Rajaratnam, 1972). A task by person-nested-within-school (t x (p:s) generalizability study was conducted on data from each form to examine the extent to which generalizations to the larger domain of mathematics for school level scores are valid. The coefficients for absolute decisions were based on either 100 or 350 students so as to reflect the school with the smallest number of students and the school with the largest number of students at a particular grade level. When the number of students is equal to 350, the generalizability coefficients ranged from .80 to .97 depending upon grade level and form. When the number of persons is equal to 100, they ranged from .71 to .95. These results provide support for using the QCAI to make decisions about schools' absolute scores. It should be noted that all but one school has a least 200 students per grade level.

To examine the generalizability of individual student scores, person x task generalizability studies were conducted for each form. The resulting generalizability coefficients ranged from .71 to .84 when the number of tasks was equal to nine (Lane, Liu, Ankenmann, & Stone, 1996). To examine errors due to potential unreliability of raters, person x task x rater generalizability studies were also conducted. The results of these analyses indicated that the variance components that included the rater source (i.e., rater, rater x person, rater x task, and rater x task x person variance components) were relatively small, suggesting that the use of one rater instead of two or more raters would have very little effect on the generalizability of the scores[2].

EVIDENCE FOR THE FAIRNESS OF THE QCAI

The fairness of the QCAI is examined with respect to the similarity of performance gains for various student subgroups, students' opportunity to become familiar with the nature and format of the assessment as well as to acquire the knowledge and skills measured by the assessment, and gender related differential item functioning.

Performance Gains on the QCAI

Overall performance gains for QUASAR students: Students with diverse ethnic backgrounds. The overall performance gains for students participating in the QUASAR project was examined to establish whether the QCAI, in general, was sensitive in capturing improved performance for a group of students with diverse ethnic and linguistic backgrounds. The analysis of overall changes in student performance was undertaken for the 4 QUASAR schools that began with the project in 1990. Student scores to a set of 11 QCAI tasks that appeared on both the 6th/7th and 8th grade versions of the QCAI and that were administered in each of the years of the project were used for this analysis.

The average percentage of student responses that obtained the two most proficient score levels (3 and 4) was examined over time. Student responses that obtained a level of 4 based on the focused holistic scoring procedure demonstrated correct and complete mathematical understanding of the problem, the use of appropriate solution processes and representations, and coherent, complete mathematical reasoning. Student responses that are not of sufficiently high quality to receive a score level of 4, but contain only a fairly minor error in mathematical knowledge, solution strategy, or reasoning processes would receive a score level of 3.

Student gains were examined for three longitudinal cohorts of students across the five years of the project: 1) Students tested in 6th grade in Fall 1990 and in 8th grade in Spring 1993, 2) Students tested in 6th grade in Fall 1991 and 8th grade in Spring 1994, and 3) Students tested in 6th grade in Fall 1992 and 8th grade in Spring 1995[3]. Across the administrations of the QCAI, the average number of students responding to each task ranged from 613 to 636.

Figure 2 shows the percentage of student responses that were scored at the two highest score levels across the three time periods: 1990-93, 1991-94, and 1992-95. The percentage point difference between the 6th grade student performances in Fall 1990 and 8th grade student performances in Spring 1993 is 26. The percentage point difference between the 6th grade student performances in Fall 1991 and 8th grade student performances in Spring 1994 is 31. The percentage point difference between the 6th grade student performances in Fall 1992 and 8th grade student performances in Spring 1995 is 27.

From these analyses, it is apparent that the QCAI is sensitive to measuring changes in performance from students with a diverse ethnic and linguistic background. Now that the instrument's capability of measuring improved performance has been established, it is necessary to determine if these performance gains are similar for various subgroups of students.

Figure 2

Overall performance gains for OCAI student responses at the two most proficient score levels.

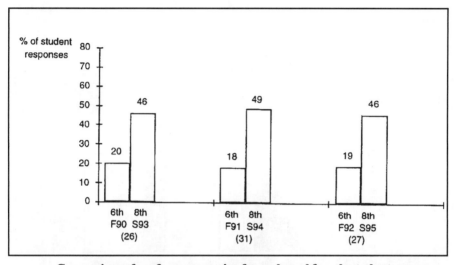

Comparison of performance gains for male and female student responses. Changes in student proficiency for male and female students were examined across the four QUASAR schools that began with the project in 1990. This analysis is based on the premise that if instruction is provided in an equitable manner at each of the schools, male and female students should have the same opportunity to increase their capacity to think and reason mathematically and therefore, demonstrate similar performance gains on the QCAI. If performance gain differences do exist for male and female student responses, the fairness of the assessment may be in question.

Similar to the previous analysis, student scores from the set of 11 QCAI tasks that appeared on both the 6th/7th and 8th grade versions of the QCAI and that was administered in each of the years of the project were used for this analysis. The average percentage of student responses that obtained the two most proficient score levels (3 and 4) was examined for each of the three longitudinal cohorts of students across the five years of the project. Across the administrations of the QCAI, the average number of female students responding to each task ranged from 251 to 329 and the average number of male students responding to each task ranged from 257 to 296.

Figure 3 provides the percentage of female and male student responses that were scored at the two highest score levels across the three time periods: 1990-93, 1991-94, and 1992-95. The percentage point differences between the 6th grade student performances in Fall 1990 and 8th grade student performances in Spring 1993 is 25 for male students and 26 for female students. The percentage point differences between the 6th grade student performances in Fall 1991 and 8th grade student performances in Spring 1994 is 31 for both female and male students. Lastly, the percentage point differences between the 6th grade student performances in Fall 1992 and 8th grade student perform-ances in Spring 1995 is 26 for male students and 27 for female students.

Figure 3

Comparison of performance gains for male and female OCAI student responses at the two most proficient score levels.

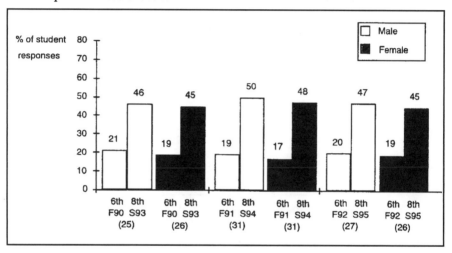

These analyses indicate that although 6th grade female students when they enter middle school were 1 or 2 percentage points below 6th grade male students, the perform-ance gains are similar for female and male students for each of the cohort analyses. Since the male and female students are receiving the same curriculum at each of the schools, these results provide evidence of the fairness of the assessment for both male and female middle-school students in the QUASAR project.

Comparison of performance gains for African American and Caucasian students. The patterns of ethnic distribution of the student population vary across schools. For the four schools that began with the project in 1990, one serves predominantly African-American students, one serves primarily Latino students, and the other two schools have student populations that are internally more ethnically diverse. Since one school serves predominantly African-American students and one serves primarily Latino students, differences detected in progress made by students in ethnic and linguistic sub-groups would be confounded with instructional program differences among the sites, if students from all four schools were included in the analysis. A more appropriate ap-proach is to examine changes in student proficiency for differing ethnic and linguistic subgroups within a school. If instruction is provided in an equitable manner at the school, all students should be expected to have similar learning opportunities. If performance differences are found for ethnic and linguistic subgroups within a school, these differences may suggest differential opportunity to learn and/or differential capacity for the assessment to capture students' mathematical thinking and reasoning.

The analysis of changes in student performance for African American and Caucasian students were undertaken in a school that served both subgroups of students (Lane, Silver, and Wang, 1995). Student scores from the set of 11 QCAI tasks that appeared on both the 6th/7th and 8th grade versions of the QCAI and that were administered in each of the years of the project were used, and the average percentage of student responses that obtained the two most proficient score levels (3 and 4) was examined for the three cohorts of students.

Figure 4 shows the percentage of Caucasian and African American student responses that were scored at the two highest score levels across the three time periods: 1990-93, 1991-94, and 1992-95[4]. At each administration occasion, Caucasians students performed better than African American students. However, the percentage point differences between the 6th grade student performances in Fall 1990 and 8th grade student performances in Spring 1993 is 40 for African American students and 36 for Caucasian students. Although 6th grade Caucasian students performed better than 6th grade African American students in Fall 1990, the Caucasian and African American students had similar gain scores across the first three years of the project.

Figure 4

Comparison of performance gains for African American and Caucasian QCAI student responses at the two most proficient score levels.

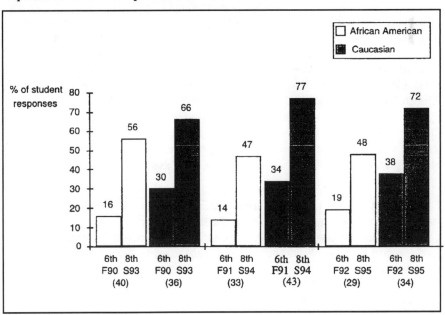

The percentage point difference between the 6th grade student performance in Fall 1991 and 8th grade student performance in Spring 1994 is 33 for African American students and 43 for Caucasian students. The gain score for African American students is 10 percentage points lower than the Caucasian students' gain score during the same time period and is 7 percentage points lower then their own gain score during the 1990-93 period. This lower gain score during the 1991-94 time period for the African American students is due to the lack of progress for 8th grade students in the 1993-94 school year (Lane, Silver, and Wang, 1995). When the 8th grade data are excluded from the analyses the percentage point differences between the 6th grade student performances in Fall 1991 and 7th grade student performances in Spring 1993 are 31 for Caucasian students and 32 for African American students. Thus, the performance gains are similar for African American and Caucasian 6th and 7th grade students during the 1991-93 time period.

The lack of gain for 8th grade African American students during the 1993-94 year appears to be due to differential opportunity to learn from the curriculum and instruction across the classes in this particular school. In order to afford more students an opportunity to take a course in Grade 8 with a clear focus on algebra, the 8th grade curriculum at this school was more differentiated in 1993-94 than in the previous year. Four 8th grade classes were designated as algebra classes, and they studied a conceptually rich curriculum intended to develop algebraic thinking and reasoning. An unfortunate consequence of this decision to create four sections of algebra at Grade 8 was that the non-algebra classes tended to contain a large percentage of students who had been less successful with challenging mathematical tasks in the past (Smith, personal communication, October 1994).

An examination of the ethnic composition of the classes receiving these two different curricula provides a likely explanation for the poorer performance gain for the 8th grade African American students, since 68% of the Caucasian 8th grade students were in the classes that were more challenging and only 30% of the African American students were in those classes. Thus, the poorer performance gains made by 8th grade African American students is likely explained by the fact that the majority of 8th grade African American students did not have the same educational opportunity as the majority of the Caucasian 8th grade students. Teachers at the school commented at the end of that year that they were disappointed in the differentiated instruction that occurred in the two sets of 8th grade classes and decided to group students heterogeneously and blend algebraic material into the curriculum for all 8th grade classes in the 1994-95 year.

The percentage point difference between the 6th grade student performance in Fall 1992 and 8th grade student performance in Spring 1995 is 29 for African American students and 34 for Caucasian students. The difference between the gap between the Caucasian students' gain score and the African American students' gain score is smaller for this cohort than the 1991-94 cohort. Although the gain score for African-American students is somewhat smaller than the gain score for Caucasian students for the 1992-95 cohort, the gain score for 8th grade African American students is similar to the gain score for Caucasian students in the 1994-95 year. Thus, the schools' effort of grouping 8th grade students heterogeneously and blending algebraic material into the curriculum for all 8th grade classes in 1994-95 benefited the 8th grade African American students.

The evidence suggests that the QCAI is capable of capturing performance gains for both African American and Caucasian students. For the first cohort analysis (1990-93), the performance gains for the African-American student responses were slightly larger than the performance gains for the Caucasian student responses. For the second cohort analysis (1991-94), the performance gains for the 6th and 7th grade African American and Caucasian student responses were similar and as previously mentioned, the lower performance gain for the 8th grade African American student responses as compared to the 8th grade Caucasian student responses was most likely due to differences in learning opportunities. For the third cohort analysis (1992-95), the 8th grade performance gains for the Caucasian and African American student responses were similar, indicating that the 8th grade curriculum and instructional changes that were made in the school now benefited both the African American and Caucasian students. The performance gains for the 6th and 7th grade African American student responses, however, were slightly lower than the performance gains for the 6th and 7th grade Caucasian student responses. Based on initial discussions with teachers at the school, there appears to be no readily apparent reason for these differences. A more in-depth examination of potential reasons for these differences is needed.

In general, these analyses provide evidence that the QCAI is capable of capturing performance gains for both African American and Caucasian students. Further, these analyses of performance gains for ethnic subgroups of students have highlighted the need to examine potential differences in learning opportunities for various groups of students when one investigates the fairness of an assessment. The results of these analyses may be influenced not only by the learning opportunities afforded to the two groups, but also the nature of the samples. First, the sample sizes were relatively small for these analyses. Across the administrations of the QCAI, the average number of Caucasian students responding to each task ranged from 19 to 25 and the average number of African American students ranged from 7 to 9. However, not each student responded to each task because each student received only one of the four forms and the 11 tasks were distributed across the four forms. Thus, the total number of students used in each analysis is about four times the average number of students responding to each task. Secondly, approximately half of the students tested in the spring of Grade 8 in these cohorts were not in the sample in the fall of Grade 6. Thus, the instability of the relatively small samples may have had an impact on the results for any one cohort analysis.

Comparison of performance gains for students in English-speaking classes and bilingual classes. The analysis of changes in student performance for students in English-speaking classes and bilingual classes was undertaken in a school that served both subgroups of students. The teacher for the bilingual classes instructed in both Spanish and English and students in the bilingual classes used both Spanish and English to communicate their mathematical thinking and reasoning. It should be noted that over 80% of the Latino students were in the bilingual classes.

Student scores from the set of 11 QCAI tasks that appeared on both the 6th/7th and 8th grade versions of the QCAI and that were administered in each of the years of the project were used for this analysis. The average percentage of student responses that obtained the two most proficient score levels (3 and 4) was examined for the three longitudinal cohorts of students across the five years of the project. Across the administrations, the average number of students in English-speaking classes who responded to each task ranged from 37 to 48 and the average number of students in Spanish-speaking classes who responded to each task ranged from 5 to 9. It should be noted that over 80% of the Latino students were in bilingual classes.

Figure 5 shows the percentage of student responses for the English-speaking and bilingual classes that were scored at the two highest score levels across the three time periods: 1990-93, 1991-94, and 1992-95. The percentage point differences between the average 6th grade student performance in Fall 1990 and average 8th grade student performances in Spring 1993 is 31 for bilingual classes and 26 for English-speaking classes. Although 6th grade students in bilingual classes were, on average, 6 percentage points below students in the 6th grade English-speaking classes in the Fall 1990, the average for 8th grade students in bilingual classes was only 1 percentage point below the average for 8th grade students in English-speaking classes in the Spring 1993.

Figure 5

Comparison of performance gains on the QCAI at the two most proficient score levels for English-speaking classes and bilingual classes.

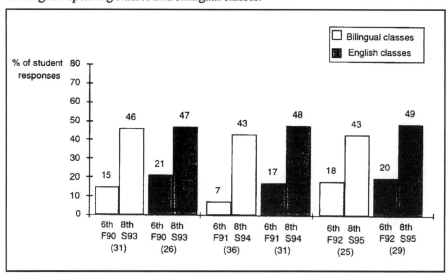

The difference between the 6th grade student performance in Fall 1991 and 8th grade student performance in Spring 1994 is 36 percentage points for bilingual classes and 31 percentage points for English-speaking classes. Although the 6th grade students in the bilingual classes were, on average, 10 percentage points behind the 6th grade students in the English-speaking classes in the Fall 1991, the 8th grade students in the bilingual classes were only 5 percentage points behind the 8th grade students in the English-speaking classes in Spring 1994.

The difference between the 6th grade student performance in Fall 1992 and 8th grade student performance in spring 1995 is 25 percentage points for bilingual classes and 29 percentage points for English-speaking classes. The 6th grade students in the bilingual classes were, on average, 2 percentage points behind the 6th grade students in the English-speaking classes in the Fall 1992. Unfortunately, the 8th grade students in the bilingual classes were 4 percentage points behind the 8th grade students in the English-speaking classes in Spring 1995.

The percentage point gains for the students in the bilingual classes were 5 percentage points higher than the students in the English-speaking classes for both the 1990-93 and 1991-94 time period; whereas, the percentage point gains for the students in the bilingual classes were 8 percentage points lower than the students in the English-speaking classes for the 1992-1995 time period. This poorer performance gain for the students in the bilingual classes in the 1992-95 time period may be a result of changes in the teaching staff for the bilingual classes. There was one bilingual teacher for the 6th, 7th, and 8th grade classes from Fall 1990 to Spring 1993. This bilingual teacher, however, was not at the school during the 1993-95 period and was replaced by different teachers each of those two years, and in the 1993-95 time period the least gain was made by students in the bilingual classes.

Overall, these analyses indicate that the QCAI is capable of capturing performance gains for bilingual and English-speaking students. The Spanish bilingual version of the QCAI presents the English and Spanish version of the task on adjacent pages so that students have the option to read the task in Spanish and/or English and to respond in either language (Lane & Silver, 1995). Validity evidence for the use of the QCAI with students from various ethnic and linguistic backgrounds was collected continuously and systematically as the instrument was being developed, administered, and refined. Thus, the way in which the instrument was developed and administered may have contributed to the fairness of the instrument for measuring performance gains for both English-peaking and bilingual students. Further, the quality of instruction provided by the bilingual teacher most likely contributed to the higher performance gains for the bilingual student responses in the first (1990-93) and second (1991-94) cohort analyses than in the third cohort analysis (1992-95). As indicated, the performance gains for the student responses from the bilingual classes were lower when the bilingual teacher left the school in 1993 and was replaced by other bilingual teachers.

Relationship Between Familiarity with the QCAI and Student Learning

The extent to which students have had the opportunity to acquire the knowledge and skills measured by an assessment may be related to the fairness of the assessment. If students have had differential access to the content and skills being assessed as well as differential familiarity with the nature and format of the assessment, the fairness of the assessment and/or learning opportunities may be questionable for some groups of students. Therefore, it is important to examine the extent to which students are familiar with the nature and format of the performance assessment.

The relationship between various consequences of the QCAI and changes in student proficiency were examined for the 1992-95 period (Parke, Lane, & Guo, 1995; Lane & Parke, 1996). Student performance gains for each of the four QUASAR schools that began with the project in 1991 were compared to the school's consequential evidence of the QCAI. The data sources for collecting evidence of the impact of the QCAI were teacher, principal, and resource partner interviews; videotapes of staff development sessions and teacher/resource partner meetings; and school artifacts such as classroom assessments and end-of-year reports.

Data from these sources were categorized into the following categories for each school: 1) teacher understanding of the QCAI criteria and what constitutes good mathematics performance; 2) student understanding of the QCAI criteria and what constitutes good mathematics performance; 3) changes in classroom assessment practices; 4) changes in the curriculum; 5) changes in instructional practices; 6) teacher and resource partner knowledge of the impact of the instructional program on student learning; 7) school administrators, district personnel, parents, and community knowledge of the QCAI and the impact of the instructional program on student performance and learning; and 8) leverage for financial support for the instructional program[5].

Performance gains were computed based on the scores that were assigned to each student response to the 11 QCAI tasks that appeared on both the $6^{th}/7^{th}$ and 8th grade version of the QCAI and that were administered in the five years of the project. The average percentage of student responses across tasks that were scored at the two most proficient score levels (3 or 4) was examined over time. The average percentage of high-level scores (3's and 4's) on 6th grade student responses in the fall of 1991 was compared with the average percentage of high-level scores on 8th grade responses in Spring 1994.

The results indicated a general relationship between student performance gain and the number and nature of the positive consequences of the QCAI. For the school with the highest student performance (34 percentage points), the impacts of the QCAI that were related to the teachers were quite numerous and varied; whereas, for the school that had the lowest performance gain (18 percentage points) the impacts were few for the teachers. For example, teachers in the school with the highest performance gain indicated that they used a variety of QCAI results and related materials (e.g., scoring rubrics, scored student responses, and public release tasks) individually or in teacher groups to help improve the curriculum, instruction, and classroom assessment as well as to gain a better understanding of the impact of the instructional programs on student performance and learning. Teachers in the school with the lowest performance gain did not indicate that they used the materials individually or in teacher groups. Moreover, teachers in the school with the highest performance gain were the only teachers that reported using the results from the QCAI reports to inform personnel in other schools and parents about the QCAI and the impact the instructional program had on student performance and learning. The number and variety of consequences for the teacher in the two schools with moderate learning gains (each with 27 percentage point gains) were between the school with the highest gain and the school with the lowest gain.

In evaluating the consequences of an assessment, Messick (1992) has argued that the focus should not be solely on the consequences of the assessment, but the consequences on the system as a whole. Further, in examining the fairness of an assessment it is important to evaluate the extent to which equitable opportunities are being provided to students. If inequitable opportunities are afforded to students, it would then be reasonable to expect differential performance gains. In these regards it is important to further examine the impact that the QUASAR project has had on the nature of the instructional activities at each of these schools.

Stein and Lane (1996) examined the relationship between student performance gains on the QCAI and the level of cognitive demands required by instructional tasks used in the classrooms[6]. They found that the school with the highest student performance gain had an instructional task profile characterized by high percentages of tasks set up by the teachers at a high level of cognitive demand, and then, for the most part, implemented by the students at a high level. By contrast, the school with the lowest student performance gain had an instructional task profile characterized by almost half the tasks set up by the teachers at a high level of cognitive demand and the other half set up at a low level of cognitive demand. Further, this school had the highest percentage of tasks implemented by the students at a procedural level. The two schools with moderate student performance gains had an instructional task profile characterized by high percentages of the tasks set up at a high level of cognitive demand with a tendency for tasks to be implemented by students at lower levels. Thus, the schools maintain the same relative position when examining student performance gains, instructional task profiles, and the nature of the consequences of the QCAI.

A variety of other factors may affect student performance gains and the nature of the consequences of the QCAI at the schools. For example, the school with the lowest performance gain had the highest turnover rate with respect to teachers, resource partners, and principals. This may have made it more difficult to implement an innovative instructional program effectively as compared to the other schools which have had more stability with respect to the teachers, resource partners, and principals. The school with the highest performance gain has had the same curriculum implemented in the classrooms since the beginning of the project; whereas, the other three schools either began the project without a curriculum in place or changed the curriculum within the project years. Thus, there are a number of factors that may have contributed to the differential consequences of the QCAI as well as the differential performance gains across schools.

Gender-Related Differential Item Functioning

The extent to which an assessment is free of statistical bias provides another source of evidence for the fairness of the assessment. Differential item functioning is a statistical procedure that is commonly used to evaluate the extent to which items function similarly for various subgroups of students at the same achievement levels. There has been an abundance of research examining gender-related differential item functioning (DIF) in mathematics for students who typically receive traditional forms of instruction, but there are few studies that have examined the extent to which gender differences are exhibited when students have had the opportunity to receive instruction that focuses on high-level mathematical thinking and reasoning. Differential item functioning needs to be examined among male and female students as they begin to have the opportunity to receive instruction that focuses on reasoning and problem-solving. Such studies require the use of performance assessments that measure students' mathematical problem solving and reasoning.

Because most of the studies that have examined gender-related DIF in mathematics performance involved the use of multiple-choice items, in-depth analyses of differences in male and female students' thinking and reasoning have not been undertaken in these studies. With the increased use of open-ended mathematics items, the opportunity now exists to examine more directly differences in male and female student performances with respect to their thinking and reasoning not only with respect to the features of tasks. The examination of gender-related DIF in mathematics performance assessments for students who are afforded quality mathematics instructional experiences may have important implications for designing and implementing innovative mathematics assessments, curriculum, and instruction.

Lane, Wang, and Magone (1996) examined gender-related differential item functioning on the QCAI using logistic discriminant functional analysis (Miller & Spray, 1993). The data analyzed in their study were from the administrations of the QCAI in all six QUASAR schools in the Spring of 1993 and the Spring of 1994[7]. Students received a different form of the QCAI on each administration. The number of students who responded to each form in the Spring of 1993 ranged from 469 to 506 and the number of students who responded to each form in the Spring of 1994 ranged from 468 to 528.

It should be noted that it was not appropriate to conduct DIF analyses for ethnic and linguistic subgroups of students. As previously indicated, the patterns of ethnic distribution of the student population vary across schools. Two schools serve predominantly African-American students, two serve primarily Latino students, and the other two schools have student populations that are internally more ethnically diverse. Since two schools serves predominantly African-American students and two serve primarily Latino students, any detection of DIF for students in ethnic and linguistic subgroups would be confounded with instructional program differences among the schools. Accordingly, DIF was only examined for gender since there was approximately an equal number of male and female students in each school.

For those items that were flagged as DIF, cognitive analyses of the student responses were conducted in order to examine differences between male and female students with respect to their thinking and reasoning. The results from these analytic analyses of the student responses were examined with respect to the criteria of the scoring rubrics. This provided information on whether particular criteria in the scoring rubrics contributed to gender-related differential item functioning. Only a few of analytic analyses will be discussed in this chapter[8].

The results indicated that out of the 42 open-ended assessment tasks, four tasks favored female students and two tasks favored male students with respect to uniform DIF[9]. The two tasks that favored male students were in the content areas of geometry and ratio/proportion. Both of the tasks included a figure and required students to show their solutions, but neither task required a written verbal response. The four tasks that favored female students were in the content areas of number sense, estimation, patterns, and ratio/proportion. As indicated, for the two ratio and proportion tasks that were flagged as DIF, one favored female students and the other favored male students. It is important to indicate that the task that favored female students is an easier task than the one favoring male students in that an appropriate solution strategy is more readily apparent. Moreover, for these two tasks in order to receive one of the two most proficient score levels students need to explicitly show their solution strategies.

The analytic analysis for the easier ratio and proportion task indicated there was not a significant gender difference with respect to selecting an appropriate solution strategy nor obtaining the correct numerical answer; however, there was a significant gender difference with respect to the amount of work shown, with male students showing less work than female students. Thus, it appears that a critical aspect that is contributing to gender-related DIF on this relatively easy task is related to the extent to which male and female students were providing their work.

The ratio and proportion task that favored male students is more difficult and an appropriate solution strategy is less apparent than it is for the easier ratio and proportion task. For the more difficult ratio and proportion task there was also a significant difference for the amount of work shown, with female students providing more work. Although not significant, for those students who showed their work, a larger percentage of male students (47%) than female students (34%) used an appropriate solution strategy and a larger percentage of male students (30%) than female students (19%) obtained the correct numerical answer. Although male students were less likely to show their work, when they did, their work demonstrated the use of an appropriate strategy more often than females.

The number sense task that favored female students required an explanation for the students' numerical answer. The analytical analysis indicated that although a larger percentage of female than male students executed their solutions successfully and provided the correct numerical answer it was not significant. However, there was a significant difference with respect to provided conceptual explanations, with female students providing more conceptual explanations that male students. This result is consistent with research that has indicated that females more often than males use written accounts of their mathematical solutions (Fennema & Tartre, 1985; Tartre, 1990).

Research has indicated that male students as compared to female students perform better on tasks that are set in a real world context (e.g., Harris & Carlton, 1993; O'Neil & Mcpeek, 1993); however the four tasks that favored female students were set in a real world context. In fact, the majority of the tasks on the QCAI are set in a real world context which reflects the current thinking in the mathematics education reform movement. Moreover, the nature of the instruction at these schools places an emphasis on mathematics thinking and reasoning, and being able to "do" mathematics in real world contexts. The context of the problem may not have been related to DIF because both male and female students in this study have had the opportunity in their classrooms to solve applied problems that are set in a realistic context. Thus, some of the features that have been associated with gender-related DIF in mathematics may not hold when the studies involve the use of performance assessments and students who have instructional opportunities that focus on reasoning and problem solving.

On the other hand, features that are unique to performance assessments may contribute to gender-related DIF. In this study, male students as compared to female students may have been at a disadvantage on a few tasks because they were not as complete in showing their solution strategies nor in providing explanations for their numerical answers. As previously mentioned, differential item functioning is a statistical finding and detection of DIF may not necessarily indicate that the items should be removed from the assessment, but rather items that exhibit DIF may have implications for curriculum and instructional changes. Additional studies examining gender-related DIF on mathematics performance assessments are needed to determine the extent to which the results in the present study are generalizable. Such studies are needed prior to making firm statements about the fairness of particular open-ended assessment tasks to male and female students or about what the implications may be for curriculum and instruction.

CONCLUSION

There are multiple sources of evidence that should be considered when one evaluates the fairness of an assessment. For an assessment that is designed to monitor the impact of instructional programs on student learning, the examination of the extent to which different subgroups of students demonstrate similar performance gains contributes to establishing the fairness of the assessment. The QCAI was designed for such a purpose and the results presented in this chapter indicate, in general, that students from various gender, ethnic, and linguistic backgrounds performed similarly when they had equitable access to quality curriculum and instruction.

This chapter emphasized the importance of not only examining performance gains, but also the importance of examining the relationship between performance gains and learning opportunities in order to establish the extent to which an assessment is fair. The results presented indicated that performance gains were related to the quality of instruction provided to students as well as to students' familiarity with the nature and content of the performance assessment. For example, consider the analysis that compared the performance gains of African American and Caucasian students in one of the QUASAR schools. The 8th grade African American students' performance gains were similar to the 8th grade Caucasian students' performance gains when they were provided with the same challenging curriculum as the Caucasian students, but when they did not have access to the more challenging curriculum and instruction their performance gains were lower than the performance gains of the Caucasian students. This analysis demonstrated that the fairness of an assessment can not solely be evaluated in terms of differences in performance outcomes of various subgroups of students, because such outcomes are dependent on the quality and nature of the opportunities provided to students.

The fairness of an assessment can also be examined in terms of the extent to which the items function differently for subgroups of students when subgroups are matched with respect to the construct being measured. Differential item functioning was detected for a small number of the QCAI items: Four of the 42 items favored female students and two of the items favored male students. An analytic analysis of the student responses to a subset of these items indicated that female students provided more conceptual explanations than male students for one item and that male students were less complete in providing their solution strategies for two items. Additional studies are needed to determine the extent to which these findings based on a small number of tasks are generalizable to other mathematics performance tasks and student populations. If similar findings are obtained in other studies, the fairness of particular tasks for male and female students may not necessarily be in question, instead such findings may have direct implications for the way in which male and female students are instructed.

In summary, several interpretations of fairness have been adopted in this chapter: Equitable access to instructional opportunities, similar performance gains for various subgroups of students when given equitable access to such opportunities, and the lack of differential item functioning. Analyses based on other interpretations of fairness, such as fairness in the design of tasks and scoring rubrics and fairness in scoring student responses, are also important[10]. It was not the intent of this chapter, however, to provide evidence related to all aspects of the fairness of the assessment, but rather the intent was to demonstrate the importance of considering multiple interpretations of fairness in testing.

References

Angoff, W.H. (1993). Perspectives on differential item functioning methodology. In P. W. Holland & H. Wainer (Eds.), *Differential item functioning*. Hillsdale, NJ: Lawrence Erlbaum.

Baker, E.L., O'Neil, H.F., & Linn, R. L. (1991). *Policy and validity prospects for performance-based assessment*. Paper presented at the annual meeting of the American Psychological Association.

Barr, R., & Dreeben, R. (1983). *How schools work*. Chicago: University of Chicago Press.

Bond, L. (1995). Unintended consequences of performance assessment: Issues of bias and fairness. *Educational Measurement: Issues and Practice, 14*(4), 21-24.

Cai, J., Magone, M. E., Wang, N., & Lane, S. (1996). A cognitive analysis of QUASAR's mathematics performance assessment tasks and their sensitivity to measuring changes in middle-school students thinking and reasoning, *Research in Middle Level Education, 19*(3), 63-94.

College Entrance Examination Board (1985). *Equality and excellence: The educational status of Black Americans*. New York: Author.

Cronbach, L.J., Gleser, G.C., Nanda, H., & Rajaratnam, N. (1972). *The dependability of behavioral measurement*. New York: Wiley.

Darling-Hammond, L., & Snyder, J. (1991). Traditions of curriculum inquiry: The scientific tradition. In P. Jackson (Ed.), *Handbook of research on curriculum*. New York: Macmillan.

Dossey, J.A., Mullis, I.V.A., & Jones, C.A. (1993) *Can students do mathematical problem solving?: Results from constructed-response questions in NAEP's 1992 mathematics assessment*. Washington, D.C.: National Center for Educational Statistics.

Doolittle, A.E. & Cleary, T.A. (1987). Gender-based differential item performance in mathematics achievement items. *Journal of Educational Measurement, 24*(2), 157-166.

Dunbar, S.B. (1987, April). *Comparability of indirect measures of writing as predictors of writing performance across demographic groups*. Paper presented at the annual meeting of the American Educational Research Association, Washington, DC.

Dunbar, S.B., Koretz, & Hoover, H.D. (1991). Quality control in the development and use of performance assessments. *Applied Measurement in Education, 4*, 289-304.

Feinberg, L. (1990, Fall). Multiple choice and its critics. *The College Board Review*, No. 157.

Fenema, E., & Tartre, L. (1985). The use of spatial visualization in mathematics by girls and boys. *Journal for Research in Mathematics Education, 16*. 184-206.

Harris, A.M., & Carlton, S.T. (1993). Patterns of gender differences on mathematics items on the Scholastic Aptitude Test. *Applied Measurement in Education, 6*(2), 137-151.

Holland, P.W., & Thayer, D.T. (1986). *Differential item performance and the Mantel-Haenszel procedure*. (Research Report No. 86-31) Princeton: Educational Testing Service.

Lane, S. (1993). The conceptual framework for the development of a mathematics performance assessment, *Educational Measurement: Issues and Practice, 12*(2), 16-23.

Lane, S., Liu, M., Ankenmann, R. D., & Stone, C. A., (1996). Generalizability and validity of a mathematics performance assessment. *Journal of Educational Measurement, 33*(1), 71-92.

Lane, S., & Parke, C. (1996). *Consequences of a mathematics performance assessment and the relationship between the consequences and student learning*. Paper presented at the annual meeting of the National Council of Measurement in Education, N.Y.

Lane, S., Parke, C., & Moskal, B. (1992). *Principles for developing performance assessments*. Paper presented at the annual meeting of the American Educational research Association, San Francisco, CA.

Lane, S., & Silver, E.A. (1995). Equity and validity considerations in the design and implementation of a mathematics performance assessment: The experience of the QUASAR project. In M. T. Nettles and A.L. Nettles (Eds.) *Equity and Excellence in Educational Testing and Assessment*, pp. 185-220.

Lane, S., & Silver, E.A. (April 1994). *Examining students' capacities for mathematical thinking and reasoning in the QUASAR project*. Paper presented at the annual meeting of the American Educational Research Association, New Orleans.

Lane, S., Silver, E.A., & Wang, N. (April 1995). *An examination of the performance of culturally and linguistically diverse students on a mathematics performance assessment within the QUASAR project.* Paper presented at the annual meeting of the American Educational Research Association, San Francisco.

Lane, S., Stone, C.A., Ankenmann, R.D., & Liu, M. (1995). Examination of the assumptions and properties of the graded item response model: An example using a mathematics performance assessment. *Applied Measurement in Education, 8*(4), 313-340.

Lane, S., Stone, C.A., Ankenmann, R.D., & Liu, M. (1994). Reliability and validity of a mathematics performance assessment. *International Journal of Educational Research, 21*(3), p. 247-266.

Lane, S., Wang, N., & Magone, M. (in press). Gender related differential item functioning on a middle school mathematics performance assessment: The use of an analytical analysis of student performance to complement a statistical DIF procedure. *Educational Measurement: Issues and Practice.*

Linn, R. L. (1993). Educational assessment: Expanded expectations and challenges. *Educational Evaluation and Policy Analysis, 15*(1), 1-16.

Linn, R. L., Baker, E. L., & Dunbar, S. B. (1991). Complex, performance-based assessment: Expectations and validation criteria. *Educational Researcher, 20*(8), 15-21.

Magone, M. E., Cai, J., Silver, E. A., & Wang, N. (1994). Validity evidence for cognitive complexity of performance assessments: An analysis of selected QUASAR tasks. *International Journal of Educational Research, 21*(3), 317-340.

Messick, S. (1989). Validity. In R. L. Linn (Ed.), *Educational Measurement* (3rd ed.) (pp. 13-104). New York: American Council on Education.

Miller, T.R., & Spray, J.A. (1993). Logistic discriminant function analysis for DIF identification of polytomously scored items. *Journal of Educational Measurement, 30*(2), 107-122.

National Council of Teachers of Mathematics (1989). *Curriculum and evaluation standards for school mathematics.* Reston, VA: Author.

Oakes, J. (1990). *Multiplying inequalities: The effects of race, social class, and tracking on opportunities to learn mathematics and science.* Santa Monica: RAND Corporation.

O'Neill, K. A., & McPeek, W.M. (1993). Item and test characteristics that are associated with differential item functioning. In P.W. Holland & H. Wainer (Eds.), *Differential item functioning,* Hillsdale, NJ: Lawrence Erlbaum Associates.

Parke, C., Lane, S., & Guo, F. (April 1995). *The consequential validity of a performance assessments in a mathematics education reform project.* Paper presented at the annual meeting of the National Council of Measurement in Education, San Francisco.

Resnick, L. B. (1990, October). *Assessment and educational standards.* Paper presented at the Office of Educational Research and Improvement Conference, The Promise and Peril of Alternative Assessment, Washington, DC.

Silver, E.A., & Lane, S. (1993). Assessment in the context of mathematics instruction reform: The design of assessment in the QUASAR project. In M. Niss (Ed.), *Assessment in mathematics education and its effects* (pp. 59-70). London: Kluwer Academic.

Silver, E. A., & Stein, M. K. (1996). The QUASAR project: The "revolution of the possible" in mathematics instructional reform in urban middle schools. *Urban Education, 30*(4), 476-521.

Smith, M. (October 1994). Personal communication.

Stein, M. K., Grover, B. W., & Henningsen, M. (1996). Building student capacity for mathematical thinking and reasoning: An analysis of mathematical tasks used in reform classrooms. *American Educational Research Journal, 33*(2), 454-488.

Stein, M.K., & Lane, S., (1996). Instructional tasks and the development of student capacity to think and reason: An analysis of the relationship between teaching and learning in a reform mathematics project. *Educational Research and Evaluation, 2*(1), 50-80.

Tartre, L. (1990). Spatial skills, gender and mathematics. In E. Fennema, & G. Leder (Eds.), *Mathematics and gender,* (pp. 27-59). New York: Teacher's College Press.

Endnotes

[1] The QCAI was administered in both the fall and Spring of the 1990-91, 1991-92, 1992-93 instructional years and only in the spring of the 1993-94 and 1994-95 instructional years. Each student received a different form of the QCAI on each administration. The forms were randomly distributed with each class in the schools participating in QUASAR in the fall of 1990, and thereafter each student received a different form on each administration occasion. The use of this sampling approach allows for the assessment of students in a relatively short time frame, thereby it keeps interruptions to the instructional process minimal; minimizes the occurrence of practice effects; avoids the problems associated with sampling only a small number of tasks; and affords valid generalizations about students' mathematical proficiency at the school level.

[2] Additional empirical evidence for the validity, generalizability, dimensionality, and scaling of the QCAI is reported in Lane, Liu, Ankenmann, & Stone (1996) and Lane, Stone, Ankenmann, & Liu (1995). Evidence was also collected to ensure that the tasks evoked cognitively complex performances and can be found in Lane, Parke, & Moskal (1992); Magone, Cai, Silver, & Wang (1994); and Cai, Magone, Wang, & Lane (1996).

[3] Due to high rates of student turnover, which are typical for schools located in poor urban communities, the cohort groups described for this analysis are not "true" cohorts. Of the students tested in the spring of Grade 8 in these cohorts, approximately half were not in the sample in the fall of Grade 6. Lane and Silver (1994) examined the performance of "true" cohorts and found that they achieved greater gains than the overall gains reported for the entire sample of students. Thus, the inclusion of all tested students in the analyses reported here is likely an underestimate of student gains.

[4] The analysis for the first two cohorts is reported in Lane, Silver, & Wang (1995).

[5] Based on the information in the transcribed interviews Lane and Parke categorized the consequences for each school independently and the interrater agreement was 88%. The discrepancies were examined by referring back to the interviews and in all cases an agreement was reached as to the placement of the consequence.

[6] This study was an extension of a study conducted by Stein, Grover, and Henningsen (in press) who found that the majority of instructional tasks in a representative sample of QUASAR project classrooms required students to think and reason and to use multiple solution strategies, multiple connected representations, and explanations.

[7] The mean scores for the forms are similar for male and female students and range from 1.20 and 1.73, and the standard deviations range from .78 to .96.

[8] Lane, Wang, and Magone (1996) provide a more thorough discussion of the analytic analyses.

[9] A total of 42 tasks were included in the analysis because between the two administrations some of the tasks were released and consequently, replaced by new tasks.

[10] Lane and Silver (1995) examine the fairness of the QCAI in terms of the design of tasks and scoring rubrics, the administration of the assessment, and the scoring of student responses.

7 Improving the Equity and Validity of Assessment-based Information Systems

Zenaida Aguirre-Muñoz
Eva L. Baker

This chapter focuses on issues of validity and equity of assessments as they guide educational policies and practices for the education of limited English proficient students. Although estimates of the number of students who are English language learners (ELLS) vary, from self-reports in the 1990 census (U.S. Bureau of the Census, 1990) to surveys conducted of school districts (Fleischman & Hopstock, 1993), their proportion is rising and may reach 10% by the end of the century. Although Spanish is the primary language for about three fourths of these students, Asian group languages – Vietnamese, Hmong, Cantonese, Cambodian, Tagalog, Laotian and Korean – are represented in large numbers. Navajo and Russian are also significantly represented.

The case of limited English proficient students is particularly instructive, for illustrates the unprecedented challenge posed by the educational reforms of the 1990s: the simultaneous call for higher standards of performance in content areas and the inclusion of children of all backgrounds in the reform movement. Although this expanded set of requirements may be regarded by some as little more than optimistic rhetoric, state and federal legislation has been enacted to create policies and practices intended to raise the attainment of limited English proficient children. The challenge is twofold: to change the perceptions of the public and teaching personnel so that these goals may be accepted; and to achieve the twin goals of increased attainment and expanded reach.

In the case of students who are not fluent in English, the situation is complicated by diverse public perceptions on the use of primary language in school. At the heart of much of the discussion is the role of language in student achievement and the expectation by a majority of the public that learning English should be a priority. Controversy exists, for instance, on the degree and length of time of maintenance of primary language in instruction. There is also a strong basic education movement in some sectors of the public, exemplified by the pressure for computationally oriented mathematics and phonics-based reading programs. These advocates take the position that the education system should demonstrate that it can teach children fundamentals before it tackles higher standards and more ambitious goals. The great success of the American system, its retention of more students through high school, is also its downfall, for the lack of demonstrable skills for many of these students is unacceptable. As the proportion rises of students in school who have home languages other than English, pressure increases for better approaches to teach and assess their learning.

Our focus is not on the desirability or relative empirical merits of bilingual, immersion, or other approaches to develop language proficiency in English. In education, there are rarely main effects. Instead, we address the problem of assessing students in content areas other than English in order to determine their levels of attainment in the subject matter. Even an approach that assists children to display mathematics competence without unnecessary language interference, for example, is controversial. But putting aside for the moment the problem of public credibility, there is considerable difficulty in meeting the technical challenge of assessment, and we must trust the results of tests if we are to act upon them.

The technical attributes of assessments, especially approaches to make them fair and accessible to student who are not fully competent in English, are of great interest nationally. Since 1990, the U.S. teaching and assessment communities have been intensely exploring new forms of assessments, and the form of these assessments greatly complicates the problem of testing in other than native languages. The newer, performance-based assessments require longer tasks, more complex cognitive processing, and deeper subject matter knowledge. They also require elaboration or explanation typically displayed through speaking or writing. These assessments are thought to be a major method to operationalize higher expectations for American children and youth. In their design, they consolidate new knowledge about student learning processes, subject matter expectations, and extrapolations from analyses of examination systems abroad. They also add new demands for students who are learning English.

Requirements for assessments of challenging content are embodied in legislation designed to impact disadvantaged children, the Elementary and Secondary Education Act (1965), Improving America's Schools Act (IASA, 1994). This legislation also requires that children who have not yet developed English competency be included in the evaluations of schools that receive federal funding. Moreover, in an effort to include students whose performance has not been reported in the past, the policies clarifying the IASA provisions require that assessment of student progress be accomplished using, where indicated, linguistically appropriate assessments for English language learners (ELLs) – students whose native language is not English and who demonstrate low English proficiency (see Section 200.1, 200.4 Exec. Order No. 12866, 1995). Although the decision of which type of assessment to administer is largely left to local school districts, many are using combinations of multiple-choice and performance tests to meet these requirements.

Performance assessments by design require both linguistic and content-related skills for their successful completion. For native speakers of English, differences in performance among different groups of students exist because of differences in familiarity, exposure to the content of the test, instruction, and motivation to complete the task (Linn, Baker, & Dunbar, 1991). ELLs have an added difficulty, as the language on the test may place them at a disadvantage (Baker & O'Neil, 1996).

The extent and nature of the impact of language skills on performance assessments remains elusive due to the paucity of research in this area. However, lessons can be learned from what is known about the impact of language skills on standardized test scores. Studies that explored the impact of language background on standardized test scores have found three factors affecting ELLs' test performance. These include: (a) limited second-language skills (Figueroa, 1990), (b) limited background knowledge of the implicit meaning of the text within a test (Haffier & Ulanoff, 1994), and (c) limited access to content-specific knowledge, such as assignment into classes with narrow curricular coverage (as argued by the work of Oakes, 1990, and Stanovich, 1991).

The first two factors influencing ELLs' test performance involve linguistic factors that provide the basis for the accommodation requirements in the IASA legislation. High-quality procedures are not available to assist in identifying students who should receive linguistic support during testing. The typical approach is to administer some measure of English language proficiency. Yet many widely used English proficiency measures have weak validity and reliability data (see Zehler, Hopstock, Fleischman, & Greniuk, 1994, for a list of reviews). These measures often lack clear construct definition, adequate scoring directions, and high-quality norms. In some cases, such as with the Bilingual Syntax Measure, validity information is not reported at all (Valdes & Figueroa, 1995). In a recent summary of research progress in the area of inclusion (Olson & Goldstein, 1997), Cheung, Clements, and Miu were reported to have documented a wide range of methods to identify and monitor ELLs' progress, including the review of archival records, home language surveys, observations, and interviews (1994, as cited in Olson & Goldstein, 1997). Yet, Hopstock and Bucaro (1993) report that 83% of local districts used English language proficiency testing to determine, in whole or in part, students with English language limitations.

Even if English proficiency identification were perfect, there would be a need to provide tests that enable ELLs who do not pass an English proficiency test to display their competence in school subjects. Why are linguistic accommodations necessary when one assesses ELLs' content understanding with complex performance assessments? Two issues related to the cognitive demands of performance assessments are important to note. First, the design of most performance assessments demands higher levels of understanding of content-specific language, or academic knowledge (conceptual as well as factual information). Attempts to assess ELLs' content understanding may result in underestimating their knowledge. Unlike basic conversational English, there is convincing empirical evidence indicating that the ability to use English for academic purposes takes several years (approximately 5 to 7 years) to develop (see Collier, 1987, 1989). While this academic language is developing, students will need help in demonstrating their knowledge acquisition, a point to be expanded upon in the next section. This situation is exacerbated by the curriculum access issue. If lower performing students are less apt to receive complex curricula, ELLs are less likely to be exposed to the academic language necessary to do well on complex performance assessments. Therefore, not only is it important to identify students appropriately and to provide ELLs with linguistic accommodations in testing situations, it is also necessary to interpret and account for educational experiences, particularly the amount and quality of content coverage and the availability of instructional resources.

LANGUAGE DEVELOPMENT ISSUES

Knowledge about second language acquisition is essential in the development of a system of linguistic accommodations directed at varying levels of English proficiency. Scholars interested in language learning generally agree that the developmental processes of primary language (L1) and second language (L2) acquisition are interrelated. The debate lies in the extent to which one language influences the other and in the methods used to measure their interrelatedness (Ascher, 1991).

Many educators and policy makers believe that children's control over the surface features of English (their fluency in conversational English) is a sufficient indicator of all aspects of English proficiency (Cummins, 1980, 1994). Once the child exhibits mastery over conversational English, efforts are made to place the child in an English-only classroom. This misunderstanding of English proficiency has had a great impact on the organization of bilingual educational programs in the U.S. In one major school district, for example, a student is placed in an English-only program if she passes an oral English test. Exiting the bilingual program is also primarily based on an oral proficiency measure.

This practice is problematic in many ways. First, it reduces English proficiency to the oral command of the language. Oral proficiency is necessary but not sufficient for educational achievement. Second, this practice suggests that conversational proficiency and academic language proficiency are synonymous. There is growing evidence that academic success is also tied to cognitive academic language proficiency (academic proficiency), also known as the cognitive demands of communication (e.g., Collier, 1987; Cummins, 1981; Wong-Fillmore, 1991), and has a different developmental trajectory.

The third concern is related to the development of academic language proficiency. Conversational English has been found to take only 2 to 3 years to master (Cummins, 1980; Gonzalez, 1986). Most bilingual programs transition students to English instruction in the third or fourth grade. Academic English proficiency, on the other hand, is acquired in approximately 5 to 7 years, depending on when the child enters the school system (Collier, 1987; Cummins, 1981). Placing ELLs in an instructional setting where English is the only form of instruction may not allow the students sufficient time to develop the academic language skills necessary for educational success.

Cummins (1994) argues that there are two principal reasons why there are major differences in the length of time needed to acquire conversational and academic language proficiency. In conversation, the learner utilizes contextual cues to facilitate the communication of meaning, cues that are largely absent in most academic settings that depend on decontextualized literacy skills and manipulation of language for successful task completion. Cummins (1994) uses an interesting example to illustrate the impact of linguistic cues:

> a cohesive device such as *however* coming at the beginning of a
> sentence tells the proficient reader (or listener) to expect some
> qualification to the immediately preceding statement. Lack of
> experience with or sensitivity to such linguistic cues will reduce
> students' ability to interpret meaning in decontextualized set-
> tings where interpersonal or non-linguistic cues are lacking. (p. 10)

Traditional assessment situations, in most instances, represent the most decontextualized contexts. Even performance assessments that attempt to provide intrinsic meaning in their assessment tasks may be decontextualized and cognitively taxing in large-scale contexts, for it is difficult for on-demand assessments to present the contextual cues found in interpersonal communicative situations. Given that most on-demand performance assessments also involve a great amount of English reading and writing, underestimates of students' content understanding are likely unless particular steps are taken to support linguistic task demands.

What factors facilitate the acquisition of academic proficiency? Based on her review of the literature, Collier (1989) proposed several generalizations about optimal age, Ll cognitive development, and L2 academic achievement. Cognitive development of Ll appears to be necessary for L2 academic language proficiency for both communicative and academic purposes regardless of age and number of hours of second language instruction. (See Collier, 1989 for review of literature.) Collier also found compelling evidence supporting the claim that negative cognitive effects in L2 acquisition are likely if Ll development is discontinued before it is complete. It is therefore reasonable to assume that L2 learning, particularly the learning of academic language, is dependent on the nature and level of Ll development (Saville-Troike, 1991).

Given the interrelatedness of Ll and L2 proficiency in academic contexts, it may also be necessary to determine the extent to which Ll proficiency impacts achievement on complex performance assessments. Information from such analysis may be useful when considering accommodation strategies for ELLS.

ACCOMMODATION STRATEGIES

The term *accommodation* denotes an adjustment to be made to the testing situation to allow the test taker to display more adequately his or her competency. The National Center for Educational Outcomes (NCEO; 1995) categorized accommodations offered for students with disabilities into four categories:

accommodations related to (a) timing, (b) setting, (c) response format, and (d) presentation. Common accommodations for students with special needs involve modifying the testing conditions, so that more time, for example, may be available for students who have difficulty in reading. In a survey of testing practices, all but 7 states report that they provide accommodations for ELLS, and 36 states permitted ELL exclusion if it is judged that the student has insufficient English competence to respond to the test (Bond et al., 1996). Seventeen states reported language accommodations of the following type: separate scheduling and testing settings, multiple or extended testing opportunities, and small-group administration. Linguistic supports were reported by some states: simplification of directions (11 states), audiotaped instructions or questions (9), use of dictionaries (9), audiotaped responses (4), other languages (4), and an alternative test (3) (CCSSO/NCREL, 1996). Expanding upon the NCEO and CCSSO/NCREL categories, let us consider a continuum of accommodation anchored at one end by students responding unaided to English language assessments and at the other, by students excluded from the testing situation.

Table 1

Continuum of Accommodations for English Language Learners

Standard Examination: and response formats	Comparable materials, setting, conditions, instructions,
Modified Setting:	Reduced distractions by administering test alone, in carrels, or in small groups
Modified Time:	Extended testing period
Modified Directions:	Simultaneous oral directions in English; simplified English directions; non-verbal supports in directions (pictures & schematics); translated directions into L1; bilingual directions provided in writing and/or orally; demonstration of sample item
Multiple Trials:	Permitting more than one administration opportunity
Adapted Test Materials:	Dictionaries or special-purpose glossaries; simplification or partial translation (key words or concepts); fully translated stimulus materials, including texts, problems; culturally adapted materials, using comparable content
Response Options:	Oral response in English; written response in English; written Spanish response; oral Spanish response; supplement to written response by oral explanation
Modifications in Scoring and Interpretation:	Special scoring procedure rubrics, adjustments; special identification of students receiving accommodations
Combinations:	Incorporating one or more adjustment or accommodation

The foregoing list pertains to tasks that are intended to be the same for all students, that is, a written response to a provided poem, a set of mathematical word problems using one unknown, or the completion of a science experiment according to specified procedures. Using these accommodations creates a series of concerns related to validity and its important subset, fairness. To begin, there is the need to determine and logically weight the advantage provided to the student against at least two factors. First, the testing authority needs to consider the cost of including the student by involving multiple accommodations against the risk of excluding the child. In order to make a better decision, at least two pieces of information should be considered. One is the degree of proficiency in English, in order to determine whether relatively minor accommodations will suffice. There is no reason to provide a full range of accommodations that take additional time and that separate students from their peers if only modest assistance is needed. In addition, the students' L1 proficiency should be known. One of the most needed diagnostic devices is a tool to establish L1 proficiency for ELLs. There is no sense in administering fully translated test materials if the student has low levels of L1 literacy.

Second, the use of combinations of accommodations raises the question of comparability of results for a given test taker. If test results are normed, the likelihood is small that results will be directly interpretable if multiple accommodations are used for a given student. In the case of norms available for translated or bilingual versions, it is incumbent upon the testing authorities to determine that the norming group is appropriate for interpreting the results of the tested students. Norming for these tests may be based on calculations from tests administered in English or on tests administered in other countries (e.g., Mexico or Spain). This assumes that the population of students in those countries is similar to the population of students in the United States and that the contexts are also comparable (Figueroa, 1990; Valdes & Figueroa, 1995). Even when norming data for U.S. populations is available for students with Spanish-language backgrounds, they are less likely to be at hand for students from many other language backgrounds.

Related to interpreting performance with respect to norms is the more global issue of validity. Even when norms are not used, there is a question of validity – that is, whether it can be demonstrated that the same construct has been measured by accommodated forms, and whether it can be shown that factors irrelevant to the construct are not intruding in the estimates of student competence. No easy solutions exist to these problems, particularly for performance tasks where explanation and elaboration are intrinsic parts of performance. Similarly, validity inferences may be compromised for tasks that in themselves are based in relatively sophisticated language skills, whether they involve encoding (i.e., reading comprehension; analysis of historical, literary, or scientific text) or the construction and expression of competence in writing and speaking.

Validity interpretations also become particularly troublesome if modifications in scoring rubrics are made. The difficulty of demonstrating that the measures are assessing the same construct in such cases is formidable and unlikely to be realized on the schedule needed for regular assessment of progress. Finally, there is the question of credibility of results and the perception of fairness. Students who are not provided accommodations (such as extended time, dictionaries, or oral directions) may perceive themselves at a disadvantage. Students who are provided accommodations may not wish to have their records marked to indicate that special adjustments in testing materials or conditions were provided.

RESEARCH ON ACCOMMODATIONS

Published studies that examine the impact of linguistic factors on performance assessment scores are few. This work is concentrated in classroom-level assessments (e.g., Pierce & O'Malley, 1992; Rosebery, Warren, & Conant, 1992) and therefore provides strategies that are not feasible for large-scale testing. Nevertheless, the demand for alternative assessments has grown among language and content educators who want more accurate measures of their students' knowledge (LaCelle-Peterson & Rivera, 1994; Short, 1993). Educators who want to measure students' content knowledge are faced with the difficulty of disentangling linguistic factors from content knowledge, as well as dealing with the problem of extensive variation in language proficiency.

One study that directly examined the effects of linguistic complexity of test items on ELLs' test performance was conducted by CRESST on NAEP math items (Abedi, 1994). Although NAEP items are not performance assessments, this study is noteworthy in that it attempted to identify and modify specific linguistic features of test items that may contribute to content-irrelevant difficulties ELLs often encounter. In the first phase of this study, the linguistic complexity of the 1992 NAEP items was examined. ELLs' test scores were lower than other students and the differences were greater for those items identified as being more linguistically complex. In this part of the study, students were also asked to complete background questionnaires. Abedi found that students who reported that they received English as a Second Language (ESL) instruction had considerably lower math scores than other students. No significant differences were found between this group and other students on other background variables such as socioeconomic status. Although the exact nature of the impact of language on performance was indeterminate, these findings provide evidence for the assertion that the language of test items may contribute to underestimates of ELLs' content knowledge.

In the second phase of this study, one linguistic accommodation was tested, the simplification of linguistic features contained in the items. Students who enrolled in average- and low-level mathematics courses and who received the standard version of the math assessment scored significantly lower than those who received the linguistically modified version. Differences were found across categories of ethnicities; however, when the type of mathematics class was statistically controlled, these differences were not significant. A hierarchical linear modeling analysis was then conducted; interesting patterns emerged. Language-related variables were shown to be more effective than the model with the original item score as the outcome variable. These patterns, however, did not reach statistical significance.

The lack of significance was attributed to three limitations. The first limitation is related to the limited number of NAEP items available for the study. Subscale analyses could not be conducted in this field test because only 10 items were used and the p values indicated that some of these items were either too difficult or too easy. Moreover, they did not obtain a good range of the types of linguistically complex items and the range of linguistic features that would be more desirable for this type of study. The third limitation was the variation in how students were classified as ELLs. School district information about students' language background was also incomplete, outdated, or invalid in many instances.

BEYOND ACCOMMODATION

It is possible that manipulating surface features of tests and making minor modifications of test conditions are the best that can be accomplished with the present state of the art. Nonetheless, we believe that for these approaches to be successful, substantial problems of interpretation, practicality, and credibility need to be overcome. As an alternative, we propose an approach that moves beyond accommodations to a consideration of theories related to knowledge representation and cognitive structure as a strategy to address the task of assessing students from varied language backgrounds. We will consider expert-novice distinctions and the use of concept maps as an additional strategy to assessing ELLs' subject matter understanding.

KNOWLEDGE REPRESENTATION

Underlying the assessment framework for our proposal are theories of knowledge representation, including mental models, schema theory, and structural knowledge. Representing knowledge in memory is tied to how knowledge is encoded, organized, and integrated into existing knowledge structures. Mayer (1984), for example, describes three cognitive processes necessary for meaningful learning: selection, organization, and integration. The selection of relevant information is the first process learner must employ. Individuals must then organize this information into a knowledge structure that binds together the pieces of information. In the final integration stage, individuals must make connections between new information and relevant existing information.

Mental models

Mental models are another way of conceptualizing the representation of knowledge. Mental models are defined as learner-constructed models or structures that are based on existing knowledge. The importance of previously acquired knowledge implies that the construction of mental models is contingent upon the existence of one's individual experiences. The ability to retrieve relevant information and to apply this knowledge to novel situations is also necessary in the construction of mental models (Seel, 1995). Mental models are created when the learner wants to better understand new objects or events (Norman, 1988; Seel, 1995). Moreover, they can simplify learning by allowing an individual to assimilate incoming information with existing knowledge (Seel, 1995).

Schema theory

Schema theory also describes how information is organized and represented and how cognitive structures facilitate the use of knowledge (Glaser, 1984; Rumelhart, 1980). The term "schema" (Bartlett, 1932) has been defined generally as a mental structure that represents some set of related information (Anderson, 1984; Rumelhart, 1980) and is used to interpret new, related experiences. Educational theorists who adhere to this knowledge-based model of human cognition contend that knowledge is organized into structures known as schemata (or schemas) and posit that the form and content of all new knowledge is in some way shaped by our prior knowledge (Anderson, 1984; Brewer & Nakamura, 1984). Students, for example, bring their *cultural* schema to the study of civilizations. They have certain expectations concerning the kinds of information a history *culture* map contains and the types of questions a culture map can answer.

Rumelhart and Norman (1981) regarded schemata as specialized cognitive networks that have been accumulated through experience and are used to carry out daily tasks. These cognitive networks are viewed as the instruments that organize and relate both declarative knowledge (i.e., factual and conceptual knowledge) and procedural knowledge (i.e., the cognitive activities necessary for integration of knowledge) (Anderson, 1984). New schemata are created when an individual compares existing schemas with new information (Rumelhart, 1980). In this process schemata are modified to reflect the novel experiences.

For example, when a child learns about democratic principles in her 5th grade social studies class, a schema is constructed about democracy that is strictly tied to the American democratic model (as the American model is generally emphasized at this grade level). In the 7th grade, this student studies the Roman Empire and learns that some of the American democratic principles have been modeled after ideas taken from the Romans. From these situations, the child builds a new schema that accommodates the novel perceptions that are at variance with her previous information about democracy. As an individual encounters more examples of the same concept, the pieces of information that comprise the schema become more integrated, and, as well more generalized (Brown, Kane, & Ehols, 1986; Holyoak, Junn, & Billman, 1984). Thus, schemas that comprise our store of prior understanding provide the basis for comprehending, remembering, and learning information (Rumelhart, 1980).

Structural knowledge

Structural knowledge, although defined in many ways, refers to a form of knowledge representation (Jonassen, Beissner, & Yacci, 1993). Whereas schemas organize declarative and procedural knowledge, structural knowledge refers to knowing how the concepts within a domain are interrelated (Diekhof, 1983, as cited in Jonassen, Beissner, and Yacci, 1993). Schema theory posits that human memory is organized semantically and that schemas, by definition, are organized into (semantic) networks of interrelated concepts. Jonassen, Beissner, and Yacci (1993) argue that these semantic networks are representations of structural knowledge. These structures contain and invoke related knowledge about a concept together with the situations where such knowledge can be used. The challenge in assessment contexts is to design assessments that both elicit a student's structural knowledge and allow the test taker to accurately convey his or her knowledge structure.

An important body of research is the work that demonstrates differences between experts and novices in cognitive structure. This research has influenced examinations of cognitive structure. For instance, considerable evidence exists that demonstrates that experts represent their knowledge in deeper, principled patterns and have flexible and generalized knowledge structures (Chi, 1985; Chi & Ceci, 1987; Chi & Koeske, 1983; Chi, Glaser, & Farr, 1988). The flexibility of their knowledge structures allows experts to encode new information more quickly than novices (Chase & Simon, 1973; Wineburg, 1991a, 1991b). In contrast, the knowledge structures of novices tend to focus on surface features and contain more superficial relationships between concepts (e.g., Chi, 1985; Chi & Glaser, 1983; Chi, Glaser, & Farr, 1988). As novices become experts, their knowledge structures begin to resemble expert knowledge structures in their level of integration and abstraction as well as their degree of organization (Royer, Cisero, & Carlo, 1993).

Concept mapping task

One alternative to essay construction as a measure of conceptual understanding is a schematic representation, commonly called a concept map. Concept maps are designed to be less discourse-dependent. Although studies that directly examine this assertion have not been conducted, there is some evidence indicating that students' knowledge may be underrepresented by their performance on multiple-choice tests or essays (Baker, Niemi, Gearhart, & Herman, 1990). This situation is particularly true for ELLs.

Concept maps emerged from research on structural knowledge (Jonassen, Beissner, & Yacci, 1993; Rumelhart & Norman, 1988; Rumelhart & Ortony, 1977) and thus purport to represent a student's knowledge structure in a given domain (see section on knowledge structures). A concept map is a graph of a given content domain (or subset thereof) consisting of nodes that represent important concepts or ideas and labeled links that depict the relationship between a pair of concepts (nodes).

Early research with concept maps was originally designed to elicit learning strategies in students (e.g., Anderson, 1979; Anderson & Armbruster, 1981; Dansereau & Holley, 1982) and has since then demonstrated its usefulness in instructional and assessment settings (e.g., Herl, Niemi, & Baker, 1996; Horton, McConney, Gallo, Woods, Senn, & Hamelin, 1993; Lambiotte & Dansereau, 1991; Novak 1995; Ruiz-Primo, Schultz, & Shavelson, 1996).

In recent years, there has been a growing interest in the use of concept maps in assessment settings. Lomask, Baron, Greig, & Harrison (1992), for example, used teacher-constructed maps from student essays and judged them on the basis of their match with expert maps. Training teachers to draw concept maps from student essays has a practical advantage for large-scale contexts in that students did not have to be trained to draw their own maps. However, this practice raises cognitive-theoretical and methodological issues concerning the student's structural representation (Shavelson, Lang, & Lewin, 1994).

A more common procedure for map construction involves paper-and-pencil tasks that ask students to construct their own map. Herl, Niemi, and Baker (1996), for example, instructed 11th grade U.S. history students enrolled in general and Advanced Placement courses to construct concept maps on the Great Depression and compared them to concept maps generated by experts in the field. Herl et al. found that experts performed higher than either of the two student groups and had higher structural scores (a measure of the similarity between clusters of concepts in a semantic network) than either group. A similar pattern was found between Advanced Placement students and students enrolled in general history courses.

When researchers interpret the scores of concept maps, issues related to comparability should be considered. Comparability of administration conditions refers to the additional demands placed on the test administrator that emerge from the performance task (e.g., group work, experimentation, etc.). Concept mapping represents a response modality, and a set of cognitive demands that reduce the dependence upon complex discourse. However, at the outset, concept mapping tasks may pose greater variability in administration because this kind of task includes an instructional lesson, and more questions are likely to arise due to the novelty of the task. How the test administrator handles student questions is largely left to the individual, thereby increasing variability in testing administration.

The key test will be whether concept mapping introduces or restricts construct-irrelevant variance. If test takers do not possess the necessary ancillary or enabling skill requirements of a given performance task, a test can be said to be biased if particular groups of "examinees are deficient in a test's ancillary abilities" (Haertel, & Linn, 1996, p. 63). Ancillary abilities refers to the set of skills or abilities required for successful completion of a task that are not explicitly part of what is to be assessed. Among these skills are students' understanding that it is important to show their best work; their willingness to do so; ability to understand the task requirements; and their mastery of the communication skills necessary to produce measurable responses (Haertel, & Linn, 1996; Linn, Baker, & Dunbar, 1991).

Ability to understand the task requirements and mastery of communication skills are critical areas when we test ELLs in English. To the extent that concept maps are dependent on English, scores for ELLs may not be comparable to scores for native speakers of English because the relative contributions of distinct ancillary abilities to the construct measured may depend on the language background of the test taker (Haertel, & Linn, 1996). We believe that there are ways to provide stimulus materials in forms that maintain their cognitive complexity and avoid bias. Nonetheless, our hunches are vastly insufficient to recommend an approach. Research is under way to determine the extent to which language background characteristics impact scores on concept maps and other forms of performance assessments, to assess the feasibility of the application of a concept-mapping approach to ELLs, and to determine whether valid inferences of ELLs' content understanding can be drawn from their scores on performance assessments.

References

Abedi, J. (1994). *Language background as a variable in NAEP Mathematics performance: NAEP TRP Task 3d: Language background study.* Los Angeles: University of California, National Center for Research on Evaluation, Standards, and Student Testing.

Anderson, T. H. (1979). Study skills and learning strategies. In H. F. O'Neil. Jr., & C. D. Spielberger (Eds.), *Cognitive and affective learning strategies.* New York: Academic.

Anderson, J. R. (1984). Spreading activation. In J. R. Anderson & S. M. Kosslyn (Eds.), *Essays in learning and memory.* New York: W. H. Freeman & Company.

Anderson, T. H., & Armbruster, B. B. (1981). Studying. In P. D. Pearson (Ed.), *Handbook on reading research.* New York: Longman.

Ascher, C. (1991). Testing bilingual students: Do we speak the same language? *PTA Today*, March.

Baker, E. L., Niemi, D., Gearhart, M., & Herman, J. (1990). *Validating a hypermedia model of knowledge representation.* Paper presented at the annual meeting of the American Educational Research Association, Boston.

Baker, E. L., & O'Neil, Jr., H. F. (1996). Performance assessment and equity: A view from the USA. [CD-ROM]. *CRESST: 5 Years of Research.* Los Angeles: University of California, Center for the Research on Evaluation, Standards, and Student Testing.

Bartlett, F. C. (1932). *Remembering: A study in experimental and social psychology.* New York: Cambridge University.

Bond, L. A., Council of Chief State School Officers, & North Central Regional Educational Laboratory. (1996). *Statewide assessment of students with disabilities.* Oak Brook, IL: North Central Regional Educational Laboratory.

Brewer, W. F., & Nakamura, G. V. (1984). *The nature and function of schemas* (Tech. Rep. No. 325). Cambridge, MA: Bolt, Beranek and Newman. (ERIC Document Reproduction Service No. ED 248291)

Brown, A. L., Kane, M. J., & Echols, C. H. (1986). Young children's mental models determine analogical transfer across problems with a common goal structure. *Cognitive Development, 1*(2),103-121.

Chase, W. G., & Simon, H. A. (1973). Perception in chess. *Cognitive Psychology, 4*,55-81.

Cheung, O., Clements, B., & Miu, Y. C. (1994). *The feasibility of collecting comparable national statistics about students with LEP.* Washington, DC: National Center for Education Statistics.

Chi, M. T. (1985). Interactive roles of knowledge and strategies in the development of organized sorting and recall. In S. F. Chipman, J. W. Segal, & R. Glaser (Eds.), *Thinking and learning skills, Volume 2: Research and open questions.* Hillsdale, NJ: Lawrence Erlbaum Associates.

Chi, M. T., & Ceci, S. J. (1987). Content knowledge: Its role, representation, and restructuring in memory development. *Advances in Child Development and Behavior, 20,* 91-143.

Chi, M. T., & Glaser, R. (1983). The measurement of expertise: Analysis of the development of knowledge and skill as a basis for assessing achievement. In E. L. Baker, & E. S. Quellmalz (Eds.), *Educational testing and evaluation: Design. analysis, and policy.* Beverly Hills, CA: Sage.

Chi, M. T., Glaser, R., & Farr, M. J. (1988). *The nature of expertise.* Hillsdale, NJ: Lawrence Erlbaum Associates.

Chi, M. T., & Koeske, R. D. (1983). Network representation of a child's dinosaur knowledge. *Developmental Psychology, 19* (1),29-39.

Collier, V. P. (1987). Age and rate of acquisition of second language for academic purposes. *TESOL Quarterly, 21,* 617-641.

Collier, V. P. (1989). How long? A synthesis of research on academic achievement in a second language. *TESOL Quarterly, 23*(3), 509-532.

Council of Chief State School Officers and North Central Regional Educational Laboratory. (1996). *1996 State student assessment programs database.* Oak Brook, IL: North Central Regional Educational Laboratory.

Cummins, J. (1980). Entry and exit fallacy in bilingual education. *NABE Journal, 4*(3), 25-59.

Cummins, J. (1981). Age on arrival and immigrant second language learning in Canada: A reassessment. *Applied Linguistics, 2,* 132-149.

Cummins, J. (1994). Primary language instruction and the education of language minority students. In C. F. Leyba (Ed.), *Schooling and language minority students: A theoretical approach.* Sacramento, CA: Evaluation, Dissemination and Assessment Center, School of Education California State University, Los Angeles.

Dansereau, D. F., & Holley, C. D. (1982). Development and evaluation of a text mapping strategy. In A. Flammer & W. Kintsch (Eds.), *Discourse processing*: Amsterdam: North Holland.

Diekhoff, G. M. (1983). Testing through relationship judgments. *Journal of Educational Psychology, 75,* **227-233.**

Elementary and Secondary Education Act of 1965., 20 U.S.C. §§ 236 *et seq.,* 821 *et seq.*

Exec. Order No. 12866, 34 C. F. R. 200, 201, 203, 205, and 212 (1995).

Figueroa, R. A. (1990). Assessment of linguistic minority group children. In C. R. Reynolds & R. W. Kamphaus (Eds.), *Handbook of psychological and educational assessment of children: Intelligence and achievement.* New York: Guilford.

Fleischman, H. L., & Hopstock, P. J. (1993). *Descriptive study of services to limited English proficient students, Volume 1: Summary of findings and conclusions.* Arlington, VA: Development Associates, Inc.

Glaser, R. (1984). Education and thinking: The role of knowledge. *American Psychologist, 30,* 93-104.

Gonzalez, L. A. (1986). *The effects of first language education on the second language and academic achievement of Mexican immigrant elementary school children in the United states.* Doctoral dissertation submitted to the University of Illinois at Urbana-Champaign.

Haertel, E. H., & Linn, R. L. (1996). Comparability. In G. W. Phillips (Ed.), *Technical issues in large-scale performance assessment* (pp. 59-78). Washington, DC: U.S. Department of Education, Office of Educational Research and Improvement.

Hafner, A. L., & Ulanoff, S. H. (1994). Validity issues and concerns for assessing English learners: One district's approach. *Education-and-Urban-Society. 26*(4), 367-89.

Herl, H. E., Niemi, D., & Baker, E. L. (1996). Construct validation of an approach to modeling cognitive structure of experts' and novices' U.S. history knowledge. *Journal of Educational Research, 89*(4), 206-218.

Holyoak, K. J., Junn, E. N., & Billman, D. 0. (1984). Development of analogical problem solving skill. *Child Development, 55*(6), 2042-2055.

Horton, K. J., McConney, A. A., Gallo, M., Woods, A. L., Senn, G. J., & Hamelin, D. (1993). An investigation of the effectiveness of concept mapping as an instructional tool. *Science Education, 77*(1), 95-111.

Hopstock, P. J., & Bucaro, B. J. (1993). *A review and analysis of estimates of the LEP student population.* Arlington, VA: Development Associates, Special Issues Analysis Center.

Improving America's Schools Act of 1994, Pub. L. No. 103-382, 108 Stat. 3518 (1994).

Jonassen, D. H., Beissner, K., & Yacci, M. (1993). *Structural knowledge: Techniques for representing, conveying, and acquiring structural knowledge.* Hillsdale, NJ: Lawrence Erlbaum Associates.

LaCelle-Peterson, M. W. & Rivera, C. (1994). Is it real for all kids? A framework for equitable assessment: Policies for English language learners. *Harvard Educational Review, 64*(1), 55-75.

Lambiotte, J. G., & Dansereau, D. F. (1991). Effects of knowledge maps and prior knowledge on recall of science lecture content. *Journal of Experimental Education, 60*(3), 189-201.

Linn, R. L., Baker, E. L., & Dunbar, S. B. (1991). Complex, performance assessment: Expectations and validation criteria. *Educational Researcher 20*(8), 15-21.

Lomask, M., Baron, J., Greig, J., & Harrison, C. (1992). *ConnMap: Connecticut's use of concept mapping to assess the structure of students' knowledge of science.* Symposium presented at the annual meeting of the National Research in Science Teaching; Cambridge, Massachusetts.

Mayer, R. E. (1984). Aids to prose comprehension. *Educational Psychologist, 19*(1), 30-42.

National Center on Educational Outcomes. (1995). *Compilation of state's guidelines for accommodations in assessments for students with disabilities* (Synthesis Report 18). Minneapolis, MN: Author.

Norman, D. A. (1988). *The psychology of everyday things.* New York: Basic Books.

Novak, J. D. (1995). Concept mapping: A strategy for organizing knowledge. In S. M. Glynn & R. Duit, (Eds.), *Learning science in the schools: Research reforming practice.* (p. 229-245). Mahwah, NJ: Lawrence Erlbaum Associates.

Oakes, J. (1990). *Multiplying inequalities: The effects of race, social class, and tracking on opportunities to learn mathematics and science.* Santa Monica, CA: Academic.

Olson, J. F., & Goldstein, A. A. (1997). *The inclusion of students with disabilities and limited English proficient students in large-scale assessments.* Washington, DC: U.S. Government Printing, Office.

Pierce, L. V., & O'Malley, J. M. (1992). Performance and portfolio assessment for language minority students. *NCBE Program Information Guide Series, 9.*

Royer, J. M., Cisero, C. A., & Carlo, M. S. (1993). Techniques and procedures for assessing cognitive skills. *Review of Educational Research, 63*(2), 201-243.

Rosebery, A. S., Warren, B., & Conant, F. R. (1992). Appropriating scientific discourse: Finding from language minority classrooms. *The Journal of the Learning Sciences, 2*(1), 61-94.

Ruiz-Primo, M., Schultz, S. E., & Shavelson, R. J. (1996). *Concept map-based assessments in science: Two exploratory studies* (CRESST deliverable to OERI). Los Angeles: University of California, Center for the Research on Evaluation, Standards, and Student Testing.

Rumelhart, D. E. (1980). Schemata: The building blocks of cognition. In R. J. Spiro, B. C. Bruce, & W. F. Brewer (Eds.), *Theoretical issues in reading comprehension* (pp. 33-58). Hillsdale, NJ: Lawrence Erlbaum Associates.

Rumelhart, D. E., & Norman, D. A. (1981). Analogical processes in learning. In J. R. Anderson (Ed.), *Cognitive skills and their acquisition.* Hillsdale, NJ: Lawrence Erlbaum Associates.

Rumelhart, D. E., & Norman, D. A. (1988). Representation in memory. In R. C. Atkinson, R. J. Hemnstein, G. Lindzey, & R. Duncan Luce (Eds.), *Stevens' handbook of experimental psychology, Vol. 1: Perception and motivation; Vol. 2: Learning and cognition* (2nd ed.) pp. 511-587. New York: John Wiley & Sons.

Rumelhart, D. E., & Ortony, A. (1977)., The representation of knowledge in memory. In R. C. Anderson, R. J. Spiro, & W. E. Montague (Eds.), *Schooling and the acquisition of knowledge.* Hillsdale, NJ: Lawrence Erlbaum Associates.

Saville-Troike, M. (1991). Teaching and testing for academic achievement: The role of language development. *NCBE Focus: Occasional papers in bilingual education. 4.*

Seel, N. M. (1995). Mental models, knowledge transfer, and teaching strategies. *Journal of Structural Learning, 12*(3), 197-213.

Shavelson, R. J., Lang, H., & Lewin, B. (1994). *On concept maps as potential authentic assessments in science* (CSE Technical Report 388). Los Angeles: University of California, National Center for Research on Evaluation, Standards, and Student Testing.

Short, D. J. (1993). Assessing integrated language and content instruction. *TESOL Quarterly, 27*(4), 627-56.

Stanovich, K. E. (1991). Discrepancy definitions of reading disability: Has intelligence led us astray? *Reading Research Quarterly, 26*(l), 7-29.

U.S. Bureau of the Census. (1990). *The foreign born population in the United States.* Washington, DC: U.S. Government Printing Office.

Valdes, G., & Figueroa, R. A. (1995). *Bilingualism and testing: A special case of bias.* Norwood, NJ: Ablex.

Wineburg, S. S. (1991a). On the reading of historical texts: Notes on the breach between school and academy. *American Educational Research Journal, 28*(3), 495-519.

Wineburg, S. S. (1991b). Historical problem solving: A study of the cognitive processes used in the evaluation of documentary and pictorial evidence. *Journal of Educational Psychology, 83*(l), 73-87.

Wong-Fillmore, L. (1991). When learning a second language means losing the first. *Early Childhood Research Quarterly, 6*, 323-346.

Zehler, A. M., Hopstock, P. J., Fleischman, H. L., & Greniuk, C. (1994). *An examination of assessment of limited English proficient students.* Task Order Report No. D070, Special Issues Analysis Center.

8 Performance Assessment & Issues of Differential Impact: The British Experience – Lessons for America

George F. Madaus
Anastasia E. Raczek
Sally Thomas

In the late 1980s, a powerful movement, alternatively labeled authentic, alternative, performance or, incorrectly, new assessment, emerged to contest the hegemony of standardized multiple-choice testing (e.g., Mitchell, 1992, Wiggins, 1989). (We use the simple term "assessment" in referring to this movement). Proponents of assessment believe that student learning and progress are best appraised, not by having students select answers, but by having them supply an extended response, generate material for portfolios, perform exhibitions, carry out experiments, or produce a tangible product that can be evaluated on its merits.

Reflecting, in part, a shift from a transmissionist or behaviorist view of learning to a constructivist one, advocates argue that these alternative forms of assessment will help students develop the conceptual and analytical skills needed to prepare them for future vocational success (Garcia & Pearson, 1994)[1]. Among the benefits attributed to such assessments are: the potential to drive reform the reform movement built around world-class standards; clear models of accepable outcomes for teachers; the elimination of negative test-preparation effects associated with multiple-choice tests; a positive influence on instruction and learning; the ability to measure higher order skills; and the potential to motivate unmotivated students.[2]

When such assessment transcends classroom use by teachers – which we wholeheartedly endorse – and is instead linked to high-stakes policy uses like promotion, graduation, higher education eligibility, future job opportunities, or teacher or system accountability, then we need a more methodical examination of any claims. This chapter presents an initial attempt to look at one beneficial claim within a high-stakes context. That is, alternative forms of assessment are fairer for all students[3] and will narrow achievement gaps between different groups (e.g., defined by gender, race, ethnicity, socio-economic status) since they will force teachers to take into account students' different learning styles or problem-solving approaches (Meisels, Dorfman, & Steele, 1995; Wiggins, 1989).[4]

This chapter describes the *relative attainment* of gender, low income, linguistic, and special needs groups as measured by teacher judgments and the performance assessments administered in 1992 to seven year olds as part of the National Curriculum in England and Wales. England and Wales provided an unique opportunity to study the operation of a large-scale, high-stakes performance assessment system which used instruments with the characteristics of the "authentic assessments" described above.[5] In 1992, National Curriculum assessment in the United Kingdom included two primary methods: teacher judgments of student performance and student achievement on performance-based tasks. At the time of the study, the 1992 National Curriculum Standard Tasks for seven year olds provided the model closest to U.S. proposals for performance-based assessment in which identical assessments are proposed for all students at a given level.[6] The British experience was a naturally occurring experiment that allowed us to explore group equity or fairness claims made for authentic assessment in the context of high-stakes at least in terms of *initial implementation, for a single age cohort*. We could not make direct comparisons of group performance across the multiple-choice and assessment formats, but we could compare teacher evaluations of different student groups on the National Curriculum and their performance on assessment tasks geared to that curriculum.

It is important to reiterate that our data is limited to seven year olds, and was gathered in the early stages of the program. Nonetheless, the English experience offers clues for our country about what we might expect in terms of group differences using assessment techniques geared to state standards or frameworks. The reader needs to keep in mind that these results must be understood in the context of England having gone through four years of extensive planning, developing curriculum framework, crafting hierarchical achievement goals for students, informing parents about the National Curriculum and the accompanying assessments, providing comprehensive, expensive inservice training around the National Curriculum and the assessment techniques, and involving teachers in the pre-testing of those techniques. In other words, these were not "dropped from the sky" assessments.

First we will outline the structure of the British National Curriculum and its assessment system as it operated in 1992.[7] Both have recently been altered considerably. For example, there has been a revision to more traditional types of testing – short answer, multiple choice, fill-in-the-blank – for political, efficiency, cost, and administrative reasons unrelated to fairness and equity concerns which is our focus. Further, in

1996/97 parents will receive test results as standardized scores set against a national average rather than in terms of the curriculum level their child had attained (Abrams, 1996). These revisions and the reasons for them are beyond the scope of this chapter. Suffice it to say what transpired over the past four years in England and Wales is a cautionary tale for America in terms of designing, implementing, and managing standards-based reform with accompanying high-stakes assessments. Next, we present the conclusions of our review of the limited literature on whether different assessment methods, i.e., multiple-choice and performance, operate differently for various student subgroups. Finally, we examine 1992 data for different groups of seven-year-old students on the U.K. assessments called Standard Tasks, and compare that performance to teacher assessments also geared to the National Curriculum.

NATIONAL CURRICULUM ASSESSMENT IN THE U.K.

As part of the *Education Reform Act of 1988*, England and Wales implemented a multi-layered National Curriculum, with a complex web of targeted skills and methods for assessing them. An original aim of the reform was to ensure that "all pupils, regardless of sex, ethnic origin and geographical location, have access to broadly the same good and relevant curriculum and programme of study" (Department of Education & Science, 1988, quoted in Troyna & Hatcher, 1991, p. 291). Assessment referenced to the mandated curriculum was *originally* intended to meet four criteria (TGAT, 1988). First, it was to be criterion- rather than norm-referenced, so that students could be measured against fixed national standards. Specific skills, or Attainment Targets, were established within each subject to be assessed – initially the core subjects of English/Welsh, Math, and Science. Second, the assessment was to be formative, supporting learning by informing both students and teachers about student progress. Third, it was to be used for accountability purposes. The assessments were intended, in part, to inform parental school- choice decisions by providing them with relative performances of schools and Local Education Authorities on the National Curriculum (Nuttall & Stobart, 1994). Finally, national assessment was designed to measure student progress toward mastery of the National Curriculum over the successive years they are in school. The last two criteria ensured that the Standard Tasks became a "high-stakes" assessment system.

The content of the National Curriculum was divided into four age-based "Key Stages" covering the period of compulsory education in the U.K.:

- Stage 1 spanned ages 5 to 7 –comparable to U.S. elementary Grades K-2;

- Stage 2 ages 7 to 11– comparable to U.S. elementary Grades 2-6;

- Stage 3 ages 11 to 14 – comparable to U.S. middle school, Grades 6-9;

- Stage 4 ages 14 to 16 – comparable to U.S. high school, grades 9-11.

Students were to be assessed at the end of each Key Stage. In 1992, when data for this study were collected, specific skills within each Attainment Target, called Statements of Attainment, were defined to represent given levels within each subject – 10 in all. Each level approximately corresponded to two years of schooling. Figure 1 shows how students were expected to achieve at higher levels as they progressed through the Key Stages; most children within a particular Key Stage should perform within a particular range of levels.

Figure 1

U.K. National Curriculum student achievement levels between ages 7 and 16.

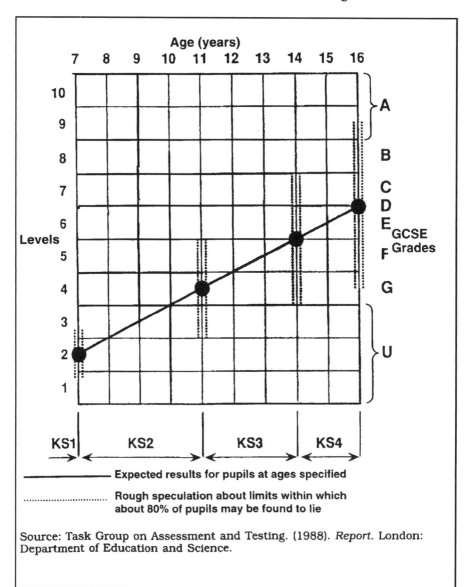

Source: Task Group on Assessment and Testing. (1988). *Report*. London: Department of Education and Science.

For example, at Key Stage 1 (age 7) about 80% of students were expected to achieve Level 2. Level 10 was defined by quite difficult Statements of Attainment, and few students were expected to attain it. Statements of Attainment were defined for each subject, and became more complex as the levels progress. Table 1 provides examples of this.

Table 1

Examples of 1992 Statements of Attainment for Levels 1-3 for Attainment Targets in English, Mathematics and Science

ENGLISH	READING (AT2)
Level 1	Recognize print has meaning, recognize words/letters, talk about content of a story.
Level 2	Read accurately, use picture and context cues, predict possible endings to a story.
Level 3	Read aloud fluently with appropriate expression from familiar stories, read silently.
	WRITING (AT3)
Level 1	Use pictures, symbols, isolated letters, words, phrases to communicate meaning.
Level 2	Complete sentences, structure sequences of events in chronology and with a rudimentary understanding of story structure.
Level 3	Complete sentences with correct punctuation. More complex stories beyond simple events, range of non-chronological writing, ability to discuss,redraft work.
	SPELLING (AT4)
Level 1	Differentiate between drawing and writing, numbers and letters, write some letter shapes.
Level 2	Spell correctly monosyllabic words, recognisable spelling of a range of words.
Level 3	Spell correctly polysyllabic words, recognise regular patterns for vowel sounds and common letter strings, beginning to check own spelling for accuracy.
	HANDWRITING (AT5)
Level 1	Begin to form letters.
Level 2	Produce legible letters.
Level 3	Begin clear and legible joined up writing.
MATH	NUMBER OPERATIONS (AT3)
Level 1	Add or subtract, using objects where numbers involved are no greater than 10.
Level 2	Know and use addition and subtraction facts up to 10.
Level 3	Know and use addition and subtraction number facts to 20. Know and use multiplication facts up to 5x5.
	HANDLING DATA - COLLECT, RECORD & PROCESS DATA (AT12)
Level 1	Select criteria for sorting objects.
Level 2	Help design a data collection sheet.
Level 3	Extract specific information from tables, lists; enter information in simple database.
	HANDLING DATA - PROBABILITIES (AT14)
Level 1	Recognise possible outcomes of simple random events.
Level 2	Understanding the uncertainty, certainty, and impossibility of certain events.
Level 3	Simple understanding of uncertainty, knowing the more likely outcome.
SCIENCE	TYPES AND USES OF MATERIALS (AT6)
Level 1	Describe objects in terms of simple properties.
Level 2	Understand the effect of heat and cold, and recognise similarities and differences in properties between objects.
Level 3	List similarities and differences, understand difference between natural , synthetic.
	EARTH AND ATMOSPHERE (AT9)
Level 1	Knows there are a variety of weather conditions and can describe changes.
Level 2	Knowledge of seasonal changes, and that weather effects lives.
Level 3	Understand common meterological symbols, knowledge of the weathering of rock and buildings.

For example, within the 1992 "Writing for Meaning" Attainment Target, Statements of Attainment associated with Level 1 included "Use pictures, symbols or isolated letters, words or phrases to communicate meaning," while Statements of Attainment associated with Level 3 included "Produce, independently, pieces of writing using complete sentences, mainly demarcated with capital letters and full stops or question marks" (DES, 1992a, p. 14). The two assessment techniques of teacher judgments of student progress and student performance on Standard Tasks or Tests were used to assess Levels of Attainment for these Attainment Targets.

First a brief description of the Teacher Assessment system. The National Curriculum specifies what should be taught in each subject through Curriculum Orders disseminated to all teachers. For assessment, teachers focused on the Statements of Attainment for deciding how well students have attained the specified knowledge or skills in the National Curriculum. Teachers were advised to use multiple sources of information in making their judgments, using assessment which promotes a wide range of classroom activities. It has been suggested that this system is not much different from what teachers have always done, except, perhaps, for more emphasis on what children have learned instead of what has been taught, more explicit specification of attainment criteria, and more formal record-keeping (Shorrocks, 1993).

The Standard Tasks were performance-based exercises built for the (now) Department for Education by external contractors. They were administered and scored by the classroom teacher; the scoring was moderated by Local Education Authority representatives. The Standard Tasks were intended to simulate typical classroom activities so that theoretically the children might not even realize they are being assessed (Nuttall, 1992). The assessment tasks required active engagement by students; many were observational situations meant to provide direct evidence concerning constructive and productive aspects of student attainment (Myford & Mislevy, 1994).

Performance on every Standard Task was judged by the teacher using pre-defined scoring criteria called "Evidence of Attainment" that were supplied along with other assessment materials. Students were scored on the level they reached in the task, based on how many objectives (Statements of Attainment) they attained. Recording procedures for the Standard Tasks were so complicated that extensive scoring documentation accompanied the testing materials distributed to teachers. Appendix 1 provides an example of 1992 Key Stage 1 scoring rules for English Writing Attainment Targets 3 (Writing), 4 (Spelling), and 5 (Handwriting).

An example of a Key Stage 1 (age 7) math task is illuminating. In assessing the Attainment Target "Using and applying mathematics," children were asked to work in groups of four to invent a game that involved the use of computational skills, such as addition and subtraction. Students were provided with dice, counters, pens or pencils, paper, and a timer, and could also request additional materials. The informational material supplied to the teachers suggested that:

"Games should not be limited to board games, but could include for example, bouncing a ball according to the number of times on a dice; balancing objects on top of one another in a set time determined by the dice. What is important for the assessment is that the way the game progresses should involve calculation, and that children should not spend too much time decorating the material but rather on thinking about differences in rules and alternative methods of scoring" (DES, 1991a, p. 23).

Teachers were to observe the game development process, encourage children to "discuss what the game should be like, its rules and scoring [and] play the game several times in order to make changes and adaptations to improve it, including checking the rules" (DES, 1991b, p. 22); they simultaneously recorded children's attainment in terms of Statements of Attainment corresponding to assessment activities.

REVIEW OF ASSESSMENT METHOD AND DIFFERENTIAL GROUP PERFORMANCE

Given some of the claims made for performance-type testing, it is important to take a closer look at whether different forms of assessment have been shown to be more beneficial for particular groups of students. As Garcia and Pearson (1994) point out, "If the consequences of our current assessment practices result in double jeopardy for low-income students, then we as a profession will need to redouble our own efforts to make sure that the consequences of submitting oneself to examination are positive rather than negative" (p. 338). As part of this study we completed an extensive literature review to shed light on the question, "Are different forms of assessment more or less beneficial for particular groups of students?" (Thomas, Raczek, & Madaus, 1996). However, because of space limitations, we can only outline the conclusions here. First, an important caution. When significant performance differences are found between groups – what the courts call adverse impact – it is important to keep in mind that such differences can result from a number of factors including: biases in the conceptualization of the domain being assessed; the scoring protocols used; the administration of the assessment[8]; differential access to opportunity to learn; or differential contextual/background factors of examinees. Or, the differential results can reflect genuine group differences in whatever trait is being assessed (Linn & Bond, 1994). The studies we reviewed, and our own data, generally speak only to the question of adverse impact, not to causes of unequal performance such as general inequalities and inequities in the educational system or in the larger society.

What did we conclude from our review? First, it is clear that how different assessment methods might work for different groups of students has not been extensively studied, especially within a high-stakes testing context.[9] Although there is some indirect research bearing on the question, we found very few published studies that directly compared differential performance across multiple choice and performance or essay tests designed to measure the same domain.

It has been asserted that multiple-choice tests operate differentially for boys and girls since girls often perform less well than boys on standardized multiple-choice tests in some subjects (Bolger & Kellaghan, 1990; Harding, 1980; Murphy, 1982; Murphy, 1991). A number of hypotheses have been suggested to explain this finding. Girls' lower performance may be related to the response format, since guessing can confer advantage to examinees, and females are generally less likely to guess and more likely to choose "I don't know" as a response option (Hanna, 1986; Hudson, 1986; Linn, Benedictis, Delucchi, Harris, & Stage, 1987). Also, girls may tend to reflect on the ambiguities present in multiple-choice distracters and therefore have difficulty finding a single correct answer (Murphy, 1991). Those few studies that directly examined male/ female differences tend to support the hypothesis that males and females perform differently by measurement method, with the multiple-choice format disadvantaging girls (Bolger & Kellaghan, 1990; Breland, et al., 1994; Jovanovic, Solano-Flores, and Shavelson 1994; Mazzeo, Schmitt, & Bleistein 1993). However, these studies suggest that the specific content of the test items is as important, if not more so than the item's format.[10]

British students from economically disadvantaged backgrounds often perform less well on tests, including performance-based tests of the National Curriculum (Edwards & Whitty, 1994; National Commission on Education, 1993; Sammons, 1994; Willms, 1986), but we found no research that suggested how different assessment methods might lessen or worsen differences across socio-economic status. There is some evidence of a negative relationship between SES and performance on the Standard Tasks, at least in the primary grades provided by one English study which found pressure had mounted to avoid enrolling children from poorer backgrounds because of their potential for poor performance on the Standard Tasks (National Union of Teachers & University of Leeds, 1993).

It does *not* seem, from our review, that performance testing is *necessarily* more equitable for minority students, although – and this is important – assessment that values diverse perspectives in problem solving may provide more opportunities for a fairer evaluation than standardized multiple-choice tests. Bilingual students generally perform less well than native English speakers on tests, including the National Curriculum assessments (Gipps & Murphy, 1994). Although teachers in the U.K. perceived that the heavy reliance on discussion made the performance tasks more difficult for second language students than English speakers, they also thought that these tasks were more appropriate than traditional tests, partly because of the increased opportunity for direct teacher/student interaction (Gipps, 1994). Interaction with the teacher in a normal classroom environment allowed more opportunity for a task to be explained and may have provided more possibilities for bilingual students to demonstrate attainment than a written test would have (Gipps, 1994).[11] Finally, special needs students perform less well than other students on performance-based assessments in the U.K. and opinions varied about the appropriateness of such tasks for special needs students (National Foundation for Educational Research, 1992b; Dearing, 1995).

STUDENT PERFORMANCE ON THE 1992 NATIONAL CURRICULUM ASSESSMENTS IN THE UNITED KINGDOM

We turn now to our analysis of the 1992 national assessment results for 17,718 seven-year olds at Key Stage 1, enrolled in 590 schools in one large English Local Education Authority.[12] These analyses look at the impact of four student characteristics on student attainment scores in English, mathematics and science: gender, entitlement to free school meals - a measure of low family income, English as a second language, and having a statement of special educational needs.[13] We also look at the effects of a school-level variable – the percentage of students in each school entitled to free meal benefits.[14] We used this school-level variable to measure the overall socio-economic context for each school. We examined student achievement using two different methods of assessment: (i) Teacher Assessments, and, (ii) Standard Task assessments. In both types of assessment students were evaluated on a scale of 0 to 4; working towards level 1 (treated as level 0) being the lowest level and level 4 being the highest for students of this age group.[15]

We focus on National Curriculum assessment results in the nine Attainment Targets for which we had both teacher assessment and Standard Task data. In English these topics were reading (EAT2), writing (EAT3), spelling (EAT4) and handwriting (EAT5); in mathematics: number operations (+, -, *, /, contained in MAT3); collecting, recording and processing data (MAT12) and probabilities (MAT14); and in science the topics were types and uses of materials (SAT6) and earth and atmosphere (SAT9).[16]

Results

Appendix 2 presents unadjusted mean scores for students grouped by gender, eligibility for free lunch, language status, and having a statement of special educational needs. Correlations between the Teacher and Standard Task assessments showed fairly strong positive relationships between the two modes of assessment, ranging from 0.92 for the two Reading assessments to 0.77 for the Probability assessments in math.

Our primary analytic technique was multilevel modeling, or hierarchical linear modeling. Hierarchical Linear Modeling is designed for analysis of hierarchically structured data, for example data collected at the individual student level, and at the school level (Paterson & Goldstein, 1991). This technique also allows us to study differences between the performance of groups of students, such as males and females, while taking into account other possible differences, for example, due to their age.[17]

First, do different groups of students perform differently on the U.K. Teacher Assessments and Standard Tasks, when other background factors are taken into account? To make direct comparisons between the results for the two assessment methods across the different subjects, we transformed the results from the 0 to 4 "Levels" scale to standardized scores. In this standardized metric, values from 0 to about 0.2 indicate a small difference between groups, values over 0.2 and less than about 0.7 a moderate difference between groups, and values over 0.7 indicate a large difference between groups. We compared the two different methods of assessment directly by measuring the relative influence of student characteristics on Teacher Assessments in comparison to Standard Tasks. Figures 2, 3, and 4 present the differences in assessment scores between groups in standard deviation units when all other student characteristics are taken into account (for the variable percent of school eligible for free meals, entries represent the influence, in standard deviation units, for one unit change in the variable).

The multilevel model results indicate that, for the most part, there is differential performance by gender, income, language, special needs, and age groups across Standard Tasks and Teacher Assessments. Generally, girls perform at a higher level than boys on English and mathematics overall, and in all three subjects, students entitled to free lunch and those whose first language is not English performed at a lower level than their comparison groups. Students with a statement of special educational needs perform at a substantially lower level than those without a statement. The school factor of percentage of students entitled to free school meals had a negative impact across the three subjects.

Differences in English Attainment between Groups of Students

Let's look specifically at each Attainment Target by subject. First, for English, results for each of the four Attainment Targets show that, controlling for other background characteristics, the differences between the girls' and boys' scores are significant, ranging from 0.21 to 0.25 standard deviations in favor of the girls. The equivalent figures for the English assessments by Standard Task were 0.20 to 0.24.

Figure 2

Variation in Teacher Assessment and Standard Task scores associated with student characteristics: Multi-level modelling results for English Attainment Targets

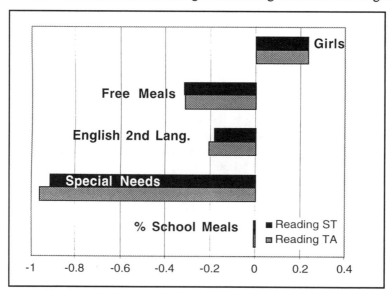

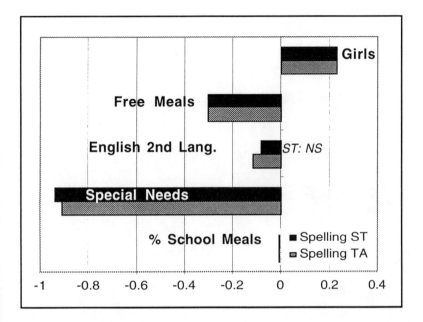

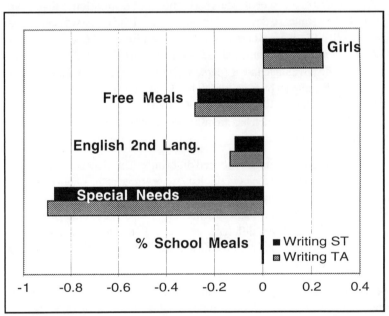

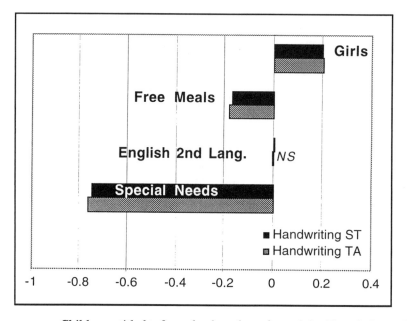

Children entitled to free school meals performed significantly lower than those not, between 0.28 to 0.32 standard deviations in the English Teacher Assessments, except on handwriting (EAT5), where there was a slightly smaller effect of 0.18. Equivalent figures for the assessments by Standard Task ranged from 0.17 to 0.32, all significant. The school level disadvantage factor (percent eligible for free school meals) also had a significant negative impact of approximately 0.01 standard deviations across all Teacher Assessments and Standard Task assessments. That is, the proportion of children in a given school eligible for free lunch has an influence on outcomes, above and beyond an individual student's economic status.

English as a second language produced differing effects depending upon the methods of assessment and different topics in English. Across three of the English Teacher Assessments, E2L students performed 0.12 to 0.21 standard deviations below non-E2L students. The equivalent figures for the assessments by Standard Task were 0.08 to 0.18. Interestingly, there was no significant difference between E2L and non-E2L students on Spelling assessed by Standard Task, and on both the Teacher Assessment or Standard Task assessments in handwriting.

On every assessment, regardless of method, Special Educational Needs students performed significantly less well than students not identified with a statement of special needs. Students with a statement of Special Educational Needs performed almost a full standard deviation below other students in the English Teacher Assessments and Standard Task assessments, except in handwriting (EAT5), where the difference was somewhat smaller.

Differences in Mathematics Scores between Groups of Students

The impact of gender was much smaller on student attainment in mathematics than for English.

Figure 3

Variation in Teacher Assessment and Standard Task scores associated with student characteristics: Multi-level modelling results for mathematics Attainment Targets

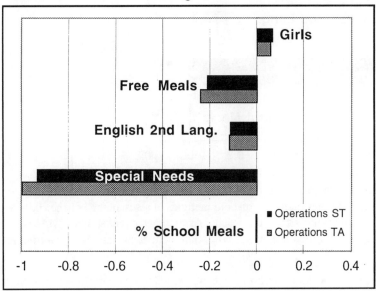

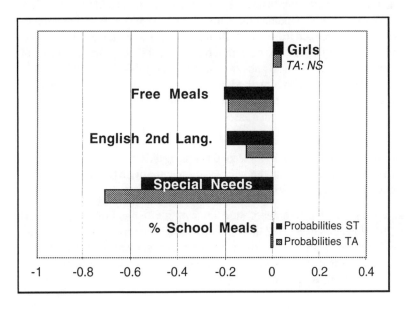

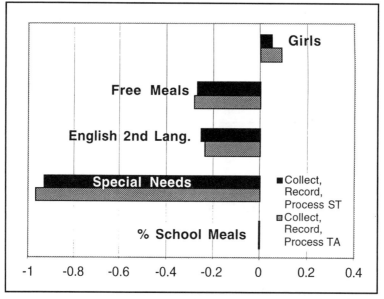

In Number Operations and Collecting, Recording, and Processing data, girls scored very slightly higher than boys on both methods of assessment; between 0.04 to 0.09 standard deviations higher. For the Teacher Assessment of probabilities (MAT14T), there was no significant difference between the attainment of girls and boys, controlling for other factors.

Students eligible for free school meals performed significantly lower than other students across all mathematics topics tested by Teacher Assessment and Standard Task assessments, even when other student characteristics were considered. Mathematics achievement differences ranged from .19 to .28 of a standard deviation on Teacher Assessments and .21 to .27 of a standard deviation on Standard Tasks. The proportion of students in a school eligible for meal subsidies also had a significant, negative, effect across all math assessments for both methods; a decrement of almost .01 of a standard deviation was associated with each 1% increase in schoolwide free lunch eligibility, the same effect size observed for the English assessments.differences in math ranged from .11 to .26.

Students who spoke English as a second language did less well on average than native English speakers across all mathematics assessments, with the smallest differences in math ranged from .11 to .26.

As on the English assessments, students with a statement of special educational needs performed much less well than others on all science and math Teacher Assessments and Standard Tasks. The relative performance for students with special educational needs was .56 to 1.0 of a standard deviation lower; the least difference was noted for the math probability Attainment Target.

Differences in Science Scores between Groups of Students

The impact of gender on student attainment in science was even smaller than it was for math. The difference between boys and girls in both Types and Uses of Materials assessments (SAT6S) was not significant. The effect for Earth and Atmosphere was statistically significant, but quite small.

Figure 4

Variation in Teacher Assessment and Standard Task scores associated with student characteristic: Multi-level modelling results for science Attainment Targets

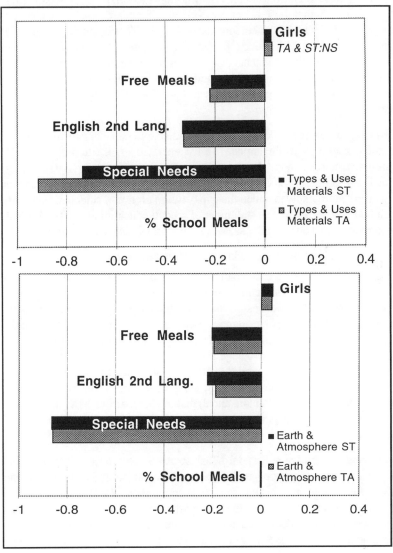

Students eligible for free school meals performed significantly lower than other students across both science topics tested by Teacher Assessment and Standard Tasks. Free school meals differences on the two Teacher Assessments were .22 and .19 of a standard deviation and on the two Standard Tasks were .22 and .20 of a standard deviation. The school-level meal subsidy variable also had a significant, negative, effect on science assessments for both methods. English language learners did less well on average on both science topics. Again, as on all of the other assessments, special needs students performed much less well than others on all science assessments.

Figures 2 to 4 summarize not only our findings in terms of group mean differences, but also show whether the Teacher Assessment or Standard Task assessment exhibited a larger coefficient for each student characteristic. That is, the figures present which assessment method, within one topic, resulted in a greater separation between groups. For example, the bar for Teacher Assessment can be compared with the bar for Standard Task assessment in Science: Types and Uses of Materials to determine which produced a wider gap between Special Needs and not Special Needs students – here, Teacher Assessment increased the gap.

Overall, for 13 out of 63 comparisons, Teacher Assessment resulted in greater differences between groups, while Standard Tasks generated larger differences between groups for only four comparisons.[18] However, for the most part, Teacher Assessment and Standard Task assessment worked similarly. Nonetheless, in some instances, Teacher Assessments were more likely to widen the gap between groups of students, especially for those who do and do not have a statement of special educational needs, although such differences still exist on a smaller scale in terms of the Standard Task assessments.

Examining the Impact of Standard Tasks on Teacher Assessment

Our last set of analyses measured the impact of student intake factors and Standard Task scores on Teacher Assessments. In other words, we measured, on average, how much of teachers' assessments were associated with student background characteristics on the one hand, and students' performance on the equivalent Standard Tasks, on the other. If the two methods of assessment do, in fact, measure the same thing, then student characteristics such as gender or language should not have much of an influence on Teacher Assessment above and beyond the effect of a student's Standard Task score. Keep in mind, though, that the structure of these analyses assumes 1) the two assessment methods are measuring the same domain, and 2) that the Standard Tasks are a relatively "objective" measure of student performance in comparison to the more "subjective" Teacher Assessment.

We found that students' Standard Task scores account for between 58% and 94% of the variation between schools in the Teacher Assessments of the same topic. But after Standard Task results have been taken into account, there is still between 6% and 42% remaining unexplained variation in student attainment measured by the Teacher Assessment. Indeed, when student characteristics are added to Standard Task attainment in a model predicting Teacher Assessments, each student background characteristic (such as gender and Free School Meals) still has a small but significant impact on Teacher Assessment. That is, once student achievement, as measured by Standard Task, is controlled for, gender, economic disadvantage, second language status, and special needs status are still significantly related to Teacher Assessment results, although the magnitude of the effects is much smaller than that displayed in Figures 2-4. For example, students' entitlement to free lunch has, on average, a significant negative impact of between 0.02 to 0.06 of a Level on Teacher Assessment above and beyond their Standard Task scores for the same topic.

LESSONS FOR AMERICA

The British National Curriculum is a large, well funded, carefully planned and pre-tested attempt at standards and assessment-based reform. As such, and despite important structural, societal, and educational differences between the two countries, American policy makers can benefit from an inspection of what has happened in England. We briefly suggest some possible lessons from England. First, there are a few important lessons that, while independent of the differential group attainment data just presented, we would be remiss not to at least mention.

(1) A large majority of English teachers report that the National Curriculum, its associated assessments, and in-service training made them reconsider the curriculum, their teaching, and student learning in new, and positive ways (Gipps, et. al., 1991; Dearing, 1993). Standards-based reform can produce similar effects in the United States. In fact, survey evidence from Maryland (Koretz, Mitchell, Barron, & Keith, 1996), anecdotal evidence from California and Kentucky, and teacher testimony from the experience of preparing for the National Board of Professional Teaching Standards certification (Haynes, 1995) supports the existence of this epiphany effect on teachers associated with standards/assessment-based reform.

(2) The British experience calls into question the use of assessment procedures for formative and diagnostic purposes on the one hand and summative and evaluative purposes on the other. In England and Wales, the high stakes use in the government's school choice plan was seen as fostering a consumerist rather than educational discourse about results. In Scotland, which also implemented standards/assessment-based reform, the absence of high-stakes summative descriptions of individuals and schools offered a greater chance for the assessments to contribute to the improvement of teaching and communication between teachers and parents (Madaus. & Kellaghan, 1993). In England the high-stakes uses quickly swamped the formative and diagnostic aspects of the National Curriculum reform.[19] We can expect the same phenomena here (Koretz, Madaus, Haertel, & Beaton, 1992).

(3) In 1996, tasks for seven year olds in England will take less time and will involve more tests of the paper-and-pencil variety, which can be used by the whole

class at the one time, including an optional written group reading test (see for example: SCAA, 1995 and Dillon, 1995). The recent retreat in England from direct assessment of complex performances to a concentration on measuring attainment of basic skills suggests that, for reasons of administrative convenience, classroom manageability, and cost,[20] the life expectancy in the United States of complex "authentic" assessments in high-stakes programs may be short. California's experience with scoring the CLAS and the associated costs of that effort is a case in point. Matthew Arnold's metaphorical use of the tide on Dover Beach – as it ebbs so it will return – is apropos to the restoration in England of more efficient measures. The tide of efficiency in measurement will in all likelihood return here in the United States as well.

Let us return to the focus of this chapter – will "authentic" assessments reduce differences in attainment between different categories of students? Recall we found significant differences in attainment between important groups of English students on two separate but related assessment techniques: Standard Tasks, which have the characteristics of the assessments called for in the United States, and Teacher Assessments of the same domains.

Equity issues around the use of the Standard Tasks emerged early. One study found that there was pressure on schools to avoid enrolling children from poorer backgrounds, "summer babies" who are young for their age group, children with special educational needs and those speaking English as a second language, because of their potential for poor performance on the Standard Tasks (Shorrocks, 1993).

In England the suggestion has been made that the "[Standard Task]-type activity with its emphasis on active, multi-mode assessment and detailed interaction between teacher and pupil may, despite the heavy reliance on language, be a better opportunity for minority and special needs children to demonstrate what they know and can do than traditional, formal tests with limited instructions" (Gipps, 1994, p. 9).[21] This may be, but group differences persisted between the gender, socio-economic, language, and special needs groupings of students on both the Standard Tasks and the Teacher Assessments.

Based on the English experience, our best estimate is that in the United States group differences in attainment will persist regardless of the mode of measurement. In fact, because disparities are much wider in the United States than in England in school funding, in availability of pre-school education for the poor, and in other key social support services like health care, housing, and child support, our use of "authentic" assessment techniques most likely will produce group differences quite a bit larger than the British results reported here.

It is important to keep in mind that these data came from the first operational implementation of the assessments, and not from a mature program with a tradition of authentic assessment. It may well be that the group disparities diminish or disappear altogether as the assessment program becomes institutionalized and a tradition of past assessment exercises becomes part of the lore of teachers and students. (Evidence from external examination systems however, casts doubt on such an assumption.) Also keep in mind that the data reflect the performance of seven year olds only. It may be that the group differences may decrease or increase as students get older. (Results from the *initial* implementation of the National Board of Professional Teaching Standards (NBPTS) Early Adolescence/English Language Arts assessments (EA/ELA) indicate adverse impact for federally protected groups of adults (Bond et al., 1994).)

Despite these caveats, the English results, at the very least, point to the need to carefully monitor group differences in light of equity claims made about the assessment technology. Our results are a caution to those in the United States making such equity claims.

Authentic assessment used in the low-stakes context of the classroom may, we think, provide an opportunity for children who do not traditionally do well on multiple-choice tests to "show their stuff." But this hypothesis – and it is just a hypothesis – also needs to be carefully investigated.

Whatever happens in classroom assessment, focusing on a high-stakes performance assessment system as a vehicle for improving equity in education is likely to do little. The needs of children facing disadvantage are simply not addressed through standards and assessments alone. We should, of course, strive for assessments in which the "concerns, contexts and approaches of one group do not dominate" (Gipps, 1994, p. 5). We should also study the extent to which test constructors "are heavily but subtly influenced by their cultural understandings" and how "those who take the test are similarly influenced but by different cultural understandings" (Hambleton & Murphy, 1992, p. 12). Most importantly, we need to move beyond standards and cutting-edge assessments and consider the different life and classroom experiences of diverse student groups and how these factors impinge on school attainment. It is disturbing how Goal 1 of the Goals 2000 legislation – opportunity to learn and delivery standards – has all but disappeared from the policy radar screen.

The adoption of "authentic" assessments geared to "world class" standards is envisaged by many as a prime mechanism of educational reform. That vision includes equity claims that such assessments will narrow present measured attainment gaps between members of disparate groups of students. Such claims must be critically examined, rationally, empirically, and – since the assessment technology is considerably older than the multiple-choice technology – historically. We should not be xenophobic and dismiss the experience of England, Scotland, Northern Ireland and Australia with standards and assessment-based reform with a glib, "theirs is a different culture and system." The United States stands to learn much about such issues of practicality, cost, infrastructure, in-service training and most importantly equity and fairness from the experiences of other countries with standards and assessment-based reform.

References

Abrams, F. (1996, July 4). Quick-fire questions to test maths. The Independent, p. 7.

Bolger, N., & Kellaghan, T. (1990). Method of measurement and gender differences in scholastic achievement. *Journal of Educational Measurement, 27*(2), 165-174.

Bond, L., Cooper, C., Freedman, S., Haertel, E., Jaeger, R., D, Linn, R., et al. (1994, May). *A comparison of two strategies for scoring the exercises in the National Board for Professional Teaching Standards' Early Adolescence Language Arts Assessment package. Report submitted to the National Board for Professional Teaching Standards*. Detroit MI: National Board for Professional Teaching Standards.

Breland, H. M., Danos, S. O., Kahn, H. D., Kubota, M. Y., & Bonner, M. W. (1994). Performance versus objective testing and gender: An exploratory study of an Advanced Placement History Examinaton. *Journal of Educational Measurement, 31*(4), 275-293.

Dearing, R. (1993). *The National Curriculum and its assessment: An interim report*. London: School Examinations and Assessment Council, National Curriculum Council.

Dearing, R. (1995). *The National Curriculum and its assessment: Final report*. London: School Examinations and Assessment Council, National Curriculum Council.

Department of Education & Science. (1991a). *Assessment record booklet: 1991 KS 1*. London: School Examinations and Assessment Council.

Department of Education & Science. (1991b). *Teacher's book: 1991 Key Stage 1*. London: School Examinations and Assessment Council.

Department of Education & Science. (1992a). *Standard Assessment Task teacher's handbook: 1992 Key Stage 1*. London: School Examinations and Assessment Council.

Dillon. (1995). *Guide to the national curriculum*. London: Oxford University Press.

Edwards, T., & Whitty, G. (1994). Education: Opportunity, equality and efficiency. In A. Glyn & D. Milibrand (Eds.), *Paying for inequality* (pp.44-64). London: Rivers Oram Press.

Garcia, G. E., & Pearson, P. D. (1994). Assessment and diversity. *Review of Research in Education, 20*, 337-391.

Gipps, C. (1994, April). *What do we mean by equity in relation to assessment?* Paper presented at the annual meeting of the American Educational Research Association, New Orleans.

Gipps, C., & Murphy, P. (1994). *A fair test? Assessment, achievement and equity*. Buckingham: Open University Press.

Gipps, C., McCallum, B., McAllister, S., & Brown, M. (1991). *National assessment at seven: Some emerging themes*. Paper presented at BERA conference, University of London, Institute of Education and Centre for Educational Studies King's College.

Hambleton, R. K., & Murphy, E. (1992). A psychometric perspective on authentic measurement. *Applied Measurement in Education, 5*(1), 1-16.

Haynes, D. (1995). One teacher's experience with National Board Assessment. *Educational Leadership, 52*(2), 58-60.

Jovanovic, J., Solano-Flores, G., & Shavelson, R. J. (1994). Performance-based assessments: Will gender differences in science be eliminated? *Education and Urban Society, 26*(4), 352-366.

Kellaghan, T., MadaU.S., G. F., & Raczek, A. E. (1996). *The use of external examinations to improve student motivation*. AERA Public Monograph Series. Washington, DC: American Educational Research Association.

Koretz, D. M., Madaus, G. F., Haertel, E., & Beaton, A. E. (1992). *Statement before the Subcommittee on Elementary, Secondary and Vocational Education, February 19, 1992.* RAND, Boston College and Stanford University.

Koretz, D., Mitchell, K., Barron, S., & Keith, S. (1996). *Perceived effects of the Maryland School Performance Assessment Program.* Final Report to U.S. Department of Education, Office of Educational Research and Improvement. Washington, DC: National Center for Research on Evaluation, Standards, and Student Testing, and RAND.

Linn, R. & Bond, L. (1994). *Studies of the extent of adverse impact of certification rates on federally protected groups and the extend to which assessment exercises are free of bias and unfairness: A report submitted to the National Board for Professional Teaching Standards.* Detroit, MI: National Board for Professional Teaching Standards.

Madaus, G. F. & Kellaghan, T. (1993). The British experience with 'authentic' testing. *Phi Delta Kappan, February,* 458-459, 462-463, 466-469.

Mazzeo, J., Schmitt, A. P., & Bleistein, C. A. (1993). *Sex-related performance differences on constructed response and multiple-choice sections of Advanced Placement examinations.* College Board Report No. 92-7. Princeton, NJ: The College Board.

Meisels, S. J., Dorfman, A., & Steele, D. (1995). Equity and excellence in group-administered and performance-based assessments. In M. T. Nettles & A. L. Nettles (Eds.), *Equity and excellence in educational testing and assessment* (pp. 243-261). Boston: Kluwer Academic Publishers.

Mitchell, R. (1992). *Testing for learning: How new approaches to evaluation can improve American schools.* New York: The Free Press.

Myford, C. M., & Mislevy, R. J. (1994). *Monitoring and improving a portfolio assessment system.* Princeton NJ: Educational Testing Service.

National Commission on Education. (1993). *Learning to Succeed.* London: Heinemann.

National Foundation for Educational Research-Bishop Grosseteste College (1992b). *National Curriculum Assessment at Key Stage 1: 1992 evaluation: Children with statements of special educational needs.* London: School Examinations and Assessment Council.

National Union of Teachers & University of Leeds. (1993). *Testing and assessing 6 and 7 year olds: The evaluation of the 1992 Key Stage 1 National Curriculum Assessment. Final Report.* London: The College Hill Press LTD.

Nuttall, D. (1992). Performance assessment: The message from England. *Educational Leadership, 49,* p. 54-57.

Nuttall, D. L. & Stobart, G. (1994). National Curriculum assessment in the U.K. *Educational Measurement: Issues and Practice, 13*(2), 24-27, 39.

Paterson, L., & Goldstein, H. (1991). New statistical methods of analysing social structures: An introduction to multilevel models. *British Educational Research Journal, 17*(4), 387-393.

Reed, T. C. Y., & Pumfrey, P. D. (1992). Dialect interference and the reading attainments of British Pakistani and ethnic majority pupils. *Research Papers in Education, 7*(1), 27-52.

Sammons, P. (1994, April). *Gender and ethnic differences in attainment and progress: A longitudinal analysis of student achievement over nine years.* Paper presented at the annual meeting of the American Educational Research Association, New Orleans.

School Curriculum and Assessment Authority. (1995). *Report on the 1995 Key Stage 1 tests and tasks in English and Mathematics.* London: SCAA.

Shorrocks, D. (1993). *Implementing National Curriculum assessment.* London: Hodder & Stoughton.

Task Group on Assessment and Testing (1988), *Report.* London: Department of Education and Science.

Thomas, S., Raczek, A. E., & Madaus., G. F. (1995). *Differential impact of performance assesment: The British experience.* Report prepared for the Ford Foundation. Chestnut Hill, MA: Center for the Study of Testing, Evaluation, and Public Policy.

Wiggins, G. (1989). A true test: Toward more authentic and equitable assessment. *Phi Delta Kappan, 70*(9), 703-713.

Willms, D. (1986). Social class segregation and its relationship to pupils' examination results in Scotland. *American Sociological Review, 51,* 224-241.

Endnotes

[1]Behaviorism approaches education as a process of breaking up complex processes into component parts and then teaching each part until students exhibit a desired behavior. On the other hand, a simplified description of constructivism is that individuals actively construct their own knowledge. In this paradigm, knowledge building requires the active mental engagement of the learner; public understanding of complex processes is not best achieved by decomposition into sub-processes, but rather through understanding how sub-processes interact within a context (Resnick & Resnick, 1992).

[2] For claims about the value of authentic assessment, see, for example, Boykoff-Baron, 1990; Educational Leadership, 1992; FairTest, 1992; Garcia and Pearson, 1994; Grace & Shores, 1992; Guay, 1991; Herman, Aschbacher, & Winters, 1992; LeMahieu, 1992 (personal communication, December 23, 1992); Mitchell, 1992; Newmann, 1991; Popham, 1993; Wiggins, 1989, 1990, 1993; Wolf, 1992. For a review of motivation theory and assessment, see Kellaghan, Madaus., and Raczek (1996).

[3]There is considerable evidence that multiple-choice standardized tests, in math and science, at least, do impact negatively on classes with large numbers of minority students. One student found that the best-selling standardized multiple-choice tests in the United States failed to adequately sample high level concepts and skills (Lomax, West, Harmon, Viator & Madaus, 1992). As part of the same study, a national survey of math and science teaches revealed that teachers of classes with high proportions of minority students were more likely to "engage in extensive test prepartion activities and for longer periods of time, align their curriculum and assessment practices to the test, state their students' scores were below expectations and feel pressured to improve scores, and believe these tests go against their own ideals of good practice" (Lomax, West, Harmon, Viator & Madaus, 1992, p. 1).

[4] Related equity claims for authentic assessment are more subject-specific. For example, alternative methods may improve girls' standing in science, not through the assessment method per se, but by influencing teacher behavior toward pupils (Jenkins & MacDonald, 1989; Jovanovic, Solano-Flores, & Shavelson, 1994; National Center for Improving Science Education, 1989). The argument is that "tests that rocus on a range of science skills will motivate teachers to spend time helping all students to develop these skills¼In this way, the classroom environment may became an 'equilizer' " (Jovanovic, Solano-Flores, & Shavelson, 1994, p. 362).

[5] Many researchers in the U.K. (e.g., Gipps & Murphy, 1994) do not make strong equity claims in relation to authentic assessment.

[6] The Key Stage 4 General Certificate of Secondary Education examination (GCSE), which includes multiple assessment techniques (such as teacher-assessed coursework, protfolios, oral assessment, written exams) is not administered in the same form to all secondary students – students may elect to take higher or lower levels of the GCSE in different subjects (Cresswell, 1994; Elwood, 1994). This makes interpretation of subgroup performance complex.

[7] Originally we had intended to analyze 1993 data across several age levels. However, as a result of a teacher boycott of the assessment system due in part to its unmanageability, 1993 data were unavailable. Further, in response to technical manageability and political problems (Gipps, 1993; Kellaghan & Madaus, 1995; Madaus & Kellaghan, 1993) the system as originally conceived has been modified extensively (Dearing, 1993).

[8] For example see Madaus & Kellaghan (1993) for a description of lack of standardization within and across sites associated with the 1991 administration of the Standard Tasks.

[9] In 1994, Gipps and Murphy completed a comprehensive review of student subgroup performance on U.K. assessments. However, most reports they reviewed had small sample sizes and did not distinguish Standard Tasks from teacher-assessed components.

[10] To summarize, three studies (Bolger & Kellaghan, 1990; Breland, et al., 1994; Mazzeo, Schmitt, & Bleistein, 1993) found that the performance gap between male and female secondary students was less on free-response exams than multiple choice. Jovanovic, Solano-Flores, and Shavelson (1994) attributed differential performance by elementary girls and boys on different assessments to item content and differential student experience, rather than test format; the AP studies also found gender variability in performance due to item content and English composition ability. The different conclusions about the relationship of gender and testing method reached by Jovanovic, Solano-Flores, and Shavelson and other studies may be because they considered different age groups - advance secondary students taking certificate exams and high-achieving, high school students versus elementary school students. Also the experiences of girls in a general student population or a highly selective one may differ; similarly, what girls are taught in Ireland and the U.S. may differ. And, finally, girls in America are more accustomed to the multiple-choice format than are girls in Ireland.

[11]Some research suggests that oral reading assessments may be more advantageous for second language students than written (Reed and Pumfrey, 1992).

[12] For a small number of students, data were missing for particular Attainment Targets; thus, for multi-level analysis where comparisons were made at the school level, students with missing data were excluded, as were those in special schools or schools with fewer than five students. The multi-level analytic sample was comprised of 16,840 students in 538 schools.

[13] Student age is also included in our models, but we do not focus on that variable here.

[14] The school-level variable of mean age in the student's grade is also included in models, but not reviewed here.

[15] The assigned level for each Attainment Target was the Standard Task level achieved, if an Standard Task was administered (since Standard Task assessment always over-rides Teacher Assessment) or simply the Teacher Assessment level for those Attainment Targets in which Standard Tasks were not administered.

[16] The Standard Task was optional for four attainment targets (MAT12, MAT14, SAT6, SAT9), but out of these at least two tasks had to be administered (one in mathematics and one in science).

[17] These analyses also estimate the amount of variation in student scores that is attributable to schools once an adjustment is made for student characteristics - often called the "effectiveness" of schools. However, we do not report those results here.

[18] The results indicate that although there were significant gender-related differences on seven of the nine Attainment Targets, only on the mathematics Attainment Target of collecting, recording, and processing data (MAT12) was the impact of gender greater on Teacher Assessment than Standard Task Assessment. Students' entitlement to Free School Meals, a characteristic significantly associated with lower scores on all Teacher Assessments and Standard Tasks, only had a greater impact on one Teacher Assessment (Number Operations) relative to the Standard Task. The impact of the school percentage of students entitled to free school meals was mostly similar for the Teacher Assessments and Standard Task Assessments across the nine attainment targets.

There were more differences in attainment between Teacher Assessments and Standard Tasks for English as a Second Language (E2L) and non-E2L students; in Reading, Writing and Spelling, Teacher Assessment resulted in larger gaps between these groups, while Math: Collect, Record and Process Data, Probabilities, and Science: Earth and Atmosphere assessed by Standard Tasks produced larger gaps. It is for Special Needs students that the two assessment methods produced the most different results. The prediced difference betweeen Special Needs and non-Special Needs students was greater on seven teacher assessments (EAT2, AT3, EAT5, MAT3, MAT12, MAT14, SAT6) and one Standard Task (EAT4).

[19] In examining this issue, the BERA group concluded that the absence of high-stakes summative descriptions of individuals and schools in Scotland offered a greater chance for the assessments to contribute to the improvement of teaching and communication between teachers and parents than did the high-stakes SATs in England and Wales.

[20] Among the specific issues that arose were the need for extra support and staff in schools, the need for procedures to minimize the disruption of school and classroom organization, and the difficulty (and perhaps undesirability) of imposing standardized conditions of administration that would permit comparability of results across schools. One thing that has become clear from the British experience is that there is no quick and easy way of rating large numbers of performance-based tasks.

[21] By some reports, bilingual students seemed uncomfortable in age seven Standard Tests pilot testing, especially because several tasks required group discussions: "Misunderstanding of instructions was a serious problem for bilingual pupils: they appeared to relax and respond better when questions were rephrased in the mother tongue; they became more motivated and handled tasks more confidently. Teachers felt that the bilingual children found it particularly difficult to show their true ability in maths and science. This was largely due to the difficulty of assessing oral responses in science interviews and the difficulties these children experienced in the group discussion element of science and maths investigations (Gipps, 1994, p. 8).

Appendix 1

Examples of scoring rules for 1992 Key Stage 1 Task Assessment of English Attainment Targets 3 (Writing), 4 (Spelling), and 5 (Handwriting)

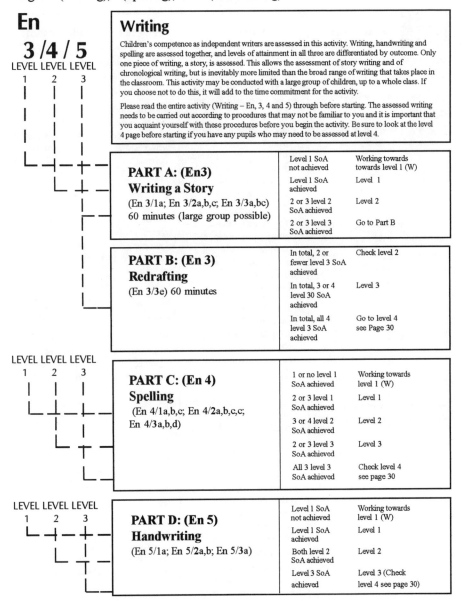

Text reprinted with permission from: Department of Education & Science. (1992). Standard Assessment Task teacher's handbook: 1992 Key Stage 1;. London: School Examinations and Assessment Council. Page 20

Appendix 1

Examples of scoring rules for 1992 Kay Stage 1 Standard Task Assessment of English Attainment Targets 3 (Writing), 4 (Spelling), and 5 (Handwriting)

En3 What to do	SoA	Evidence of Achievement
Part A: Writing a Story • Set up a purpose and an audience for the children's story writing • Help the children to decide upon a subject and a title for their stories • Ask the chidlren to write a story using En 3 *Pupil Sheet* if you wish • Once the assessments have been made, children may make their stories into books or display them or read them to their audience	En 3/1a Use pictures, symbols or isolated letters, words or phrases to communicate meaning En 3/2a Produce independently, pieces of writing, using complete sentences, some of them demarcated with capital letters and full stops or question marks En 3/3a Produce independently, pieces of writing using complete sentences, mainly demarcated with capital letters and full stops or question marks	1. Writes isolated letters/words and tells you what they say or 2. Writes independently; separate 'ideas' or sentences can be identified uses at least *two* capital letters and at least *two* full stops correctly or 3. Writes independently; ideas expressed in recognisable sentences; more than half the sentences correctly punctuated; in a long pieve any passage of 10 sentences may be assessed for punctuation
Only children achieving at least two of the level 3 assessments in writing (En3) so far need carry on to Part B	En 3/2b Structure sequences of real or imagined events coherently in chronological accounts En 3/3b Shape chronological writing, beginning to use a wider range of sentence connectives than 'and' and 'then'	2. Order of events is plausibly chronological or 3. In addition to 2, a range of sentence connectives or phrases is used to relate one event to another
	En 3/2c Write stories showing an understanding of the rudiments of story structure by establishing an opening, characters, and one or more events En 3/3c Write more complex stories with details beyond simple events and with a defined ending	2. The piece is a narrative with more than one character, at least one event and an opening or In addition to 2, the piece has some further detail, such as description of setting or feelings or motives of characters (more than just a few words), and a defined ending

Text reprinted with permission from: Department of Education & Science. (1992). Standard Assessment Task assessment record booklet: 1992 Key Stage 1. London: School Examinations and Assessment Council. Page 14.

Appendix 2

Mean student achievement (and Standard Deviations) on English Attainment Targets by assessment method and student background factors

Group (Sample Size)†	READING [Attainment Target 2]		WRITING (for meaning) [Attainment Target 3]		SPELLING [Attainment Target 4]		HANDWRITING [Attainment Target 5]	
	Teacher Assessment Mean Level	Standard Task Assessment Mean Level	Teacher Assessment Mean Level	Standard Task Assessment Mean Level	Teacher Assessment Mean Level	Standard Task Assessment Mean Level	Teacher Assessment Mean Level	Standard Task Assessment Mean Level
Gender								
Boy (N=8985)	1.84 (0.72)	1.87 (0.74)	1.65 (0.65)	1.64 (0.66)	1.77 (0.70)	1.84 (0.71)	1.82 (0.58)	1.83 (0.59)
Girl (N=8691)	2.04 (0.71)	2.07 (0.73)	1.85 (0.64)	1.83 (0.67)	1.96 (0.66)	2.04 (0.68)	1.96 (0.53)	1.96 (0.54)
Free School Meals (SES)								
Not FSM (N=13235)	2.04 (0.70)	2.07 (0.72) *	1.83 (0.64)	1.81 (0.66)	1.96 (0.66)	2.04 (0.67)	1.95 (0.53)	1.95 (0.54)
FSM (N=4029)	1.61(0.71)	1.62 (0.72)	1.48 (0.64)	1.45 (0.65)	1.56 (0.68)	1.63 (0.70)	1.70 (0.59)	1.70 (0.60)
English Second Lang.								
Not E2L (N=15707)	1.98 (0.71)**	2.01 (0.73) **	1.78 (0.65)**	1.76 (0.67)**	1.90 (0.67)*	1.97 (0.69)**	1.91 (0.55)	1.91 (0.56)
E2L (N=1554)	1.52 (0.70)	1.55 (0.71)	1.43 (0.62)	1.43 (0.63)	1.53 (0.68)	1.63 (0.69)	1.69 (0.58)	1.70 (0.58)
Special Education Needs								
Not SEN (N=16939)	1.96 (0.71)**	1.99 (0.73) **	1.77 (0.64)**	1.75 (0.66)**	1.89 (0.67)**	1.96 (0.68)**	1.90 (0.54)**	1.91 (0.55)**
SEN (N=322)	0.81 (0.70)	0.83 (0.70)	0.78 (0.66)	0.77 (0.66)	0.76 (0.72)	0.79 (0.75)	1.00 (0.76)	1.04 (0.73)

† This is the maximum N for this subject. Sample size within groups may be up to 1% less across assessments due to missing data.

** = significant main effect for this factor p<0.01 (5-way ANOVA, listwise deletion of missing values)

* = significant main effect for this factor p<0.05 (5-way ANOVA, listwise deletion of missing values)

Appendix 2

Mean student achievement (and Standard Deviations) on Mathematics Attainment Targets by assessment method and student background factors

Group (Sample Size)†	NUMBER OPERATIONS (+, -, x, ÷) [Attainment Target 3]		HANDLING DATA: COLLECT, RECORD AND PROCESS DATA [Attainment Target 12]			HANDLING DATA: PROBABILITIES [Attainment Target 14]		
	Teacher Assessment Mean Level	Standard Task Assessment Mean Level	Teacher Assessment Mean Level	Standard Task Assessment (OPTIONAL) Mean Level	N for Optional ST Assessment	Teacher Assessment Mean Level	Standard Task Assessment (OPTIONAL) Mean Level	N for Optional ST Assessment
Gender								
Boy (N=8986)†	1.78 (0.68)	1.71 (0.76)	1.87 (0.69)	2.04 (0.77)	6244	1.86 (0.71)	2.36 (0.82)	2958
Girl (N=8687)	1.84 (0.64)	1.77 (0.71)	1.94 (0.65)	2.10 (0.71)	5948	1.91 (0.67)	2.39 (0.78)	2935
Free School Meals (SES)								
Not FSM (N=13235)	1.89 (0.64)*	1.82 (0.72) *	1.99 (0.65)	2.16 (0.71)	9171	1.97 (0.66)	2.45 (0.78)	4417
FSM (N=4029)	1.56 (0.67)	1.48 (0.71)	1.65 (0.68)	1.79 (0.76)	2765	1.64 (0.72)	2.15 (0.83)	1317
English Second Lang.								
Not E2L (N=15704)	1.84 (0.65)**	1.77 (0.73) **	1.94 (0.66)**	2.10 (0.73)**	10840	1.93 (0.67)**	2.42 (0.79)	5289
E2L (N=1555)	1.50 (0.68)	1.42 (0.73)	1.60 (0.68)	1.74 (0.75)	1094	1.49 (0.74)	1.96 (0.83)	444
Special Education Needs								
Not SEN (N=16938)	1.83 (0.64)**	1.91 (0.72) **	1.93 (0.65)**	2.10 (0.71)**	11677	1.91 (0.67)**	2.40 (0.78)**	5648
SEN (N=321)	0.68 (0.74)	1.04 (0.76)	0.84 (0.78)	0.88 (0.83)	258	0.77 (0.81)	1.27 (1.07)	84

† This is the maximum N for this subject. Sample size within groups may be up to 1% less across assessments due to missing data.

** = significant main effect for this factor p<0.01 (5-way ANOVA, listwise deletion of missing values)

* = significant main effect for this factor p<0.05 (5-way ANOVA, listwise deletion of missing values)

Appendix 2

Mean student achievement (and Standard Deviations) on Science Attainment Targets by assessment method and student background factors

Group (Sample Size)†	SCIENCE: TYPES & USES OF MATERIALS [Attainment Target 6]			SCIENCE: EARTH & ATMOSPHERE [Attainment Target 9]		
	Teacher Assessment Mean Level	Standard Task (OPTIONAL) Mean Level	N for Optional ST Assessment	Teacher Assessment Mean Level	Standard Task (OPTIONAL) Mean Level	N for Optional ST Assessment
Gender						
Boy (N=8981)†	1.96 (0.69)	2.14 (0.76)	4056	1.96 (0.57)*	2.12 (0.63)	5024
Girl (N=8684)	1.99 (0.66)	2.17 (0.74)	4009	2.00 (0.53)	2.17 (0.59)	4804
Free School Meals (SES)						
Not FSM (N=13228)	2.06 (0.65)	2.23 (0.72)	6153	2.04 (0.53)	2.21 (0.59)**	7270
FSM (N=4023)	1.73 (0.70)	1.88 (0.78)	1769	1.80 (0.60)	1.95 (0.63)	2290
English Second Lang.						
Not E2L (N=15704)	2.02 (0.65)**	2.20 (0.72)	7232	2.02 (0.53)**	2.19 (0.60)**	8727
E2L (N=1555)	1.56 (0.75)	1.64 (0.85)	690		1.80 (0.59)	830
Special Education Needs						
Not SEN (N=16938)	2.00 (0.66)**	2.17 (0.73)**	7770	2.00 (0.53)**	2.17 (0.58)**	9371
SEN (N=321)	0.96 (0.82)	1.11 (0.85)	151	1.00 (0.78)	1.09 (0.81)	187

9 The Case for Affirmative Action in Higher Education

William H. Gray III
Michael T. Nettles
Laura W. Perna
Kimberley C. Edelin

HISTORY: ORIGINS OF AFFIRMATIVE ACTION

Affirmative action in the United States is rooted in a succession of presidential Executive Orders spanning more than three and a half decades and the past eight Presidents of the United States. From President Kennedy through President Clinton, each American President has issued an Executive Order to address the 350 years of racial injustice that Black Americans have endured in America. President Kennedy's 1961 Executive Order 10925 marked the first time that the nation's Commander in Chief sought to establish a national affirmative action policy. Responding to many years of racial inequality in employment, education, public accommodation, and other aspects of society, President Kennedy sought to ensure that primarily African Americans but also other disadvantaged groups gain access to employment opportunities that had been the exclusive province of White Americans throughout the nation's history.

President Kennedy's Executive Order (10925) established a committee on equal employment opportunity to examine the federal government's employment practices and to "consider and recommend additional affirmative steps to be taken by executive departments and agencies to realize the national policy of nondiscrimination within the executive branch of government." The following excerpts from President Kennedy's Executive Order provide the rationale that he and his successors have used in establishing affirmative action policies:

> • discrimination based upon race, creed, color, and national origin is "contrary to the Constitutional principles and policies of the United States,"

• "it is the plain and positive obligation of the United States Government to promote and ensure equal opportunity for all qualified persons, without regard to race, creed, color, or national origin, employed or seeking employment with the Federal Government and on government contracts,"

• "it is in the general interest and welfare of the United States to promote its economy, security, and national defense through the most efficient and effective utilization of all available manpower," and

• that "a review and analysis of existing Executive orders, practices, and government agency procedures relating to government employment and compliance with existing non-discrimination contract provisions reveal an urgent need for expansion and strengthening of efforts to promote full equality of employment opportunity."

This was a time when African Americans were denied opportunities on the basis of their race, and the affirmative action policy was authorized as a step toward ending de jure and de facto discrimination against Blacks. These principles from Kennedy's Executive Order have endured throughout the next three decades, but the need for affirmative action has perhaps been best expressed by the nation's 36th President, Lyndon Baines Johnson, in his keynote address on June 4, 1965 at the 97th annual commencement of Howard University. In that commencement address President Johnson stated the following:

You do not take a person who, for years, has been hobbled by chains and liberate him, bring him up to the starting line of a race, and then say, "you are free to compete with all the others," and still justly believe that you have been completely fair. Thus it is not enough just to open the gates of opportunity. All our citizens must have the ability to walk through those gates.

Lyndon Johnson's 1965 Executive Order 11246, which followed his historic Howard University address, strengthened the national policy by establishing the Equal Employment Opportunity Commission (EEOC) under Title VII of the 1964 Civil Rights Act. The Executive Order also required federal government agencies "to provide equal opportunity" in employment, "to prohibit discrimination in employment because of race, creed, color, or national origin," and "to promote the full realization of equal employment opportunity through a positive, continuing program." In President Johnson's administration, federal contractors were required to "take affirmative action to ensure that minority applicants [for employment] are employed, and that employees are treated [during employment] without regard to their race, creed, color, or national origin." In 1967 the Order was amended by Executive Order 11375 to prohibit discrimination based upon sex.

In what is known as Revised Order #4, President Richard Milhous Nixon established an even stronger national affirmative action policy. Nixon's policy mandated federal nonconstruction contractors, including universities, to develop, implement, and document a written affirmative action compliance program. Under Nixon's affirmative action policy, employers were required to conduct analyses of deficiencies in the utilization of minorities and women, and to set goals and timetables for correcting the deficiencies and achieving "prompt and full utilization of minorities and women, at all levels and in all segments of its work force where deficiencies exist." Goals were defined as significant, measurable, and attainable targets rather than rigid and inflexible quotas.

Education and training were new features added by President Nixon to the national policy. Among the factors to be considered in determining whether minorities were underutilized in any job group were "the existence of training institutions capable of training persons in the requisite skills; and the degree of training which the contractor is reasonably able to undertake as a means of making all job classes available to minorities." This was the first explicit indication that education and training were essential and central elements of the nation's affirmative action policy. President Nixon made it clear that educational institutions had a vital role to play in ensuring that the workforce had quality candidates to employ. In a 1969 Presidential Memorandum to heads of departments and agencies about equal employment opportunity in the federal government, President Nixon stated the following:

> No more serious task challenges our nation domestically than the achievement of equality of opportunity for all our citizens in every aspect of their lives regardless of their race, color, religion, national origin or sex… we must, through positive action, make it possible for our citizens to compete on a truly equal and fair basis for employment and to qualify for advancement within the Federal service.

Nixon implemented the first direct affirmative action policy under what is known as the "Philadelphia Plan." Under this plan, Nixon emphasized that federal contractors in Philadelphia were to utilize affirmative action to create more jobs for minorities. This was the first time preferences were used by the federal government to ensure "minority group representation in all trades."

In 1977 Congressman Parren J. Mitchell (Democrat), from the Baltimore City district of Maryland, sponsored two bills (H.R. 4961 and H. Amdt. 18) that were later signed into law by President Carter which further established the policy and practice of "leveling the playing field" for Black Americans. One bill (H.R. 4961) increased assistance under the Small Business Investment Act of 1958 to small businesses owned or controlled by minorities and provided statutory standards for contracting and subcontracting by the federal government pertaining to minority businesses. The second (H. Amdt. 18) required that at least 10% of the dollar amount of every public works contract from the federal government be set aside for the procurement of materials and supplies from minority businesses.

By the end of the 1970s policies supported by five Presidents (Kennedy, Johnson, Ford, Nixon and Carter) and by every session of Congress from the 87th in 1961 through the 96th in 1980 had clearly established that federal contractors and other organizations receiving funding from the federal government were required to take affirmative steps to provide equal opportunities for African Americans.

AFFIRMATIVE ACTION IN HIGHER EDUCATION

Much of the history of higher education in America is marked by racial segregation and the exclusion of African Americans. Etched in our recent memory is the infamous scene from 1963 of Alabama's Governor George Wallace blocking the doors of the University of Alabama to prevent two African Americans (Vivian Malone and James Hood) from attending their first day of classes even after they were admitted through an admissions process that involved no preferences, exceptions, or affirmative action. We also recall 1962 when Mississippi's Governor, Ross Barnett, challenged the U. S. Supreme Court's order to admit James Meredith to the University of Mississippi. Meredith also met Ole Miss' admissions requirements and required no preferences, not even a racial preference. Yet Governor Barnett, like Governor Wallace, could not accept the absence of preferences for White citizens, preferences that America had adhered to for 350 years. So instead he sought to continue denying the rights of Blacks.

While a small number of African Americans enrolled in universities in the North (e.g. Yale, Harvard, Oberlin, Ohio State, Michigan and Iowa State) early in the 20th century, the beginning of the widespread elimination of racial barriers coincided with the enactment of the national affirmative action policies in the 1960s and 1970s. The cases of the University of Alabama and Ole Miss are just two vivid examples of actions taken by colleges and universities throughout the nation to provide access for African American students who had historically been denied opportunity regardless of whether they had achieved the requisite admission test scores, grades, and other criteria.

The first challenge to affirmative action in higher education that resulted in an opinion by the U. S. Supreme Court was the 1978 landmark case of *Regents of the University of California v. Bakke*. In this case, the Supreme Court appeared to support affirmative action by upholding "race" as a legally acceptable criterion for colleges and universities to include in their admissions process, but only when used along with other criteria, such as test scores, high school grades, geography, alumni status, and special talents. Writing on behalf of the majority of the Court, Justice Lewis F. Powell articulated the Supreme Court's view of the importance of diversity in higher education and the appropriateness of affirmative action to achieve it in the following words:

The attainment of a diverse student body is a constitutionally permissible goal for an institution of higher education; however, ethnic diversity is only one element in a range of factors which a university may properly consider in attaining the goal of a heterogeneous student body; although a university must have wide discretion in making sensitive judgments as to who should be admitted, constitutional limitations protecting individual rights may not be disregarded.

While Justice Thurgood Marshall concurred with Justice Powell and the majority of the Court, he found the need to express his perspective about the individual rights element of the Court's ruling. Because of the many years of racial discrimination suffered by African Americans, not because of their individual and personally distinctive characteristics but rather because they were members of the Black race, Justice Marshall found racial group remedies to be appropriate. Justice Marshall's point of view is expressed in the following 1978 quote following the Supreme Court's decision in the Bakke case:

> It is unnecessary in twentieth century America to have individual Negroes demonstrate that they have been victims of racial discrimination; the racism of our society has been so pervasive that none, regardless of wealth or position, has managed to escape its impact. The experience of Negroes in America has been different in kind, not just in degree, from that of other ethnic groups. It is not merely the history of slavery alone but also that a whole people were marked as inferior by the law. And that mark has endured. The dream of America as the great melting pot has not been realized for the Negro, because of his skin color he has never even made it into the pot.

As a consequence of the affirmative action exercised by the nation's colleges and universities during the 1970s, 1980s and 1990s, the nation has witnessed unprecedented growth in African American participation in higher education overall and in access to predominantly White colleges and universities.

Figure 1 shows that, since 1976 (the first year for which national data by race are available), the number of African Americans and Hispanics enrolling in the nation's predominantly White colleges and universities has increased dramatically (by 41% and 203% respectively). The increase for White students over the same period was 13%. The rate of increase in African American and Hispanic undergraduate enrollment in all of the nation's colleges and universities was roughly the same rate as at non-HBCUs between 1976 and 1996. Today about 1,352,600 of the nation's 12,259,400 undergraduates are African American. About 15% of all African American undergraduates are attending Historically Black Colleges and Universities (HBCUs).

The number of bachelor's degrees awarded to African Americans by non-HBCUs increased by 62% between 1976 and 1995 (see Figure 2). Over this same period, the number of bachelor's degrees awarded increased by 182% for Hispanics, 328% for Asians, and 10% for Whites. African Americans received 85,161 of the 1,160,134 bachelor's degrees awarded in 1994-95. About 28% of all bachelor's degrees awarded to African Americans are from HBCUs and 72% are awarded by predominantly White universities. These data suggest that affirmative action has helped to increase access to higher education for African Americans.

Figure 1

Increase in the Number of Undergraduates Attending Colleges and Universities Nationwide: 1976 to 1996

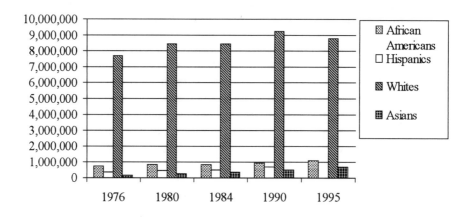

Figure 2

Increase in the Number of Bachelor's Degrees Awarded by Colleges and Universities Nationwide: 1976 to 1995

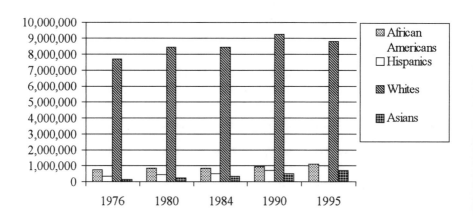

The increase in the number of White students attending and receiving degrees from HBCUs reveals yet another indication of gains related to affirmative action. The affirmative action debate pays too little attention to the growth in the number White students attending and receiving degrees from HBCUs. Figure 3 shows that White undergraduate enrollment at HBCUs increased by 69% between 1976 and 1995, compared with a 17% increase for African Americans. The number of bachelor's degrees awarded to White students by HBCUs increased by 72% over the same period, compared with a 15% increase for African Americans. Whites received 3,060 of the 28,327 bachelor's degrees awarded by HBCUs in 1994-1995.

Figure 3

Changes at Historically Black Colleges and Universities in Undergraduate Enrollment and Bachelor's Degrees Awarded: 1976 to 1995

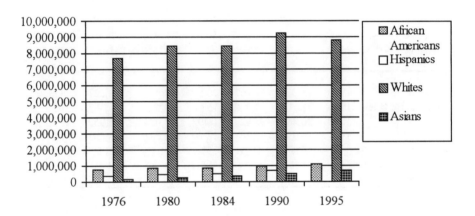

Table 1 shows that, over the past three decades, African Americans and Hispanics have experienced an increase in access to some of the nation's most prestigious predominantly White colleges and universities. These increases may be attributed to affirmative action policies in student admissions. The number of African American undergraduates enrolled increased between 1980 and 1997 by 24% at Harvard University, 62% at the University of Mississippi, 68% at the University of California at Berkeley, and 50% at the University of Texas at Austin. Hispanic enrollment increased by 117% at Harvard University, 614% at the University of Mississippi, 237% at the University of California at Berkeley, and 74% at the University of Texas at Austin.

Table 1

Trends in Undergraduate Enrollment at Selected Colleges and Universities by Race: Selected Years from 1970 to 1997

Institution	Year	Total	White	Black	Hispanic	Asian	Other
Harvard University	1970	NA	NA	NA	NA	NA	NA
	1980	6,552	5,008*	449	232	307	556*
	1990	6,622	4,289	509	417	980	427
	1997	6,630	2,782	555	503	1,180	1,610
% Change 1970-97		NA	NA	NA	NA	NA	NA
% Change 1980-97		1%	-44%	24%	117%	284%	190%
University of	1970	6,358	NA	151	NA	NA	NA
Mississippi	1980	7,852	7,082	560	7	43	160
	1990	8,595	7,672	630	18	46	229
	1997	8,3007,046		907	50	104	193
% Change 1970-97		31%	NA	50%	NA	NA	NA
% Change 1970-80		6%	-.5%	62%	614%	142%	21%
University of	1970	18,264	11,107	709	405	2,227	945
California,Berkeley	1980	21,110	13,948	758	823	4,367	610
	1990	20,860	8,762	1,492	3,024	5,962	469
	1997	20,930	6,574	1,270	2,771	8,565	613
% Change 1970-97		15%	-41%	79%	584%	285%	-35%
% Change 1970-80		-.8%	-53%	68%	237%	96%	.5%
U. of California	1970	19,610	14,745	1,390	1,120	2,120	235
Los Angeles	1980	21,235	14,930	1,040	1,380	3,760	125
	1990	23,745	11,135	1,615	4,875	6,740	389
	1997	23,270	8,195	1,440	4,035	9,220	380
% Change 1970-97		19%	-44%	4%	260%	335%	62%
% Change 1980-97		10%	-45%	38%	192%	145%	204%
University of	1970	NA	NA	NA	NA	NA	NA
Texas, Austin	1980	36,599	31,432	901	3,010	427	829
	1990	37,152	26,793	1,481	4,638	2,836	1,404
	1997	38,861	24,219	1,353	5,234	4,783	1,272
% Change 1970-97		NA	NA	NA	NA	NA	NA
% Change 1980-97		6%	-23%	50%	74%	1020%	53%

Notes: * Estimate

NA = not available

Fall 1970 enrollment data for UCLA are for Fall 1973

Over the same period Asian enrollment increased by 284% at Harvard University, 142% at the University of Mississippi, 96% at the University of California at Berkeley, 1020% at the University of Texas. By contrast the number of White undergraduates declined by 44% at Harvard University, 0.5% at the University of Mississippi, 53% at the University of California, Berkeley, and 23% at the University of Texas at Austin.

THE CURRENT DEBATE ON AFFIRMATIVE ACTION IN HIGHER EDUCATION

The Supreme Court's ruling to uphold the legal standing of "race" as one among several factors in the admissions process has been a guide to colleges and universities in establishing affirmative action as part of their admissions policies and in awarding a small fraction of their scholarships. Legal challenges in the states of Maryland, Texas, California and Michigan pose a threat to the affirmative action policies of the past three decades as well as to the progress that has been made thus far. Within the past two years bills have been proposed in 13 state legislatures to abolish affirmative action programs. The U.S. House of Representatives will soon consider an amendment to the Higher Education Act, sponsored by California Republican Frank Riggs, that would prohibit colleges and universities from considering race, sex, color or national origin in the admissions process. Later this year voters in the state of Washington will consider whether to eliminate affirmative action programs. Several other cases raise new questions about how race can be used as a criterion for pursuing the racial diversity that the nation's colleges and universities want to achieve. These include: the anti-affirmative action case of *Podberesky v. Kirwan* (1994) prohibiting the use of race in awarding Banneker Scholarships at the University of Maryland, the Federal Court's decision in the case of *Cheryl Hopwood v. Texas* (1996) prohibiting the use of different test scores and other criteria in granting admissions to White, African American and Latino applicants, and the Federal Court's 1997 ruling in support of California's public referendum Proposition 209.

After seeing the devastating effect of *Hopwood v. Texas* on enrollment at the University of Texas and at the urging of the University of Texas System, Texas Attorney General Dan Morales has taken the first step toward appealing a March 1998 ruling on the case. The ruling awarded $776,000 to the lawyers who represented the plaintiffs in the *Hopwood* case and included an injunction preventing the University of Texas from considering race in the admissions process. University of Texas officials hope such action may ultimately lead the U.S. Supreme Court to reexamine the 1996 decision. State officials in Texas seem at last to be alarmed at the effect of the Court's ruling in the *Hopwood* case. Before the decision in 1996, there were 65 African Americans admitted for the entering class at the University of Texas law school and 31 enrolled. In the fall of 1977, only 11 African Americans were admitted and only 4 enrolled. The state of Texas is 14% African American.

Prior to California's referendum on Proposition 209, the colleges and universities in California were becoming models of racial and ethnic diversity. Access for African American students to higher education, particularly the most elite public colleges and universities in California, has declined as a consequence of these anti-affirmative action policies. Table 2 shows that the number of African American applicants admitted to the University of California system as a whole declined by 18% between Fall 1997 and Fall 1998, the year after the changes in admission policies that were required by Proposition 209 were implemented.

The decline in access for African Americans appears to be somewhat greater at the more selective campuses within the University of California system. For example, the number of African American applicants accepted for admission declined by 67% at Berkeley and 43% at UCLA between Fall 1997 and Fall 1998. Only 2% of all applicants admitted at the University of California, Berkeley were African American in Fall 1998, down from 7% in Fall 1997. Similarly, the number of Latino applicants admitted declined by 53% at UC Berkeley and 33% at UCLA. The number of admitted White applicants declined by 9% within the University of California overall, but by only 2% at UC, Berkeley and 5% at UCLA. Asians now represent 37% of all students admitted to UC, Berkeley and 41% of all students admitted to UCLA.

Table 2

Change in the number of applicants admitted to the University of California before (Fall 1997) and after (Fall 1998) Proposition 209

Race/Ethnicity	**System**			**Berkeley**			**Los Angeles**		
	Fall 1997	Fall 1998	% change	Fall 1997	Fall 1998	% change	Fall 1997	Fall 1998	% change
Total	100% 42,863	100% 44,393	4%	100% 8,450	100% 8,034	-5%	100% 10,172	100% 10,186	0%
African American	4% 1,509	3% 1,243	-18%	7% 562	2% 191	-66%	5% 488	3% 280	-43%
American Indian	1% 336	1% 318	-5%	1% 69	0% 27	-61%	1% 81	0% 46	-43%
Asian	34% 14,421	32% 14,427	0%	35% 2,925	37% 2,998	2%	41% 4,154	41% 4,187	1%
Latino	13% 5,685	12% 5,294	-7%	15% 1,266	7% 600	-53%	15% 1,497	10% 1,001	-33%
White	41% 17,680	36% 16,109	-9%	32% 2,725	33% 2,674	-2%	33% 3,383	32% 3,209	-5%
Other/ Unknown	8% 3,232	16% 7,002	117%	11% 903	19% 1,544	71%	6% 569	14% 1,463	157%

Table 2 (continued)

Change in the number of applicants admitted to the University of California before (Fall 1997) and after (Fall 1998) Proposition 209

Race/Ethnicity	Davis Fall 1997	Davis Fall 1998	Davis % change	Irvine Fall 1997	Irvine Fall 1998	Irvine % change	Santa Cruz Fall 1997	Santa Cruz Fall 1998	Santa Cruz % change
Total	100%	100%	4%	100%	100%	3%	100%	100%	11%
	16,859	17,549		11,382	11,701		9,257	10,233	
African American	3%	2%	-36%	3%	2%	-19%	2%	2%	-2%
	518	332		303	246		223	219	
American Indian	1%	1%	-18%	1%	0%	-14%	1%	1%	17%
	122	100		66	57		82	96	
Asian	45%	47%	9%	47%	45%	-1%	25%	25%	9%
	7,596	8,260		5,389	5,309		2,316	2,516	
Latino	10%	7%	-20%	12%	11%	-9%	13%	12%	7%
	1,626	1,302		1,412	1,291		1,159	1,245	
White	33%	29%	-10%	33%	29%	-10%	53%	43%	-10%
	5,615	5,064		3,770	3,375		4,915	4,448	
Other/ Unknown	8%	14%	80%	4%	12%	222%	6%	17%	204%
	1,382	2,491		442	1,423		562	1,709	

Source: News releases: University of California, Berkeley (3/31/98) Los Angeles, (3/31/98), Davis (3/16/98), Santa Cruz (4/6/98)

WHY SOME OPPOSE AFFIRMATIVE ACTION IN HIGHER EDUCATION

In order to attempt to understand the anti-affirmative action movement that has emerged in recent years and the policies that yield such a reversal of fortune and opportunity for African Americans, Latinos, economically disadvantaged citizens and the nation, it is important to try to hear the logic that the opponents of affirmative action have used to explain their position. On the surface, the opponents of affirmative action like Ward Connerly in California, could simply be demanding a return to an era prior to the 1964 Civil Rights Act when African Americans had very limited access to higher education and employment opportunities.

The opponents of affirmative action, in *Podberesky v. Kirwan* (1994), *Cheryl Hopwood v. Texas* (1996), Proposition 209 (1996), and the most recent cases, *Gratz and Hamacher v. University of Michigan* (1997) and *Grutter v. University of Michigan Law School* (1997), make the following general arguments, each one of which is a myth:

• minorities and women can compete without preferences;

• my children should not be penalized for something they did not do;

• not every White person is advantaged and not every minority is disadvantaged;

• affirmative action means that less qualified individuals are preferred;

• admissions test scores and grade point averages are fair and objective measures of merit;

• affirmative action has negative effects on college success and graduation rates;

• Blacks who enter under affirmative action suffer negative psychological effects; and

• discrimination in any form, including preferences, is wrong.

We would like to address each of these points because otherwise it may be difficult for many Americans who have supported the merits of affirmative action for the past 37 years to avoid being seduced by the flawed logic of its opponents. If affirmative action is abolished, the outcomes will be detrimental not just to African Americans, but also to the nation. These mythical arguments against anti-affirmative action prey upon the fears of some Americans who feel that their own personal opportunities are now being threatened by affirmative action. Turning to blame the victims of over 350 years of injustice and exclusion instead of embracing the need to repair the damage inflicted over these past three and half centuries is not a good solution for the United States of America.

The first anti affirmative action argument claims that minorities and women can compete without preferences

Only during the past four decades has the nation begun to take the necessary corrective actions to restore the basic legal and human rights that have been denied to African Americans for much of America's history. Selected events from *The Timetables of African American History* (1995) illustrate the unique plight of African Americans compared to other groups in America:

• In 1811, Christopher McPherson, an affluent free Black, was jailed and then sent to the Williamsburg Lunatic Asylum because he opened a night school for free Blacks in Richmond.

• In 1823 the state of Mississippi prohibited teaching reading and writing to Blacks, as well as meetings of more than five slaves or free Blacks.

• In 1834 the state of South Carolina prohibited the teaching of free and enslaved Black children.

• In 1838 the state of Ohio prohibited state funds to be used to educate Black children.

• In 1847 the state of Missouri passed a law prohibiting the education of Blacks. The first school for Blacks in the state of Missouri was not organized until 1864.

• It was only in 1862 that the first Black woman earned a bachelor's degree from an accredited American college (Mary Jane Patterson, Oberlin College). This was 226 years after the founding of America's first universities — more than two centuries in which the benefits of higher education were enjoyed exclusively by White Americans.

• In 1868, four years after the Emancipation Proclamation, the Alabama state legislature voted to segregate its schools.

• It was in 1870, nearly 100 years after the signing of the Declaration of Independence and 83 years after the adoption of the U.S. Constitution, that the 15th Amendment granted Black men the right to vote.

• Black women, along with all women, did not gain the right to vote until 1920 under the 19th Amendment.

• More than 50 years after ruling that "separate but equal" facilities were constitutional in *Plessy v. Ferguson* (1896), the United States Supreme Court ruled in *Brown v. Board of Education of Topeka* (1954) that segregated schools were "inherently unequal" and, therefore, unconstitutional.

• After more than three years of legal action, the NAACP forced the University of Alabama to enroll its first black student, Autherine Lucy, in 1956.

• In 1962 Governor of Mississippi Ross Barnett tried unsuccessfully to prevent James H. Meredith from enrolling in the University of Mississippi, even though the United States Supreme Court ordered his admission.

• The poll tax, a requirement long used to prevent Blacks from voting, was finally outlawed in 1964 under the 24th Amendment.

• The first Black to head a major public predominantly White university was Clifton Reginald Wharton, Jr. in 1969 (Michigan State University).

• In 1973 Barbara Sizemore became the first African American woman to head the public schools of any major U.S. city (Washington, DC).

• Not until 1987, 106 years after its founding, did Spelman College, an all-woman historically Black college, appoint a Black woman as its president (Johnetta B. Cole).

• In 1990 a state court judge in Gwinnett County, Georgia ruled that a 39-year old law prohibiting members of the Ku Klux Klan from wearing hooded masks in public was unconstitutional.

• It was not until 1992 that the first African American woman, and the third African American period, was elected to serve in the United States Senate (Carol Mosely Braun).

These historical events portray the enduring discrimination and unfair treatment of African Americans and the need for interventions to correct the many injustices of the past and present. Affirmative action is one appropriate measure for bringing about incremental improvements.

A second criticism of affirmative action that we often hear is the following: My children should not be penalized for something they did not do

Whites born in the United States within the past twenty years are now applying for college admissions. While these youngsters have not lived and participated in a de jure segregated society, they have benefited and continue to benefit from the de facto segregation that exists in the United States today and the vestiges of our historically segregated society.

In their 1997 book *Black Wealth/White Wealth* Drs. Melvin Oliver of the Ford Foundation and Thomas Shapiro of Northwestern University point out vast differences in the assets and wealth of Blacks and Whites who are considered to be of equal class, educational and employment status. For example, among white collar Americans who are considered to be of upper class, Whites have an average net worth of $77,850 compared to an average net worth of $17,499 for Blacks (Oliver and Shapiro, 1997). Hoffman and Novak, researchers at Vanderbilt University, have found that only 13.3% of Black households with income below $40,000 own a computer, compared with 27.5% of white households. Moreover, Black students who do not have computers at home have less access than White students to computers in other locations like their schools. These kind of gaps are prevalent at each educational, occupational, and class level and reflect the intergenerational advantage that White Americans have over African Americans, as well as the vestiges of de jure racially segregated history in America.

The racial composition of some occupational categories in America today also reflects the de facto segregation that continues to exist in the United States and that provides greater support for White youngsters than for Black youngsters. For example, despite the fact that the population of the U.S. is 70% White American:

- 100% of the nation's governors are White
- 89% (8 out of 9) of Supreme Court justices are White
- 98% of the nation's commercial airline pilots are White
- 96% of the nation's geologists are White
- 96% of the nation's dentists are White
- 94% of the nation's lawyers are White
- 94% of the nation's aerospace engineers are White
- 92% of the nation's economists are White
- 91% of the nation's architects are White

Source: *The Riverfront Times*, from the Bureau of Labor Statistics

The opportunities that White youngsters are disproportionately afforded, such as the quality of schools they attend, the quality of their home neighborhoods, and the employment options which they are afforded, are not unrelated to the wealth of their parents, grandparents, and great grandparents that many started earning from the economies of slavery and de jure segregation. The spoils of today's de facto segregated society are related to social class and the quality of the nation's schools that are distributed to people according to their race and class. For example, at almost 61% of elementary and secondary public schools in the United States, fewer than 5% of the students are African American. African Americans represent the majority of students in 10% of the nation's schools (Nettles & Perna, 1997b). African American students attend public schools that are racially segregated largely because they live in neighborhoods that are racially segregated. For example, in Philadelphia in 1980, White residents lived in neighborhoods that were 67.5% White. By contrast, African American residents lived in areas that were 99% Black (Massey, Condran, & Denton, 1987). Racial segregation, poverty, and schooling are interrelated.

The schools with the highest representation of African Americans are also the schools that have the highest rates of poverty. For example, public elementary schools that are 5% or less African American have 39% of students receiving free or reduced fee lunch. By contrast, in the schools where between 6% and 49% of the students are African American, 58% require free or reduced fee lunch. And, at the schools with 50% or more African American enrollment, 84% of students need free or reduced fee lunch. Remedial math and reading programs are also more likely to be offered in schools with a majority of African American students.

African American young children are more likely than any other group to have Head Start as their option for pre-school. In 1992, almost one-third (31%) of African American three-and four-year olds who were enrolled in pre-school attended Head Start, compared with 12.7% of all three- and four-year olds. While African American young children begin school as eager to learn as students of other racial/ethnic groups, there appears to be an early gap in their vocabulary skills. African American and White preschoolers achieve similar scores on tests of motor and social development (100.0 versus 102.6) and verbal memory (96.2 versus 97.7), but African American preschoolers score much lower than Whites on tests of vocabulary (74.6 versus 98.2). This is likely to be related to the differential quality of pre-school options available to children of various races in America.

Nearly one-third of African Americans (30%) and Hispanics (32%) attend public elementary and secondary schools in large central cities, compared with only 5% of Whites (Nettles and Perna, 1997b). The following data from a recent report published in *Education Week* in collaboration with the Pew Charitable Trusts, illustrate the plight of urban schools:

• urban students are far less likely to graduate on time than non-urban students;

• 43% of minority children attend urban schools. Most of them attend schools in which more than half of the students are poor and that are predominantly, if not completely, minority;

• the poorest students are at greatest risk. In urban schools where most of the students are poor, two-thirds or more of the children fail to reach even the "basic" level on national tests of reading, writing, math and other subjects;

• urban school districts are twice as likely as non-urban districts to hire teachers who have no license or who have only an emergency or temporary license;

• most urban students lack access to the rigorous curricula, well-prepared teachers, and high expectations that would make better achievement possible. Performance is worst in high-poverty urban schools, where the majority of students are poor;

• of the 49 urban districts that responded to their survey of 74 large city districts, 15 reported that it would take $500 million or more to restore their buildings to good condition.

Source: *Quality Counts,* 1998

The issue of school funding is particularly relevant to the discussion of urban education and the education of African American and Hispanic youngsters. Table 3 shows the per pupil expenditures for several school districts throughout the nation. Per pupil expenditures are lower in urban school districts than suburban districts. Expenditures are also lower in school districts with the highest minority student representation. For example, in Detroit, where minority students comprise 79% of the enrollment, the per pupil expenditure is $7,364, whereas the per pupil expenditure is $11,934 in the predominantly White suburb of Bloomfield Hills. The 89% minority school district of Bridgeport, Connecticut spends $6, 989 per pupil, whereas the 20% minority Greenwich school district spends $10,909 per student. The opponents of affirmative action argue that "you cannot throw money at schools" to solve the problem of academic achievement. But a recent court case before the Supreme Court of New Jersey (Abbot vs. Burke, 1990) provides evidence that the poorer the school district, the worse the quality of education, and that increased school funding is necessary to address many of the problems encountered in urban schools.

Table 3

Per Pupil Expenditures and Racial Composition of Selected School Districts

State	School Year	District	Per Pupil Expenditures	% Minority Student Enrollment
Michigan	1995-1996	Detroit	$7,364	79%
		Bloomfield Hills	$11,934	11%
Washington, DC and Maryland	1996-1997	Washington, DC	$6,888	96%
		Montgomery County	$8,644	45%
Connecticut	1996-1997	Bridgeport	$6,989	89%
		Greenwich	$10,909	20%
Massachusetts	1993-1994	Boston	$4,496	83%
		Cambridge	$10,791	60%
Pennsylvania	1996-1997	Philadelphia City	$6,860	80%
		Lower Merion	$11,056	12%

A third anti-affirmative action argument holds that not every White person is advantaged and not every minority is disadvantaged

While not every White person in the United States is advantaged and not every Black American is disadvantaged, if you are African American in the United States today you are more than three times as likely to be poor than if you are a White American. In 1996, only 8.6% of non-Hispanic Whites were living in poverty, compared with 28.4% of Blacks and 29.4% of Hispanics (Lamison-White, 1997). The rates of poverty for African American and Latino youngsters are even more abysmal. In 1996, 40% of African Americans and Latinos under 18 years of age were living below the poverty line, compared with 15% of White children (Bureau of the Census, 1997). African American and Latino youth are also more likely to live in distressed neighborhoods or in concentrated poverty than their White counterparts. In 1994, 25% of African American and 10% of Latino young adolescents were living in distressed neighborhoods, compared with 2% of Whites (Casey, 1994).[1] Further, African Americans and Hispanics are more likely to be chronically poor.[2] In 1992 and 1993, 15.1% of African Americans and 10.3% of Hispanics were poor in all 24 months of those two years, compared with only 3.1% of Whites (Bureau of the Census, 1994). It is important to examine poverty rates in connection with affirmative action because children from low income families fare less well in school than children from more affluent families (Brooks-Gunn, Duncan, Klebanov, & Sealand, 1993).

African American and Hispanic youngsters are also more likely to attend schools where the majority of students are poor. Michael Nettles and Gary Orfield (in progress) report that students who attend high poverty schools are disadvantaged because the education they receive involves a much lower level of competition than that received by students in more affluent schools. The problem of high poverty schools is "intimately tied" to racial segregation. About 8% of the schools in the United States have between 80% and 100% Black and Latino students and, among schools that are 90% to 100% African American and/or Latino, almost nine-tenths (87.8%) are predominantly poor and only 3% have less than one-fourth poor children. A student in a segregated minority school is 16 times more likely to attend a concentrated poverty school (Nettles and Orfield, in progress).

A fourth myth about affirmative action is that affirmative action means that less qualified individuals are preferred

After controlling for other factors related to the probability of being admitted (test scores, grades, social class, etc.), Black applicants are about 14% more likely than White, Asian, and Hispanic applicants to be accepted for admission into the nation's 120 most selective colleges and universities. The probability of an applicant being admitted into the next tier of 222 very competitive colleges and universities is unrelated to race after controlling for such factors as socioeconomic status, test scores, high school grades, curricular program, extracurricular activities, and educational expectations. Analyses of college admissions decisions among 1992 12th graders using the National

Educational Longitudinal Study (NELS) database show that only about 1 in 4 African Americans require affirmative action to be admitted to the nation's 120 most selective colleges and universities. This means that 3 out of 4 are entering these institutions with scores and high school preparation similar to their Asian and White counterparts.

These analyses show that race is only one of many factors that is considered in the admissions process, and that race is a consideration only at the most selective colleges and universities. Even at the most elite colleges and universities where preferences are granted to African Americans, African Americans represent only 4% of the entering class. This underrepresentation shows why affirmative action is required to ensure diversity in the nation's colleges and universities. At the vast majority of colleges and universities, no preference is granted to African Americans based upon their race or membership in an underrepresented minority group.

Moreover, although the analyses suggest that a White or an Asian may be rejected while an equally qualified African American is admitted, this is not necessarily the case. In fact, White and Asian applicants who are rejected for admission are more likely to be rejected in favor of students of their same race who are granted preferences based upon their ties to prominent alumni, individuals who reside in particular counties or states, or individuals who have demonstrated superior athletic excellence or musical talents than they are to be rejected by a Black or Hispanic applicant. These are human attributes that colleges and universities find to be important preferences beyond race.

A fifth argument against affirmative action states that admissions test scores and grade point averages are fair and objective measures of merit

In arguing against preferences that favor African Americans, opponents of affirmative action suggest that college admissions decisions should be based upon a narrow definition of merit in which high school grades and standardized admissions test scores are the primary criteria used for selection. They argue that high school grades and standardized admissions test scores:

• are the best indicators of student achievement;
• provide a clear indication of student preparation for succeeding in college; and
• are fair for students of all races and social class backgrounds.

The best available evidence does not support this argument. First, there are huge gaps in the average college admissions test scores of African Americans, Asian Americans, Hispanics, and Whites taking the tests and the average scores of African Americans are the lowest. In 1996, for example, the average score on the verbal component of the SAT was 434 for African Americans, compared to 526 for Whites, a gap of 92 points. On the math component, the average score was 103 points lower for African Americans than for Whites (423 versus 526). Thus, when the verbal and math parts of the SAT are combined, average scores are nearly 200 points lower for African Americans than for their White peers. Because Asians averaged 495 on the verbal section of the

SAT and 560 on the math section, average scores for African Americans are 219 points lower than the average scores for Asians who took the test. Average scores are about 70 points lower for Mexican Americans and Puerto Ricans than for Whites on the verbal section of the SAT and about 70 points lower on the math section.

When socioeconomic status is held constant, Asian Americans may not be more educationally successful than African Americans. Table 4 shows that Asian SAT test-takers come from families with higher incomes than Black and Hispanic test-takers. Asian SAT test-takers are also more likely than all other groups of test takers to be enrolled in an academic track in high school (see Table 5). Only one-third of Black high school seniors who took the test were enrolled in a college preparatory program, compared to 41% of Whites and 56% of Asians.

Table 4

Distribution of 1997 SAT Takers Nationally by Family Income

Race	Below $20,000	Below $30,000	Over $80,000
American Indian	17%	30%	15%
Asian Americans	24%	30%	15%
Black or African	33%	52%	7%
Mexican American	33%	50%	8%
Puerto Rican	32%	48%	9%
White	7%	16%	25%

Source: College Board and Educational Testing service, 1998

Table 5

Percentage of high school seniors who took the SAT and were in a college preparatory program

Race	Percent
Asian	56%
White	41%
Black	33%
Hispanic	25%
American Indian	19%

Source: National Center for Educational Statistics, 1996 Digest of Educational Statistics.

Although average test scores are lower for African Americans than for Whites and Asians, many African Americans are qualified to attend the nation's most selective colleges and universities. In fact, more African Americans and others from underrepresented groups were qualified for admission to the University of California, Berkeley than were admitted for the fall of 1998. Only 8,000 of the 30,000 applicants to the University of California, Berkeley were granted admission for the Fall 1998 semester. Among the rejected applications were 800 African American, Chicano, Latino, and Native American applicants who had achieved 4.0 grade point averages in high school and SAT scores of 1200 or higher.

Do these scores reflect the capacity of African Americans to perform in college, or are they more of a reflection of their family income and social class background? In 1997 52% of African American SAT-takers lived in families where the income was below $30,000 annually, compared with 37% of Asians and only 16% of Whites. One quarter (25%) of White and 19% of Asian 1997 SAT takers had family incomes of at least $80,000, compared to only 7% of African Americans (see Table 4). The correlation between SAT scores and income is .40 (Carnevale, Haghighat, & Kimmel, 1998). No factor other than high school grades in core curricula better predicts SAT scores than family income (Carnevale, et al, 1998).

Are SAT scores an accurate and good predictor of African American student performance in college? There are two ways to respond to this question which, when taken together, make the conclusion a bit ambiguous. The best evidence that we have available suggests that, as with Whites and other population groups in the United States, Black students who score higher on the SAT or ACT and other admissions test also receive higher grades in their first year of college than students with lower scores. This can be tied to the fact that, during the first year of college, students take the same courses. It is not until later in the curriculum that students choose courses and programs in the areas of their strengths and interests. This means that, while admissions tests may have predictive validity for colleges and universities when trying to estimate freshman student performance, there is much less evidence available to suggest that students with higher SAT scores are more likely to persist through college to graduation, or even that they will have higher cumulative grade point averages over the entire college curriculum.

Furthermore, when comparing the predictive validity of SAT or ACT scores for first-year grades, the College Board, the Educational Testing Service, and the American College Testing (ACT) Company are finding that test scores over-predict first-year grades for even the highest performing African American men. This may reflect the challenges African American students experience in gaining the necessary support of their college professors in college as much as it reflects their SAT scores. All of this suggests that the SAT and ACT may not only be biased against low income people and Black Americans, but that they are also less appropriate for predicting performance for African Americans than for Asians and Whites. It also means that colleges and universities need to find better criteria than admissions tests when they are estimating how Black applicants will perform in college. The tests are not as fair and objective as the proponents of Proposition 209 would have us believe.

Grades earned in high school curricula are also assumed to be fair, equitable, race-neutral and social-class-neutral measures of school achievement and readiness for college. But in fact, high school grades earned in different and racially and economically unequal schools may simply reflect student performance on different and unequal standards not the same, equal, and fair standards. African Americans, on average, attend schools with fewer resources than their White and Asian counterparts, have fewer opportunities to take rigorous college preparatory courses and Advanced Placement courses, and have less access to the best teachers. While African American children represent 16% of the school age population, they comprise only 3% of all students nationwide who enroll in Advanced Placement Calculus, only 4% of those enrolled in Advanced Placement U.S. History, and only 2% of the students enrolled in Advanced Placement Physics. We should also be asking how many African Americans have access to Advanced Placement courses in their high school, and how many are discouraged or even prohibited from taking such courses by their guidance counselors or school psychologists. In addition, over 62% of Asian and 50% of White high school students, but only about 40% of African American and Hispanic high school students, have taken high school physics. We should also be asking how many African Americans attend schools where physics — real physics taught by someone who knows physics and who has a college degree in physics — is even offered.

A sixth anti-affirmative action argument suggests that affirmative action has negative effects on success/graduation rates of college students

Bachelor's degree completion rates are lower for African Americans than for Whites and Asians. Table 6 shows that, among first-time freshmen entering California's public universities in 1990 who were admitted under regular admissions criteria, only 63% of African Americans graduated within six years, compared with 79% of Whites and Asians. Regardless of racial/ethnic group, six-year graduation rates were substantially lower for freshmen who were admitted by exception than for regularly admitted freshmen. These data illustrate the need for colleges and universities to examine the availability of their academic and social support services and the effectiveness of these services in promoting persistence to degree completion for all students.

Table 6

Six-year graduation rates for first-time freshmen entering California public universities in 1990

Admission Status	Total	African American	American Indian	Asian	Chicano	Filipino	Latino	White
Total	75%	58%	64%	78%	62%	73%	70%	77%
Regular admission	77%	63%	68%	79%	65%	74%	73%	79%
Admitted by exception	50%	45%	47%	50%	47%	41%	50%	55%

Source: Office of the President, The University of California

Merely observing that African Americans have lower degree completion rates than Whites and Asians does not prove that affirmative action has negative effects on college success. African American college students likely face barriers and obstacles to their success in college that students of other racial/ethnic groups do not. On average, African American undergraduates have greater need for financial aid than White undergraduates. Financial need is determined by a federal formula that estimates the difference between the costs of attending a postsecondary institution and the amount a family can be expected to contribute to the costs. Table 7 shows that nearly three-fourths (73%) of all African American undergraduates have some amount of financial need, compared with 57% of all Whites, 65% of all Hispanics and Asians, and 62% of all American Indians. A higher percent of African American than White undergraduates have some amount of financial need regardless of the type of institution they attended. Financial difficulty is among the most common reason that students report for leaving a college or university (Astin, 1975; Pantages and Creedon, 1978; Wenc, 1983).

Table 7

Percent of undergraduates with financial need by institutional type: 1992-93

Institutional type	African American	American Indian	Asian	Hispanic	White
Total	73%	62%	65%	65%	57%
Public 2-year	55%	52%	57%	49%	44%
Public 4-year college	74%	82%	67%	70%	63%
Public 4-year univ.	80%	68%	73%	69%	62%
Private 4-year college	86%	—	67%	93%	71%
Private 4-year univ.	85%	—	75%	84%	74%

From: Tuma & Geis, 1995

Moreover, some evidence suggests that admissions test scores and grades do not predict academic success. In her examination of students who applied to law school in 1990-91, Linda Wightman (1997) found that African Americans had substantially lower undergraduate grade point averages (one standard deviation lower) and LSAT scores (1.5 standard deviations lower) than Whites. Nonetheless, 78% of the African Americans who would not have been admitted into law school if the decision had been based solely on undergraduate grades and LSAT scores did in fact graduate from law school. Graduation rates were comparable for African Americans who would and would not have been granted admission under a model in which only undergraduate grades and LSAT scores were considered in the admissions decision (80% vs. 78%). Furthermore, African Americans and Hispanics who would not have been admitted to law school under an admission model relying solely upon undergraduate grades and LSAT scores were found equally likely to pass the bar examination as those who had the required grades and test scores.

A seventh criticism of affirmative action states that Blacks who enter under affirmative action suffer negative psychological effects (e.g., they may feel inferior).

Shelby Steele (1990) and other critics of affirmative action argue that affirmative action causes people who benefit from it to develop low self-esteem, feelings of inferiority, and feelings of being less qualified and less deserving than their peers. These are considered to be the negative psychological effects of affirmative action. Shelby Steele's evidence, however, is anecdotal and based upon his personal experiences and encounters and not based upon surveys of the views of students or employees.

Evidence generated by national surveys does not support the claim of negative psychological effects that are advanced by the opponents of affirmative action. A 1995 public opinion survey conducted by the Gallup Organization reports that those who benefit from affirmative action do not suffer negative psychological effects. Gallup's national poll of a cross-section of 1,220 employees in U.S. corporations and government asked the following question: "Have you ever felt that your colleagues at work or school privately questioned your qualifications because of affirmative action?" Almost 90% of the respondents indicated no. Of the African American respondents, three-quarters (74%) indicated no. White men, who have traditionally benefited from preferences, do not suffer from self-doubt and a loss of self-esteem as a result of preferential treatment (Plous, 1996). In a 1994 national survey of 319 White women and 71 African American men and women employees, Marylee Taylor found that 51% of employees state that their organizations use affirmative action in hiring employees and that benefiting from affirmative action did not cause them to experience negative psychological effects. Compared to White women and African American men and women in non-affirmative action workplaces, White women and African American men and women whose employers practiced affirmative action in hiring did not differ in job satisfaction, intrinsic interest in work, life satisfaction, health or happiness. Instead, Taylor discovered two positive psychological effects of affirmative action: greater occupational ambition and a higher view of people as being helpful.

Other evidence also suggests that African American students who benefit from affirmative action do not experience feelings of inferiority. Claude Steele (1990) suggests that high-achieving African American students feel pressured to prove themselves academically in order to refute the negative stereotype about Blacks being less qualified and less able than their White counterparts. Claude Steele characterizes this pressure as stereotype threat, and African American students do not internalize this threat. Many African American students who enroll in the nation's most competitive colleges and universities, where affirmative action is most prevalent, feel confident about their academic ability and are not suffering negative psychological effects from affirmative action (Steele, 1990).

The eighth criticism of affirmative action declares that discrimination in any form, including preferences, is wrong.

We exercise many subjective preferences in every aspect of American society, whether in employment, in school placement, in hiring and promoting college and university faculty, in awarding government and private sector grants and contracts, and in college and university admissions. Rarely if ever are decisions made without some element of subjective preference. Each year we witness some college and university professors achieve promotion and tenure, while other equally talented faculty, who are equally well published and accomplished, are denied promotion and tenure. Sometimes it is due to preferences expressed by promotion and tenure committees in favor of a particular perspective or skill of one faculty member over another. Or, it may merely reflect the subjective judgements by colleges and universities about faculty at a given point in time. Preferences have been a central part of faculty recruitment, promotion and tenure in higher education and in the student admissions process since the founding of Harvard University in 1636. At that time the preference was for affluent males with educated parents. The following student preferences are exercised each day in college and university admissions:

• high and low socioeconomic status;
• athletic and other special talents;
• relation to alumni and/or political leaders;
• geographic region of a state (counties) and nation;
• sex in major fields where men and women are underrepresented (e.g., women in engineering, men in nursing); and
• national recognition for personal achievements or leadership.

None of these preferences, however, seems to attract as much scrutiny and criticism as race, especially, it seems, when the preference is for African Americans. Even after Proposition 209 passed, the state legislature in California passed Title V of the California code of regulations, which permits the University of California campuses to allow exceptions (same as preferences) for 6% of the entering class based on athletic or other talents. This is evidence that neither higher education nor any other segment of America operates without preferences. Higher education has always used preferences. It has in the past, it does today, and it will continue to do so in the future.

The admission of student-athletes represents a special case of preference in college admissions, and provides us with an example of how even the most ardent proponents of so called "objective standards" use preferences. This example shows how hypocritical we can appear to be when we argue for total objectivity and no special preferences. Student athletes recruited by Division I colleges and universities are required to meet NCAA academic eligibility requirements in order to qualify to participate in Division I athletics. To meet NCAA Division I academic eligibility students must:

• graduate from an accredited high school,
• successfully complete a core curriculum of at least 13 academic courses, and
• attain a grade point average (GPA) and standardized test score combination based on a sliding scale ranging from a minimum 2.0 GPA and 1010 SAT to 2.5 GPA and 820 SAT.

The NCAA requires students to complete the following high school core curriculum in order to qualify to participate in Division I intercollegiate athletics:

• at least four years of English;
• two years of math (one year of algebra and one year of geometry, or one year of a higher-level math course for which geometry is a prerequisite);
• two years of social science;
• two years of natural or physical science (including at least one laboratory class, *if* offered by the high school); [emphasis ours]
• one additional course in English, math or natural or physical science; and
• two additional academic courses.

     The NCAA provides an exception (same as preference) to the laboratory science course requirement for students who attend high schools that do not have a science laboratory. We must ask, why is this an acceptable exception? And why are these appropriate requirements? How valid are the NCAA requirements or the exceptions that are permitted by the NCAA? Does the NCAA attempt to show the validity of its requirements by documenting that students who meet these criteria perform better in college or that students who do not meet these requirements fail to complete college? Why does the NCAA make exceptions (preferences) for students whose high schools do not have science laboratories but give no consideration to other critical elements of learning environments that many students do not have access to, such as teachers who are trained and certified in the field in which they are teaching?

     African American high school students not only have less access to science laboratories, but they are also more likely to attend schools that have fewer resources, lower quality facilities, higher rates of substitute teachers, and fewer teachers who are certified in the subjects they are teaching. Each of these factors is critical to preparing students to meet the NCAA requirements and college admissions standards. Therefore, additional exceptions would appear to be required, and should be considered, in order to level the playing field for African Americans who are seeking college admissions. This is why race is an important criterion to include in college admissions.

CONCLUSION

     Our nation needs a major commitment toward reforming K-12 education and pre-school education, particularly for African Americans. But this is the long-term, not the short-term, solution to the issues of fair and equitable access to employment and higher education for African Americans. Today, we need affirmative action to continue the progress made during the past decades. The seemingly "get tough" policies like Proposition 209 or the National Collegiate Athletic Association's eligibility requirements seem to have little effect upon improving the quality of education. Instead, they seem only to limit access for the students who need the highest quality of education the most. And, while the opponents of affirmative action, like Ward Connerly, argue against racial preferences out of one side of their mouths, they choose and advocate their own discriminatory preferences out of the other side. Proponents of Proposition 209 seem willing to allow privilege based upon athletic talent and the NCAA allows preferences for students whose high schools do not offer laboratory sciences. Why not give preferences to students who attend high schools that don't have a real physicist teaching physics or Advanced Placement courses, or who attend underfunded schools that are crumbling from years of neglect and deferred maintenance?

Many systemic reforms are required to provide high-quality K-12 education for African American children. Affirmative action policies in higher education cannot be eliminated until we take measures to ensure that all children regardless of their socio-economic status have access to the highest quality of preparation and education for college. Among the important interventions required for the elementary and secondary education of African Americans in the United States are the following:

• raise the academic standards of Head Start and other publicly supported pre-schools so that African American and poor children have access to the same high quality pre-school education as White and affluent children;
• provide all children with access to high-quality teachers who are trained and certified in the subjects that they teach;
• require elementary math, science and literacy teachers to have college degrees, licenses and certification in the subjects they teach;
• provide African American and disadvantaged children with access to high-quality curricula, especially college preparatory programs and Advanced Placement courses;
• increase funding to urban poor school districts to the level of property-rich school districts while simultaneously launching system-wide educational reform efforts in urban poor school districts; and
• decrease class and school size in large urban schools.

Ensuring that all citizens, regardless of race or sex, have access to high quality education at all levels is critical to the nation's continued economic prosperity. Our nation's workforce is not only growing increasingly dependent upon the participation of members of minority groups, but also upon the participation of individuals with higher levels of education. The non-White share of the United States population is projected to grow from about one-fourth (24.4%) in 1990 to more than one-third (35.7%) by 2020 (Bureau of the Census, 1996). Non-Whites are projected to increase their share of the civilian labor force from 21.5% in 1990 to 27% in 2005 (Smith & Johns, 1995). Women and minorities are projected to comprise two-thirds of all American workers by 2020 (Dreyfuss, 1990 in Justiz, 1994).

Even with affirmative action policies, members of minority groups, on average, are not participating equally in the nation's labor market. Unemployment rates for Blacks and Hispanics continue to be higher than unemployment rates for Whites. Family incomes are lower for African Americans and Hispanics than for Whites. African Americans and Hispanics continue to be underrepresented relative to their representation among full-time workers in executive, administrative, and managerial positions, and are over-represented in unskilled occupations, such as administrative support and clerical, private household service, machine operators and assemblers, and laborers (Nettles & Perna, 1997a). As a result of their differential status in the labor market, the percentage of children below the poverty level continues to be higher for Blacks and Hispanics (30.4% and 26.5% in 1991) than for Whites (8.8%) (Smith & Johns, 1995, p. 994).

If all citizens of our nation are not provided with access to an equal opportunity to succeed we will suffer tremendous long-term economic and social costs as a nation. These long-term costs greatly outweigh any short term effects of affirmative action-type policies that consider race among several criteria in the college and university admissions process. After World War II Congress opened the doors to opportunity for millions of Americans with the GI Bill. This was in the best interest of America. We must act now, once again, in the best interest of America to ensure that all people, regardless of race, ethnic origin, or sex, have access to opportunity as we move into the 21st century.

References

Brooks-Gunn, J., Duncan, G.J., Klebanov, P.K., & Sealand, N. (1993). Do neighborhoods influence child and adolescent development? *American Journal of Sociology, 99*, 353-395.

Bureau of the Census (1996). Population projections of the United States by age, sex, race, and Hispanic origin: 1995 to 2050.

Carnegie Council on Adolescent Development. (1995, October). *Great transitions: Preparing adolescents for a new century.* New York: Carnegie Corporation of New York.

Carnevale, A.P.P., Haghighat, E., & Kimmel, E.W. (March, 1998). *How do we choose?: An exploration of alternative decision-making in college admission.* Princeton, NJ: Educational Testing Service

Gross, Martin L. (1997). *Social and Cultural Madness in America,* (pp. 218-223)

Harkey, S. (1995). *Timetables of African American history: A chronology of the most important people and events in African-American history.* New York: Simon & Schuster.

Justiz, M. (1994). Demographic trends and the challenges to American higher education. Chapter 1 in *Minorities in Higher Education.* Justiz, M.J., Wilson, R., & Bjork, L.G. (Eds.). Phoenix: the American Council on Education and The Oryx Press.

Lamison-White, L. U.S. (1997). *Poverty in the United States: 1996.* (U.S. Bureau of the Census, Current Population Reports, Series P60-198). Washington, DC: U.S. Government Printing Office.

Massey, D.S., Condran, G.A., & Denton, N.A. (1987). The effect of residential segregation on blacks' social and economic well-being. *Social Forces, 66,* 29-56.

Nettles, M. T., & Perna, L. W. (1997a). *The African American Education Data Book, Volume I: Higher and Adult Education.* Fairfax, VA: The Frederick D. Patterson Research Institute.

Nettles, M. T., & Perna, L. W. (1997b). *The African American Education Data Book, Volume II: Pre-School through High School Education.* Fairfax, VA: The Frederick D. Patterson Research Institute.

Nettles, M.T., & Orfield, G. (in progress).

Norment, L. (1998, January). 12 most powerful blacks in corporate America and how they got there. *Ebony, .LIII (3),* 36-44.

Oliver, M. L. & Shapiro, T. M. (1997). *Black Wealth/White Wealth: A New Perspective on Racial Inequality.* New York: Routledge.

Plous, S. (1996). Ten myths about affirmative action. *Journal of Social Issues, 52,* 25-31.

Roper Center for Public Opinion – POLL Database. (Question ID: 037). [Electronic Database]. (1995). Storrs, CT: Roper Center for Public Opinion.

Rudolph, F. (1990). *The American college and university: A history,* 2nd Edition. Athens, GA: The University of Georgia Press.

Smith, J.C. & Johns, R. L., (Eds.) (1995). Statistical Record of Black America. Detroit: Gale Research Inc.

Steele, C.M. (1997). A threat in the air: How stereotypes shape intellectual identity and performance. *American Psychologist, 52,* 613-629.

Steele, C.M, & Aronson, J. (1995). Stereotype threat and the intellectual test performance of blacks. *Journal of Personality and Social Psychology, 69,* 797-811.

Steele, S. (1990). *The content of our character: A new vision of race in America.* New York: St. Martin's Press.

Taylor, M. (1994). Impact of affirmative action on beneficiary groups: Evidence from the 1990 General Social Survey. *Basic and Applied Social Psychology, 15,* 43-69.

Tuma, J., & Geis, S. (1995). Student Financing of Undergraduate Education, 1992-93. (NCES 95-202). Washington, DC: Office of Educational Research and Improvement, U.S. Department of Education.

Wenc, L. M. (1983). Using student aid in retention efforts. In *Handbook of student financial aid,* (pp. 330-346). San Francisco: Jossey-Bass Publishers, Inc.

Wightman, L. F. (1997). The threat to diversity in legal education: An empirical analysis of the consequences of abandoning race as a factor in law school admissions decisions. *New York University Law Review, 72*(1), 1-53.

Endnotes

[1] A distressed neighborhood is a Census Tract or Block Numbering Area (BNA) with at least four of the five following characteristics: 1. High poverty rate (above 27.5%); 2. High percent of female-headed families (above 39.6%); 3. High percent of high school dropouts (above 23.3%); 4. High percent of males unattached to the labor force (above 46.5%); 5. High percent of families receiving public assistance income (above 17.0).

[2] In this report, "chronically poor" was defined as being poor in each month of 1992 and 1993.

Epilogue

The ephemera of academic production — the speeches, responses to speeches, "think" pieces, viewpoints and the like — often are consigned to dusty files after their brief public airing. Here, a cross-section of these has been resurrected to challenge the reader to probe further, to provoke new questions and encourage renewed dialogue. The more casual tone of these offerings belies their creative roots. It is the editors' hope that readers will find the stimulation in this section to carry the conversation on assessments and equity to new levels, in new directions

10 Epilogue: Part1
Tests as Barriers to Access

William H. Gray III
Michael T. Nettles
Catherine M. Millett

We have many examples throughout our history of how educational assessments have played a part in expanding opportunities for individuals. But, just as we have seen educational tests and assessments being used as vehicles for expanding opportunity, we have also observed them being used as impediments to access and progress.

We find ourselves today at a critical juncture with regard to educational testing and assessments because of the recent actions taken by various levels of government, and by colleges and universities. Not to mention all the standards setters who rely upon test scores as indicators of progress. This is why I consider your meeting here today and tomorrow to be so very important and why I hope you come away from the meeting with some actions to take us forward toward using testing and assessments to expand access and opportunity. In many ways, we appear to be moving away from using test scores as conduits of opportunity and in the direction of using them as barriers to access.

We know that one million students, for example, take the SAT each year and nearly the same number take the ACT as a requirement for admission to the nation's colleges and universities. In addition, school children in practically every grade, in every school in the nation experience some form of standards-based assessment, or standardized tests for such reasons as complying with government regulations, deciding whether they will be promoted from one grade to the next, and for judging their teachers' performance as well as their teachers' merit pay increases.

Standardized tests have been criticized for the past three decades for a variety of technical and social reasons. Two social reasons loom prominent: first, the cultural bias of their content, and second, the use of the test to discriminate unfairly against the poor, the disenfranchised, and minority people. It is a commonly accepted practice for colleges and universities to use admissions tests to screen applicants for admissions; and, in fact, they appear to accurately predict freshman year performance. But, even this practice can be criticized because the tests have lower predictive value in forecasting students' subsequent grades in college, and they have even less power when it comes to predicting graduation from college and performance in professional jobs after college. Yet, test scores are used to determine access to prized places in colleges and universities, and for employment entry and promotion opportunities for such public service professionals as fireman and policeman in cities throughout the nation.

Despite decades of steady attacks upon the discriminating content and inappropriate uses of educational tests, we continue to find the assessment industry having to respond to some of the same challenges today that were raised throughout the past three decades. I'll just mention four recent examples that have been prominently covered by the national media to show how tests are being used to reduce opportunities for employment, college admissions, college scholarships, affirmative action, and ultimately progress toward social and economic equality.

First, the police department in the city of Chicago has recently established a special commission to find alternative means to the traditional standardized tests that they have been using to promote police officers and fire fighters. This policy shift was necessary because of the numerous legal challenges to using the scores from traditional tests as the primary criterion for hiring and promoting. The mounting evidence shows that the use of tests for hiring and promoting has led to the appointment of too few African Americans and Hispanics. For example, in July of 1995, 26,000 people took the entry firefighters examination in the city of Chicago. Fifty-four percent of the examinees were either Black or Hispanic. Based on the test performance, 1,782 individuals achieved a passing score, but only 20 percent of those receiving a passing score were either Black or Hispanic. In Chicago the consequence of passing the test is receiving a position in the fire department. These are positions with a $33,000 annual salary and great fringe benefits. And for those who failed the exam in 1995, the next opportunity to apply to take the exam again and to apply for an opening may be 10 years away. Last year the city of Chicago promoted 54 police officers to become detectives on the basis of their test scores. In a police force where 40 percent of the members are Black or Hispanic, because of their test score, only three of the 54 new detectives were minorities; one was African American and two were Hispanics.

Consequently, because of their test scores, many talented, even exceptional African American and Hispanic police officers who have demonstrated exemplary service and achievements in their role as police officers are being left behind when promotions are made.

A second example comes from the Texas court case of *Hopwood v. State of Texas* (1996). This is an example of an attack upon affirmative action by the courts. The decision in this case could lead to the prohibition of admissions policies, and other programs and incentives employed by colleges and universities to attract Blacks and Hispanics to their campuses. The basic issue in the Hopwood case is access to education, specifically legal education. Four White residents in the state of Texas, including Cheryl Hopwood, the named plaintiff, charged that they were discriminated against on the basis of "race" in the admissions process at the University of Texas Law School. They objected to the separate admissions committees and the fact that African Americans and Mexican Americans who were admitted to the Law School had lower Texas Index scores (Texas Index scores are comprised of LSAT test scores plus grades). Cheryl Hopwood could have challenged the university's admission of a larger number of White students than Black students to the Law School, but she chose instead to focus her attack upon the minority admissions process. Hopwood had a higher Texas Index score than 63 of the 90 African American and Mexican American law students who entered last year, but she had a Texas Index score that was higher than 109 White students who were admitted. Interestingly, she didn't protest against the lower scores of the 109 white students.

The University of Texas Law School stated that it had the goal of admitting a class consisting of 10 percent Mexican Americans and five percent Blacks, proportions roughly comparable to the percentage of Black and Mexican Americans graduating from Texas colleges and universities. The plaintiffs argued that it was discriminatory to have the Black and Mexican American applicants' Texas Index ranked in a separate process than other applicants.

Here again, African Americans and Mexican Americans are being judged to be less qualified because of their test scores even when more of their white counterparts could be attacked on the basis of the same argument; but they are not. Furthermore, such attacks upon the minority students give the public the impression that the plaintiffs were higher achievers than all the minority students, and they were not. This continues a racist view that minorities are less qualified than their White counterparts.

In addition to its ruling that the separate admissions committees were illegal, the Fifth Circuit Court of Appeals ruled that White students can not be rejected in the admission process if their scores on the Texas Index exceed those of Blacks and Mexican Americans who are being admitted, and this might be the most frightening aspect of the Hopwood case. Interestingly, Dr. Linda Wightman of the Law School Admissions Council, who is here today, has produced data to show that the African Americans who were admitted with lower test scores prior to the Fifth Circuit Court ruling had similar rates of completing the University of Texas Law School and passing the Texas Bar Examination as their White colleagues who were admitted.

And even though all the Black students did not have lower Texas Index scores than all the Whites, the Texas Index scores have very little relationship to law school completion, Bar passage rates and successful law practice. This is a clear example of how the use of test scores as the prominent criterion in the admissions process can have the damaging effect of lowering career aspirations and achievements for minorities who are demonstrating in every way that they can succeed. This is also an example of how test scores are unjustifiably used to stereotype minorities.

A third example is the case of *Podberesky v. Kirwan* in the state of Maryland. This is a case that reveals how test performance can be used, even after students are admitted, to affect the distribution of limited financial resources. In 1985, the Benjamin Banneker Fellowship Program at the University of Maryland at College Park was established and was open to all "minority students" and provided a modest stipend. But in 1988, the eligibility requirements were changed to include only African Americans. This was a necessary change in the policy because even though the Black students who received the Banneker scholarships had higher test scores than the average University of Maryland student, on average, their test scores were slightly below the level required to receive the most prestigious and lucrative Francis Scott Key scholarships offered by the University of Maryland. The average combined SAT score for Banneker scholars in 1995 was 1136, which is well above the national average for students of every racial group and also above average score of students enrolled at the University of Maryland.

The plaintiff, Daniel Podberesky of Polish and Costa Rican descent initially applied for the University's prestigious Francis Scott Key Scholarship, which like the Banneker scholarship is a merit-based, but non-race targeted scholarship program. When Mr. Podberesky was not selected for the Key Scholarship, he applied for the Banneker merit-based scholarship for African Americans, contending that he should be eligible because of his Costa Rican lineage. When he was denied the opportunity to compete for the scholarship, he claimed that his individual rights under the Equal Protection Clause of the 14th Amendment and Title IV of the Civil Rights Act of 1964 were violated.

The Federal District Court in Maryland upheld the Banneker Fellowships as being appropriate, but later the Fourth Circuit Court of Appeals overruled the Federal District Court and declared that the Banneker scholarship program for African Americans was unconstitutional. Again, this is an example of how test scores used for ranking people can have a detrimental effect upon social progress. This program was viewed as taking one step toward eliminating de jure discrimination against Blacks in Maryland which kept Thurgood Marshall from attending the University of Maryland. The Fourth Circuit Court's ruling has become even more interesting in recent weeks in light of the case of Knight v. Alabama where a Federal Judge has ruled that it is acceptable for the state of Alabama to designate scholarships for White students to attend the historically Black colleges and universities in Alabama in order to enhance desegregation.

A fourth example comes from the case of the *United States & Ayers v. Fordice* (1994). In the 1970s, the state of Mississippi established an admissions policy requiring higher minimum composite scores on the ACT for the five historically white institutions than for the three historically black institutions. Recently, the state of Mississippi has altered its policy by establishing a uniform minimum cut score of 16 on the ACT for admission to all of its universities, both black and white. This new policy raises concern that access to higher education may be substantially reduced for the people in the state who can benefit the greatest from higher education, the poor and Black people in the state. When the state of Mississippi implements this policy, over one half of the African Americans who have been entering college each year in the state would not meet the admissions requirement.

Three of these four examples are from the southern region of the United States, but there are many instances like this that are springing up all over the nation. For example, I could have just as easily elaborated upon Julia McLaughlin's case against the Boston Latin School's strategy for ensuring that 30 per cent of its students are African American and Latino. Or the infamous University of California's decision to eliminate the affirmative action practices that helped to increase African American and Hispanic enrollments in that state's college and universities. These cases are leading to the same negative influences upon the public's perceptions and attitudes about African Americans that the Willie Horton ads had during the 1988 presidential election. I think of this barrage of recent activities surrounding testing policies for employment, educational access, and scholarships as being "Willie Horton goes to college." That is, the current testing and assessment policies are creating fear across the entire spectrum of social class and race in our society.

The Americans who have the greatest amount of resources fear that special treatment granted to poor and minority people in the name of equal opportunity or affirmative action reduces the quality of the institutions they attend and threatens to erode the privileges that have been the exclusive province of wealthier citizens. The fear of the people in the "underclass" is that the greater use of educational tests will reduce their opportunities for upward social and economic mobility, which in essence is their ability to share in the American dream. You may recall that the Willie Horton ads created a fear among Whites of Blacks in general, and among Blacks, the fear was that the whole society would look upon us in the same way that Willie Horton was presented.

The problems of educational testing pertaining to Blacks are also problems for poor people, regardless of their race. The enduring high correlation between family income and test scores does not escape the skeptic's view that standardized tests can be inappropriately used as a tool to maintain our current socioeconomic class stratification. Even a casual look at the distribution of College Admissions Test Scores, both the ACT and the SAT, each year reveals a stronger correlation between test scores and income than test scores have with any other indicators of school involvement and academic success. For example the average composite ACT score for families with annual incomes of less than $17,000 is 19 compared to a composite average of 23 for those with family incomes of $60,000 and over. Similarly, SAT takers in 1995 with family incomes of $70,000 or more had a combined score of 1004 compared to a combined score of 813 for those with family incomes of less than $20,000.

Table 1
SAT Performance by Income, 1995

Income	Number	Percent	Verbal Mean Score	Math Mean Score
INCOME				
Less than $10,000	47,396	5%	354	415
$10,000 - $20,000	88,696	10%	380	433
$20,000 - $30,000	111,774	13%	405	454
$30,000 - $40,000	133,976	15%	420	468
$40,000 - $50,000	108,921	12%	431	482
$50,000 - $60,000	99,552	11%	440	493
$60,000 - $70,000	75,918	9%	448	502
$70,000 or more	220,394	25%	471	533

Source: College Bound Seniors: 1995 Profile of SAT Program Test Takers

Table 2
ACT Performance by Income, 1995

Income	Number	Percent	Mean Composite Score
$17,999 or less	65,160	15%	19.2
$18,000 - $29,999	75,198	18%	20.8
$30,000 - $41,999	91,458	21%	21.5
$42,000 - $59,999	92,554	22%	22.2
$60,000 and over	104,428	24%	23.0

Source: College Bound Seniors: 1995 Profile of ACT Program Test Takers

The testing and assessment companies like to illustrate the relationship between the rigor of courses that students take in high school and their test scores. I agree that these are important relationships to present, but more attention needs to be given to the strong contribution that income makes to student test performance. The family income factor is particularly alarming in light of the *New York* magazine's March 18 article titled "Give me Harvard or Give me Death" that vividly described the measures that affluent families take to ensure that their children achieve the highest possible test scores. These include hiring personal tutors sometimes at a cost of up to $500 an hour. Five hundred dollars is an amount that is equal to the average weekly income of more than half of the African American families in the United States.

Another indication of the socioeconomic challenge is found in the movement to change the medium of testing from pencil and paper to a computer format. This is likely to have a negative impact on low income and minority students. Today, only 13 percent of Black Americans live in a household with a computer, compared with 30 percent of White Americans. Moreover, while 37.5 percent of White Americans use computers at home, at work, or in public places such as public libraries, only 25 percent of Black Americans use computers in these areas. Similarly, the 1993 Census found that about seven percent of households earning less than $10,000 had computers at home compared to 62 percent of those with incomes of $75,000 or more. The *Times Mirror* 1994 survey of technology in American households revealed that among college graduates with children, almost half reported that the child used a personal computer; but only 17 percent of parents with a high school education or less reported that their children used a home computer.

Table 3
Percent of Degree Attainment by Race/Ethnicity, 1976-77 and 1992-93

Degree Level	Total	White, non-Hispanic	Black, non-Hispanic	Hispanic	Asian or Pacific Islander	American Indian/ Alaskan Native	Nonresident Alien
Associate							
1976-77	404,956	84.5	8.2	4.1	1.7	0.6	0.8
1992-93	508,154	79.9	8.3	5.9	3.3	0.9	1.8
Bachelor's							
1976-77	917,900	88.0	6.4	2.0	*1.5*	0.4	1.7
1992-93	1,159,931	81.7	6.7	3.9	4.4	*0.5*	2.8
Master's							
1976-77	316,602	84.0	6.6	1.9	1.6	0.3	5.5
1992-93	368,701	75.6	5.4	2.9	3.8	0.4	12.0
Professional							
1976-77	63,953	91.4	4.0	1.7	1.6	0.3	1.1
1992-93	74,960	81.1	*5.5*	4.0	6.9	0.5	2.0
Doctoral							
1976-77	33,126	81.1	3.8	1.6	2.0	0.3	11.3
1992-93	42,021	63.5	3.2	2.0	3.8	0.3	27.3

Source: U.S. Department of Education, National Center for Education Statistics, "Degrees and Other Formal Awards Conferred" surveys, and Integrated Postsecondary Education Data System (IPEDS), "Completions" surveys.

Efforts to repeal Affirmative Action throughout the states provide even more examples of how some Americans are seeking to reduce opportunity and access for poor and minority Americans, and how test scores may be the prime weapons that are available for them to use. Opponents of Affirmative Action appear to fear the progress that has been made by minorities in achieving the American dream, but not enough progress has been made.

Some examples of persistent social inequalities and the need for action come from higher education. Even though African Americans represent nearly 13 percent of the U.S. population, they comprise only:

- 8.3 percent of the Associate's degree recipients
- 6.7 percent of the Bachelor's degree recipients
- 5.4 percent of the Master's degree recipients
- 5.5 percent of the Professional degree recipients
- 3.2 percent of the Doctoral degree recipients

This level of representation among degree recipients resembles the levels of representation 15 years ago.

Another indicator of social inequality and the need for progress relates to the fact that 55 percent of Black families have annual incomes below $25,000 compared to 27 percent of White families. Only 17 1/2 percent of African American families have incomes above $50,000 compared to 38 per cent of White families. This is the same pattern of income differences we observed in 1970.

Table 4

Percent Distribution, by Income Level, Race and Hispanic Origin, in Constant (1993) Dollars: 1970 and 1993

Year	Number of Families (1,000)	Percent Distribution						
		Under $10,000	$10,000 - $14,999	$15,000 - $24,999	$25,000 - $34,999	$35,000 - $49,999	$50,000 - $74,999	$75,000 and over
All Families								
1970	52,227	8.2	7.3	16.6	19.6	23.6	17.3	7.5
1993	68,506	9.6	7.2	15.5	14.8	17.9	19.4	*15.5*
White								
1970	46,535	7.0	6.7	15.8	19.8	24.5	18.2	8.0
1993	57,881	7.3	6.6	15.1	15.1	18.8	20.6	16.6
Black								
1970	4,928	20.1	13.0	23.9	17.2	15.1	8.8	1.9
1993	7,993	25.8	11.4	18.6	13.7	12.9	10.9	6.6
Hispanic Origin								
1970	2,499	14.9	12.9	23.3	18.9	18.4	9.0	2.7
1993	5:9461	17.9	12.5	22.2	16.6	14.0	11.4	5.5

Source: Current Population Survey

Of the more than one million people who took the SAT and ACT last year, the distribution in performance of Black people was different from their White and other minority counterparts. Black students had the lowest scores of any racial/ethnic group on both the SAT and ACT. These two tests are only presented as examples. The same problems are observed with other tests used for education and employment.

Table 5
SAT & ACT Performance by Race/Ethnicity, 1995

Classification	Number Who Took SAT	SAT Composite Score	Number Who Took ACT	ACT Composite Score
ETHNIC GROUP				
American Indian/Alaskan Native	8,936	850	11,361	18.6
Asian/Asian Amer./Pacific Islander	81,154	956	27,784	21.6
Black/African American	103,872	744	89,155	17.1
Hispanic Latino:				
Mexican/Mexican American	36,323	802	24,431	18.6
Puerto Rican	13,056	783	24,054	18.7
White	674,343	946	650,664	21.5

Source: College Bound Seniors: 1995 Profile of SAT Program Test Takers and
The American College Testing Program, Inc.

The challenge for the testing industry is not simply to help colleges, universities, and employers to screen and select, but at the very least to be sure that people who are scoring below these levels indeed would not succeed if they were given an opportunity by the people who make decisions based upon test scores. This is especially important in the state of Mississippi, where nearly one-half of this year's African American entering class of college freshmen would not be admitted under the new minimum cut score requirement imposed by the state.

Furthermore, there is no evidence that cut-scores will improve the quality of Mississippi's colleges and universities. Surely, some will say that Mississippi's universities will have higher quality students. But can we be sure that many capable students will not be unfairly and unnecessarily denied an opportunity because their impoverished backgrounds and neglected home communities may have hindered their ability to score higher on standardized tests or to have access to advance placement courses and coaching. The *Los Angeles Times* recently reported that in California students receive bonus points in their GPA calculations just for taking Advanced Placement courses and that low income students, through no fault of their own do not have access to the variety of Advanced Placement courses that their affluent peers have. A second point in the article was that low income minority students may not have the opportunity to enhance their SAT scores by taking costly courses or purchasing test preparation books. To quote the *Times* reporter, Harry Pachon "an inflated SAT score might go nicely with the more affluent student's inflated GPA".

The millions of us who are affected by tests and assessments are not completely satisfied that these standardized tests are being used appropriately, nor that the testing industry is aggressive enough in ensuring that their products are being developed with the greatest consideration for expanding opportunities or for ensuring that the tests are used appropriately.

Here are a few questions 1 would like the industry to address.

• Specifically, how will the College Board, ETS, ACT, CTB, McGraw Hill, and other testing companies respond to this action by the state of Mississippi? Do they agree that this constitutes appropriate use of testing in that state?

• What is the testing industry's response to the Hopwood decision in Texas? Even if you applaud people like Ms. Hopwood for pursuing their civil rights, how will you correct the racial stereotyping and prevent the use of tests as weapons to attack affirmative action?

• What role does the testing industry play in making sure that Black and Latino youngsters qualify for the very best scholarships that colleges and universities have to offer?

• How should we prevent further widening of the existing racial gaps in family income that are in part the consequence of test performance?

The risk to people like me who raise these kinds of questions is that we will be labeled as being opposed to high standards, high expectations of students, and hard work by students. In fact, I am in favor of high standards, high expectations, and hard work as much as I am in favor of opportunity and equality. But, we have been in the midst of educational reform for the past 15 years since the Reagan administration published *A Nation at Risk,* and we have been setting new high standards for everybody and moving away from norm-referenced tests to criterion or standards-based assessments for the past decade. Yet, we have very little evidence to show that we have improved the academic achievement of African Americans and poor people. In fact the best evidence we have from college admissions tests, the National Assessment of Educational Progress, and other assessments is that the racial and economic gaps are widening. So for the following four reasons, I think your meeting today and tomorrow could be extremely important:

• First, to ensure fairness in the content of tests and by being more convincing to the public that people who you deem to be qualified to take your tests have a realistic expectation of successful performance on the test, and in the educational programs and occupations for which the tests are administered. Otherwise, we are wasting the time and precious resources of the people who are least able to pay.

• Second, to ensure fair and appropriate use of tests by the government. This applies to court decisions as well as state and local, and institutional policies for education and employment.

• Third, to ensure that the standards reform movement, in which the testing industry plays a prominent role, works toward improving the educational conditions and achievements of poor and minority children; not just those who have been benefiting all along. And

• Fourth, to ensure that focusing upon test scores does not detract from students' joy of learning and the self confidence they have about progressing in school and in their careers.

For each of these four areas, the evidence that we are making progress is either unavailable or unconvincing. For example, does a child who scored 15 on the ACT in the state of Mississippi not stand a chance of success at Mississippi State, or Ole Miss, or Alcorn State University, or Jackson State, or the University of Southern Mississippi? Even the most prestigious universities seem not to have a highly publicized minimum cut score. Rather, they take into account not only the additional criteria of grades and rigor of courses in high school, but also other talents such as music, drama, athletics and the potential for leadership in a variety of academic and cultural fields as well as students' social and economic backgrounds. There is even evidence that the best universities in the country reject candidates who are the highest performers on standardized tests in favor of candidates who present a diverse array of talents. I am not so concerned, however, about students with perfect SAT scores who are rejected by Harvard, Yale or Princeton. These students will simply be admitted to other higher education institutions of equal or comparable prestige, and go on to achieve social and economic status and have access to economic networks in America that are comparable to what they would have achieved had they been admitted by Harvard.

Rather, I am concerned about the poor and minority youth in the state of Mississippi and other places from poor communities with poor schools, and little support at home who have succeeded in every other way except meeting the minimum cut score or falling short on such schemes as the Texas Index because of their test scores. Given the present will of some of our government leaders, the courts, and many colleges and universities to use tests to deny access, it rests upon the shoulders of those of you in the testing and assessment community to take on more of the responsibility for ensuring that your instruments do not close the door to access and opportunity for the neediest segment of the American population.

10 Epilogue: Part 2
Educational Standards and Alternatives in Educational Reform

Edmund W. Gordon

If the purpose of the nation's attention being given to educational standards is to move the productivity of our schools toward the achievement of academic excellence in our students, including those whose status is low because of their class, ethnicity or gender, this effort is flawed. We cannot reach universal academic excellence via the route of higher standards for the mastery of academic discipline based on content alone. Even though I fully support universally high academic standards of achievement for all students, I do not think that the priority need is for a Madison Avenue style promotion of higher academic standards, while budgetary allocations for the delivery of education services shrink. All across this land, the allocation of public funds for the education of poor and low status persons is threatened and in many instances is actually declining.

I don't think we need to promote standards. I think that most of us know what high standards are. Even if higher standards were the correct priority, the current movement is flawed because it places its emphasis on achievement outcomes to the neglect of pedagogical inputs. The movement lacks symmetry in its treatment of educational inputs and achievement outcomes. I contend further that the movement may be flawed because the emphasis on standards for student mastery within each of the curriculum content areas is inconsistent with our changing conceptions of the nature of knowledge and knowing; it is inconsistent with changing conceptions of the functions of teaching; it is inconsistent with changed understanding of the processes of learning; and it is inconsistent with changing technologies for assessment. Permit me to develop some of these points.

I contend that the problem with our schools is not that we don't know what good education is or what well educated people look like or what they should know or what they should be able to do. Sixty years ago in the rural and segregated public schools of Goldsboro, North Carolina, Hugh Victor Brown, Sadie Bell Grantham, Rosa Gray,

Charity Hatcher, Beula Mae Perkins and other dedicated African American teachers, not only knew what it meant to be well educated, they also worked hard to enable most of my fellow students and me to achieve that quality of education. Before we could graduate from Dillard High School, we had to pass their version of the New York State regents examination. They knew what educated people were supposed to know and know how to do.

Kenneth Clark recounts an incident that occurred some ten years later when he was lecturing in rural South Carolina, encouraging black people to fight against segregated education. Ken was reporting some of his findings concerning the negative effects of segregated public schools. He claims that he was interrupted about half way through his talk by a parent in the audience. The man said to Ken, "Professor Clark, we already know how bad they are treating us. We know that our children are not getting the best education. What we need from you is for you to tell us how we get them to give us the education that they and we know that we need." Some thirty years later, when Doxey Wilkerson was studying the aspirations held by African American parents for their children's education, he found that these parents held high aspirations for their children's education – Wilkerson claimed that they were "unrealistically high" – but he also reported that they did not know how to turn those high aspirations into high academic achievement. Even more serious was his finding that the longer these children stayed in the public schools of Harlem, the lower were their test scores, the more their parents' aspirations dropped and the greater these parents' frustrations became. Knowing what the standards were was not their problem.

Our productivity in the education of low status children is low not because teachers and parents do not know what academic standards are or should be. Rather, low status students' achievement is low because we do not have in place a system for the enablement of academic achievement that ensures that the great majority of our students have appropriate and sufficient opportunities and supports for the development of intellective competence. It is not out- come but in- put standards that should be the priority as we try to reverse that condition. National and state efforts at the improvement of the quality of educational achievement will require more than new standards. They will require greater symmetry between the attention given to the quality of teaching, learning and assessment transactions on one hand, and the character and quality of the outcomes we expect to achieve through education.

When we turn to questions of what we are to do in teaching, learning and assessment transactions with lower class, ethnic minorities or female students, we get very confusing messages. There are many very interesting initiatives available. Some of them show considerable promise. However, the most frequently heard message seems to indicate that we don't know what to do except demand that these students try harder. Another troublesome message suggests that schools are incapable of adequately educating low status students. In a provocative work, Berliner and Biddle suggests that the crisis in education in the U.S. is a manufactured crisis. They claim as did Ron Edmonds, that the problem is not a lack of know-how, but a failure of will to distribute what we know to certain segments of the population. There are places in the U.S. where education works quite well. There are student populations whose achievement patterns are comparable to the best in the world. Could it be that a set of opportunity to learn and conditions of education standards, influenced by what these high achieving students get, might result in high achievement for most of these low status students?

The modern history of accountability in education dates back to the early 1980s with the Chief State School Officers efforts to come to agreement on a few key indicators of the quality of educational productivity in the public school sector. The focus was on reading, math, writing, and attendance. This modern history was preceded by, modest efforts at the turn of the 20th century and slightly before the middle of this century by some of the discipline-based associations and accrediting groups to specify minimal offerings in elementary and secondary schools. These earlier efforts at standardizing the curriculum also include efforts by the College Entrance Examination Board and the College Testing Service to standardize the process of and standards for admission to college. These efforts had important implications for educational-standard setting, but explicit attention given to standards for educational achievement in the U.S. is a late 20th century development.

In the mid-'60s, the then U.S. Office of Education developed the National Assessment of Educational Progress (NAEP) under the leadership of the then Commissioner Francis Kepel. Professor Ralph Tyler was commissioned to provide leadership in the development of an assessment system that could enable the nation to determine what American students know and know how to do. Although this was a major assessment effort, the determination of criteria or standards for such a system was required. NAEP emerged as the nation's principal source of information concerning the extent to which elementary and secondary schools are producing educational achievements referenced to patterns of such achievement in other nations of the world. It is this implicit concern for world class standards for educational achievement that has framed much of the current effort.

In 1990, the Chancellor of the New York City public schools issued what were, perhaps, the nation's first minimum standards for elementary and secondary schools. These standards, recommended by a blue ribbon commission, were directed at levels of productivity for the schools of the city. The standards specified attendance rates, levels of school pacification, percentages of students passing specific achievement tests, and percentage of students who passed the New York State Regents' Examinations. In addition to these out comes, the standards also provided that schools were to be held to progress standards referable to students in the bottom quarter of achievement percentiles. For those students whose achievement was lowest, schools were to be required to demonstrate specified annual gains, even if the standards for achievement were not met. Individual schools were to be held accountable for meeting these standards. The report of the commission was prophetic in that it called for greater attention to be given to symmetry between student outcomes and staff/school inputs (opportunity to learn), and to the specification of the quality of course content, and to the improvement of the instruments and procedures of assessment. While this work in NYC was driven by a concern for student, school and staff accountability, however, the effort, like others, settled for holding students more accountable than it held schools and their staffs. After 2 1/2 years of debate we were unable to agree to specify minimum standards for opportunity to learn.

In the current educational reform movement, attention has been focused on the establishment of higher standards for educational achievement, and improved instruments and procedures for educational assessment. The New York State Council on Curriculum and Assessment is an atypical example of this movement. The council has been charged with responsibility for making recommendations directed at strengthening the curriculum of elementary and secondary schools in New York State, and improving the system by which educational achievement is assessed. General concern has been expressed for ensuring that our new and higher standards are universal – i.e., that they apply to all of our students, and that they be equitable, in the sense that the imposition of these standards not treat unfairly any of our students, and especially those students with whom our schools have traditionally been less than successful. Nonetheless, like the NYC Commission on Standards, the New York State Council has not seriously engaged questions having to do with standards for institutional and professional practice. Meanwhile the Governor of New York State is asking for criminally destructive cuts in the state's budget for education and human services.

Obviously, the movement in support of higher standards, and effort directed at improved assessment have proceeded at a faster rate and with greater clarity than has concern for the provision of sufficient opportunities to learn, and the enablement of equity in educational assessment procedures. Yet any realistic examination of the demographic trends in the nation reveals that the goals of educational reform cannot be achieved without real progress in the achievement of a higher degree of equity in the educational productivity of our nation. It is thus for practical as well as moral reasons that our curriculum and assessment reforms must take seriously a commitment to symmetry and equity.

The emphasis on standards for content mastery, framed by subject matter domains is no doubt influenced by the concern for specifying what it is that our children should know and know how to do. We have tended to approach such specification through the disciplines within which knowledge and technique traditionally have been organized. However, contemporary conceptions of knowledge suggest that these boundaries are breaking down, and that many knowledge artifacts are more sensitive to differential contexts and idiosyncratic perspectives. Some investigators suggest that knowledge is neither best acquired nor optimally utilized for problem solving in discipline-based domain-specific isolation. Increasingly we recognize the trans-disciplinary nature of the most recalcitrant, as well as some of the most ordinary problems of human existence. I predict that the next struggle in the domain specific standards movement will be waged around decisions concerning what content and content domains can be left out. Already we hear teachers worrying about how to achieve comprehensive coverage in each of the subject matter areas. The emerging concern for "core or essential concepts" and the pursuit of deeper understanding through counter intuitive "less is more" strategies moves us in the right direction. But what seems even more appropriate is the introduction of curriculum designs, standards and assessment probes that combine disciplinary and transdisciplinary knowledge and understanding.

There is another set of problems inherent in a subject matter domain specific approach to standards. We continue to hear concern for the tension between local curriculum specificity and state, and especially a national curriculum. In the struggle to protect the prerogatives of local and state education authorities, we hear all too little about the implications for education of the rapid movement toward economic, political and cultural globalization. There is something inconsistent about the concurrent talk of "world class" standards and local curriculum specificity. Equally inconsistent is the concern for standards for achievement without concurrent attention to standards for the quality of the opportunities and resources necessary to such achievement.

Some students of pedagogy are suggesting that teaching and learning are less about the transfer of knowledge and skill and more concerned with the development of intellect. Practitioners who approach education from a constructivist perspective argue that the development of intellect requires that learners be involved in the discovery and construction of the meanings and relationships which inform their knowledge and understanding. In both of these developing approaches to teaching and learning a heavy emphasis on the learning of specific knowledge and technique is likely to be challenging to all but the most expert of our teachers. In my own teaching, I struggle to use disciplinary and trans-disciplinary content and the substantive issues which are grounded in such content as the vehicles for strengthening the intellective competence of my students. (I use intellective competence to mean the ability to think, to acquire, produce, transform and utilize experience, information and technique to solve problems.) We turn to the disciplines of the sciences in search of explanatory mechanisms. We examine the disciplines of the arts and humanities in search of possible meanings. It is through critical interpretation that I encourage students to make sense of and try to understand what they experience. I don't need to tell any of you who have tried to do this kind of teaching, how difficult it is. And I, at least, have the advantage of not being required to teach to a content standard. If Socratic inquiry and the development of intellective competence are to be privileged in teaching and learning, I contend that domain-specific, discipline-driven standards are dysfunctional to modern pedagogy.

Following developments in the National Assessment of Educational Progress, the nation has embraced an academic achievement standards movement that seeks to specify what modern students should know and know how to do. I have challenged this movement as being flawed and not in the best interest of low status, low achieving populations. Rather than input or outcome standards that are informed by what we want our children to know and know how to do, it may well be that our concern for outcome standards, if we must have them, should focus on what we want our children to be and to become – intellectively and socially competent, productive and compassionate human beings. Since the criteria for these competencies may not be well understood, our national and state debates might well focus on the nature of humane human competence, the conditions necessary to its achievement, and the national will to honestly pursue it for all of our people.

10 Epilogue: Part 3 Merit and Opportunity: Testing and Higher Education at the Vortex

Nancy S. Cole

The current tornado of political activity about affirmative action, voter initiatives labeled "pro civil rights," and legal rulings on college admissions policies have thrown the higher education community into the center of a troubling national debate. Testing organizations join higher education at this vortex as standardized tests are simultaneously the presumed culprit and the presumed solution for many of these difficult issues.

MERIT AND OPPORTUNITY IN TODAY'S CONTEXT

Today's debate revolves around whether consideration should be given to race, ethnicity, and gender when officials make decisions about higher education admissions. Although our society promoted affirmative action in the 1960s and 1970s, today many see it as reverse discrimination and inconsistent with our cultural sense of fair play. Many Americans believe that we should be blind to such characteristics and should admit students to college on the basis of individual accomplishment, especially as higher education is seen as an important ticket to economic success.

As a nation, we clearly value elementary and secondary education for all youngsters and guarantee free public education to Grade 12. The equity issues at these levels involve the variable quality of locally administered systems to which youngsters have access and the unequal opportunities to learn that the variable quality produces. At this lower level of education, the issue does not involve merit to qualify for access to local schools.

The nation has not presumed to provide free higher education for all students nor access to one's public higher education institution of choice. Although many state community college systems attempt to provide low tuition and easy access, more selective higher education, with higher fees and selective admissions, is also publicly supported. This latter segment of higher education is seen to be of special societal value by promoting contributions from some highly trained individuals. Notions of equity in selective higher education include concerns for selecting equitably those well prepared for advanced learning as well as those likely to build on learning to make advanced contributions to society.

An essential American value is that a person should advance in this society on the basis of his or her own accomplishment as opposed to family connections, wealth, social standing, place of birth, racial/ethnic heritage, or gender. Thus, it is not surprising that a dominant view of merit in higher education has been based on objective measures of individual accomplishment including standardized test scores. Such measures fit well with the notion of identifying individuals with strong preparation for advanced learning and those most likely to make important contributions to the nation.

These notions seemingly combined to produce a common public view of appropriate selection to identify the "best qualified" students. In 20th century higher education, testing has come to embody a dominant public notion of "merit" and the accompanying view of equity as selection using objective measures of "merit." In this view, equitable opportunity is often presumed because all children have access to education through high school to prepare themselves to compete for this valued form of education. The problem, of course, is that this prescription of opportunity does not address the impact of unequal education at earlier levels on a student's ability to compete for access to higher education (and succeed, if granted access).

Considerations of merit and opportunity as well as looming equity issues must interact with the fact that we are a nation of enormous racial/ethnic diversity. The unequal early educational preparation of all our citizens creates a dangerously wide social and economic divide. Our nation has not yet reconciled the need to assure diverse groups the opportunity to achieve advancement through higher education with current notions of individual merit that presume a prior equality of opportunity that does not in fact exist.

How does a nation deal reasonably with such a difficult set of issues? Although public discussions sometimes oversimplify the issues of merit and opportunity, at Educational Testing Service (ETS) we know that these issues are extremely complex. Contrary to the often simple public notion of merit as test scores, we know test scores should not be asked to be the sole or primary definer of "merit." We believe test scores can provide important and dependable information, but we advise against putting too much weight on tests for a number of good reasons. Contrary to the simple notion of fair opportunity to compete for higher education admissions, we know that American students have widely differing preparation for that competition, with a disproportionate number of minority students attending, mediocre schools.

Those of us at the vortex of the debates about affirmative action in higher education have a responsibility to assist the American public in its struggle with the complexities of merit and opportunity. The purpose of this statement is to provide some information to assist us in meeting this critical challenge.

THE MYTH OF TESTS AS A SINGLE YARDSTICK AND THE REALITY OF DATA

As noted, publicly accepted notions of merit for selection purposes rely heavily on objective measures of individual accomplishment. Test scores have become a widely accepted 20th century embodiment of merit for higher education admissions. As with many simple solutions to complex issues, equating test scores with merit creates a mythology that is not consistent with the reality of data.

In particular, it is a myth of test scores that almost any test will provide a single, unequivocal yardstick by which we can measure all comers. The further myth is that the right, proper, and fair way to achieve selection based on merit is by rank ordering applicants from high to low on this indisputable yardstick and selecting from the top down. Any deviation from this procedure is thought to be a clear violation of the inherent justice of this merit principle.

For this over-simple notion of merit to be correct, the data would need to support that there is *one and only one* primary ordering of people as "best qualified." But the data tell us quite unambiguously that there are multiple orderings from multiple credible yardsticks. Let's look at the data.

Individual Variation

First, we all know that some good, well qualified students do better on some types of tests than others. Some well qualified students are stronger in English, others in history, and still others in science or mathematics. If we define "well qualified" in terms of performance on a verbal or history test we will get a different rank order of those qualified than on a test of math or science. Any two credible academic tests will produce different rankings of individuals. Which is the unequivocal yardstick?

Group Variation

The myth of the single yardstick is important to the sense of fairness the public wants. If different orderings are possible, then we have to be able to defend one over the other. The lack of a single yardstick is demonstrated in even more vexing fashion by the fact that the effects on rank orderings of individuals from different subgroups will vary with the choice of test.

Consider first comparisons of females and males. Data from representative samples of high school seniors show substantial female/male differences in test performance in important academic areas as shown in Table 1. Here we see that young women do much better than young men on tests of writing and language use and young men do much better than young women on tests of mechanical and electronics content. Even if we focus on tests of language-related areas, there is not a uniform effect. Females do relatively best in writing and language use, with a smaller advantage over males in reading, and essentially none in vocabulary and reasoning.

Table 1

Gender Differences in Test Performance in 12th Grade

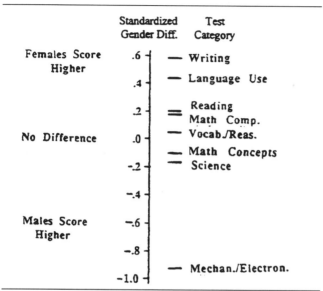

*From compilations of 74 different tests, grouped by subject category
from Willingham & Cole, in press.

Basically, these data demonstrate that if our yardstick includes tests of writing and language use, many more females will rank high than if our yardstick includes tests of math concepts and natural science. In similar comparisons of White with Black or Hispanic students, we see similar differences in the relative performance of members of these groups on tested subjects in addition to the familiar overall difference favoring Whites. Both Black and Hispanic students score best in Writing relative to Whites and worst in Math and Science. Again, the data do not support the existence of a single, unequivocal yardstick.

If Not Tests Alone, Add Grades

Because grades are often seen as a part of this imagined single yardstick, it is important to remind ourselves that adding grades to test scores does not produce this single yardstick either. In fact, the data remind us that grades and tests differ in some systematic ways. Tests measure quite specific skills at a single point in time; grades are derived from multiple performances over much longer time periods and involve a much broader set of possibly unenumerated skills. Some students do better on one; others on the other.

Group differences are involved here too. Females do better than males on grades in most subjects (see Table 2) whereas, as we saw in Table 1, for tests it depends on the subject. How much weight we put on grades and tests in the combination of the two will affect the resulting rank ordering of individuals. Again, the supposed single yardstick is in fact no single yardstick.

Table 2
Gender Differences in Grades of 12th Graders*

	Standardized Gender Diff.	School Subjects
Females Perform Better	.6	
	.4	── English
	.2	═ < Social Sci / Science / Math
No Diff.	.0	

*From seniors in 1992 in the National Educational Longitudinal Study and reported in Willingham & Cole, in press.

Using Predictions of College Grades

An important use of test scores and high school grades has been to predict college grades. Such predictions are sometimes seen as sacrosanct. Several interesting results have become apparent from many studies. First, college grades are not always comparable. Students in the same college take different courses and sections of courses for which grading standards differ. Different types of institutions have policies that apparently either encourage such diversity in course-taking and grading or discourage it (Willingham et al., 1990). These institutional policies affect the degree of prediction that test scores and high school grades achieve.

The clearest result is that prediction is better when both test scores and high school grades are used as opposed to either alone or any other variable. But it is also clear that the level of prediction achieved and the most predictive combination of test scores and grades depend on a range of events and policies regarding grading practices at a particular institution and change over time. Grade prediction does not seem to have solved our single yardstick conundrum either.

Broader Notions of Talent and Success

Academic success, like most human endeavors, involves a mix of talents and shows itself in a variety of forms. Accordingly, students might reasonably be considered "well qualified" for higher education by some other indicators such as:

• other types of academic accomplishment (winning science fairs, publishing original fiction, in-depth study of advanced topics, etc.)
• special signs of creativity (inventing a new device, creating a recognized piece of art, producing a novel and respected idea, etc.)
• effectiveness with others (working well with others toward productive ends, demonstrating leadership, showing special effectiveness as a communicator, demonstrating interpersonal skills that command respect, etc.)
• motivation (working hard and consistently toward an important purpose, showing drive and determination when faced with obstacles, clear indications of desire to learn and succeed, etc.)
• orientation to social and community concerns (productive involvement with social service activities, demonstrated understanding of community concerns, personal aspirations that include service to others, etc.)

Unfortunately our measures of these characteristics are not as objective or as dependable as test scores. However, when we construct formal measures of these talents and forms of prior success for research studies, we find that they identify some different individuals than those identified by the traditional assessments. Although there are practical problems in identifying these talents, surely they remind us of other credible yardsticks.

Implications for the Public Notion of Merit

Recognizing individual merit is an important public value. However, the data remind us that accomplishing this recognition is not so simple as implementing a single, indisputable yardstick. Those in higher education must not, for reasons of convenience or lack of information, allow the discussion of merit to take on simplistic forms that neither do justice to the importance of the principle nor the message of the data.

The absence of a single yardstick means that implementing an appropriate notion of merit with integrity will surely require both multiple measures and good judgment by committed educators. Higher education and testing organizations can help the public understand the myths and implications of the data. We can also act on this knowledge by basing our actions on multiple yardsticks and good judgment, as the important principles of merit and equity deserve.

THE MYTH OF FAIR OPPORTUNITY TO COMPETE FOR SELECTION AND THE REALITY OF DATA

Another essential American value is that every person in this nation should have a fair opportunity to succeed. Historically this value, like the value of merit, was a rejection of the notion that a person's lot in life should depend primarily on the conditions to which he or she was born. In a nation with fair opportunity, people will have a high probability of success if they work hard and learn enough, regardless of family or wealth.

The notion of fair opportunity is greatly complicated when applied to higher education since college and graduate study are late in a series of educational experiences. It is much easier to imagine what fair opportunity for higher education should mean if all people have had equal educational experiences prior to higher education. In this scenario, fair opportunity would be a fair chance to demonstrate merit on the same terms as all other applicants.

But what does fair opportunity mean when inequities exist in prior education – when the opportunities to learn and prepare for higher education are vastly different for different individuals? In considering this issue there are data relevant to some of the questions to which we need answers:

 • *Are there educational inequities prior to higher education?*

 • *Is admission in the face of prior educational inequities only giving a student the opportunity to fail?*

There are also questions for which we do not find helpful data:

 • *How should we think about merit in the face of inequitable prior preparation? In such cases, should we differentiate the meaning of merit from the traditional meaning of "best qualified"?*

In each case, however, answers to these questions challenge the myth that every student has a fair opportunity to compete in selective admissions for college or graduate or professional study. Sometimes the answers pit notions of opportunity against present public notions of merit. Nonetheless, it is useful to consider what we do know that bears on these critical questions.

Data on Inequities in Schooling

Test data clearly tell us that average student performance differs greatly by state, by school within state, and even by school within school district. Data from the National Assessment of Educational Progress indicate the state to state variation vividly (see Table 3). The test data from most large school districts, typically featured in local newspapers, show large differences in average student performance among schools.

Table 3

Proficiency in Reading Assessments for Selected States* Grade 4, Public Schools

	NAEP Scale Score
Maine	228
Wisconsin	224
Pennsylvania	215
Colorado	213
Arkansas	209
Florida	205
California	197

*Data from the 1994 NAEP (Campbell, et. al., 1996)

One may argue that such data are not conclusive about the opportunities students have to learn since it is also true that there are some good performers in almost any school. Still, the large differences among schools in student performance are strongly suggestive of different opportunities to learn. When an opportunity presents itself, most parents try to live in communities with high performing schools, indicating a strongly held common belief that there are important inequities in learning opportunities in this nation's schools.

Is Admission Without Adequate Preparation Only An Opportunity to Fail?

A traditional concern in higher education is that admitting students who do not have adequate preparation to succeed is a futile exercise. Is it not reasonable to assume that students who are far too poorly qualified for a particular college have little or no chance of success? However, we may overestimate the failure expectations for moderately qualified applicants, especially if we view applying itself as an indication of their interest and intention to succeed.

The situation of applicants whose preparation is less than ideal but good enough to support a reasonable chance of success is illustrative. Consider a hypothetical situation built from typical data. Suppose a rather selective college has an applicant pool of 5,000 students and 1,000 places available. Using test and grade data with correlations typical of selective colleges, we can compute the probability of attaining a college grade average of 2.5 (half B's, half C's) for several groups of applicants as shown in Table 4. With 1,000 places available, this college might define the highest 1,000 scorers as the "best qualified" for admission. However, the second group of scorers also has a high probability of passing. In fact, it is often the case that the second group of applicants does not have dramatically lower probabilities of success than the first group. (How close the probabilities in these different groups are will depend on the strength of the applicant pool. The data presented here is for a strong applicant pool as self-selection usually results in a reasonable match of applicants and requirements.)

Table 4

Probability of Success in College for Students of Different Ranks in Applicant Pool*

Applicants	Probability of Achieving Grade Average of 2.5
Highest 1,000 Scorers	.86
Second 1,000 Scorers	.71
Third 1,000 Scorers	.59
Fourth 1,000 Scorers	.45
Lowest 1,000 Scorers	.27

*Based on hypothetical data using, a .55 multiple correlation of high school grades and test scores with college grades and a college GPA distribution typical of highly selective colleges with able applicant pools.

My point is that the chance of succeeding at a college does not drop to zero for students slightly less qualified than the top applicants. Although people may think of students as "qualified" or "not qualified," the notion of two distinct categories is a myth. *There is actually a continuum of qualification in which the chances of success are only marginally different for those who qualify and some who fail to make the cut.* The data illustrate that typically, for many more students than those selected, we would not be "inviting failure" by their selection. It is only in more extreme cases of inadequate preparation that the invitation to fail is a seriously relevant concern.

Alternative Meanings of Merit When Prior Inequities Exist

There have been good reasons for higher education to equate "merit" with some tangible evidence of "best qualified." However, when inequitable preparation is present, it raises an appropriate distinction between the two concepts. Is it not meritorious for an individual to achieve a high (but not the highest) level of qualifications against the odds of a difficult family circumstance, extreme poverty, or a weak school? Such a person may not be the best qualified, but *might well have been* had he or she been exposed to better circumstances. I would argue for consideration of a concept of merit that acknowledges accomplishments against such odds, especially if the level of performance is sufficient to give the person a reasonable chance of success. Without some flexibility in our definition of merit, fair opportunity to compete for higher education in the face of prior inequities is a particularly cruel myth.

Of course, designing and implementing a system that takes into account such additional factors would be difficult. Which difficulties of circumstance are worthy of special merit if overcome, and which are not? How can the difficulties be gauged? Who decides?

Another nontraditional indicator of merit could be evidence of a characteristic badly needed by society. Suppose we greatly need more scientists and engineers to be successful as a nation. Should we give special consideration to an individual likely to pursue a course of study and career in science or engineering? Suppose it is essential that we have well educated minority populations for national success. Should we give special consideration to minority applicants in such a circumstance?

Managing the Complexities When the Myths are Exploded

These are issues of great complexity and difficulty; they are issues that must be raised in such a way that permits us to consider what we know and to debate appropriate action. We will need much wisdom for resolution of these issues, much frank consideration of the points on both sides, and much appreciation for the complexities that lie beneath the surface of these debates. Solving the dilemma of fair opportunity in access to higher education while preserving an appropriate notion of merit may require the wisdom of Solomon. Even without such wisdom, we can at least lead the thoughtful consideration of the issues.

These two essential and fundamental values of Americans – for merit and fair opportunity – are as key today as at any time in our nation's history. And today higher education is one of the most visible stages on which we demonstrate our national commitment to these values. As we do so, we must acknowledge the myths that seemed to make equitable the education that precedes higher education – even though acknowledging these myths makes finding solutions even more difficult.

Understanding that a single yardstick is a myth makes it clear why we must not let testing be the quick and simplistic answer when it is not the right answer. To fail to represent other worthy yardsticks of merit is a disservice to the importance of the merit issue. To presume a level playing field of fair opportunity when we know full well the field is not level is a similar disservice. Testing organizations and higher education owe the nation a deeper understanding of the complexities in reconciling the inherent value of merit and opportunity *without* the myths.

References

Campbell, J.R., P.L., Reese, C.M., & Phillips, G.W. (1996)., *NAEP 1994 Reading Report Card for the Nation and the States; Findings from the National Assessment of Educational Progress and Trial State Assessment.* Washington, D.C.: U.S. Department of Education.

Willingham, W. W. & Cole, N. S. (in press). *Gender and Fair Assessment.* Hillsdale, NJ: Erlbaum.

Willingham, W. W., Lewis, C., Morgan, R., & Ramist, L. (1990*). Predicting college grades: An analysis of institutional trends over two decades.* Princeton, NJ: Educational Testing Service.

10 Epilogue: Part 4 If You Want Equity, You Need Standards

Joan Baratz-Snowden

It is over a decade since A *Nation at Risk* and the intense public focus on our students and schools. That report put in bold perspective a singular problem with our schools: Our students were not achieving as well as they could, as well as students from other nations and as well as they need to for the future. We know the problem is complex and those who decry the sorry state of U.S. student educational achievement are usually concerned about two separate, but related, issues:

- our highest achieving students are not being pushed far enough;
- and, more importantly, there is a significant learning gap between our highest and lowest achieving students, and minority students are disproportionately represented in the low achieving groups.

A *Nation at Risk* triggered much activity – much still needs to be done to address these problems. The American Federation of Teachers (AFT) has been a major voice in school reform efforts to assure greater school achievement particularly for minority students.

Al Shanker was asked to talk about the role of standards in the reform process, particularly in regard to minority students. The AFT believes that setting high standards, creating curriculum to assist students in meeting those standards and developing assessments to determine if those standards are met is the linch pin to school improvement, particularly for minority students. Nothing is more important to assuring high achievement of all of our students than setting high standards and working to professionalize teaching. Without such standards the system is adrift, and the educational prospects of minority students, in particular, are in jeopardy.

Let me clarify what I am saying. Standards are not THE answer, but they are essential to assuring higher student achievement for minority students. As Lewis Carroll's Chesire cat was wont to say: "If you don't know where you're going, any road will take you there." That is the situation that we are in today. Without high standards for students, anything goes, and anything is accepted – and even mediocre and poor work is sometimes rewarded as excellent. We find that without the articulation of a commonly accepted set of high standards for all children, many children are allowed to proceed through the system without achieving much. They are "socially promoted," despite the fact that they know very little, and may have been taught very little. It is an unaccountable system, and poor students and minority students suffer the most.

Why is that? Many critics of the AFT position concerning the need for high standards for all students say it is unfair to hold disadvantaged students to such standards. They say that such students come to school unprepared and unable to learn, or have teachers who are ill prepared to teach them. For these reasons, they argue that if one imposes standards those children will suffer because they will be unable to meet them and be stigmatized by failure. But what kind of a favor do we do to students by putting them ahead? Who benefits from that system? Who is responsible in that system?

Certainly students suffer the most. The current issue of AFT's *Questline* contains the tale of two sisters who were graduates of the Chicago public school system. They attended school regularly, took all the courses they were supposed to, did the homework when it was assigned, which wasn't all that often, and earned A's and B's. It wasn't until they got to Malcolm X College and flunked the entrance exam that they learned that they had been horrendously short changed. They were unable to read on the 6th grade level! It was only with remedial help, *after high school graduation*, that they got the skills they needed and were able subsequently to enroll in, and successfully complete college. No standards robbed them of an education.

And what about the system? Without standards such failure to educate can be glossed over and swept under the rug. School administrators and teachers, who believe these students can't learn, can remain complacent with lower expectations and the consequent delivery of third-rate schooling. There is no accountability without standards.

Teachers routinely tell us that they are pressured by principals to pass students who have not mastered the work. They have no recourse – it is their professional assessment against the principal's authority. Without commonly agreed upon high standards, teachers have no standards other than their own to appeal to, both to get extra help for students, and to assure that other students don't get the message that effort or accomplishment is unnecessary for "success" in school. Indeed, without the standards the teachers who make the greatest effort and demand the most from their students can easily be characterized as "hard on students," and unreasonable, most especially by those – teachers and students alike – who don't wish to make the effort.

Without standards it is difficult to keep the system accountable – indeed, to demand the resources necessary to assure that students learn. The "opportunity to learn standards" is hard to argue for in the absence of standards for achievement that demonstrate the need for such standards. If everyone is learning, no matter how little, what is the fuss all about?

Content standards and assessments based on those standards are essential to the opportunity to learn standards. Assessments yield results. With clear expectations for results, it is no longer possible for the system to avoid redressing student failure. The evidence is right there. The opportunity to observe progress is there for all to see.

But there is another reason why common standards of achievement are especially critical for minority students. It is those students who are most likely to have a school career that is characterized by moving from school to school. We know that a third of children in high poverty schools are likely to change schools each year and in some schools the turn-over rate can exceed 100 percent! Without a common set of standards and accompanying curriculum such students are put at even greater risk, since what is being taught and expected in one school may not be in sync with what is taught in another school, even within the same district.

How can setting high standards be unfair for minority students? The AFT has conducted numerous surveys with parents and teachers. Over and over again parents tell us how important education is for their children – this is particularly true with parents of minority students. They know education is the ticket out. They know their kids can learn. They want the schools to teach them; to hold their children to high standards of achievement and behavior.

This is a critical point in any discussion of standards. Standards do not come out of thin air. Moses did not descend Mt. Sinai with the Ten Commandments in one hand and the standards for social studies, science, math and English in the other hand. Standards are socially constructed. To set meaningful standards it is necessary that teachers understand what students really are capable of (benchmarking to high achievement) and to understand where students are headed – what they need to know. But those standards must also be credible to parents and the public.

Parents of minority students must be involved in the standards setting process. They must understand the value of the standards for their kids' success. And when they "buy-in" to those standards – which has been AFT's experience in our work with parents – it is up to the system to deliver, with help from parents. Anything else, lesser standards for poor kids, or children of color – is unthinkable.

By *not* holding students to those high standards, and the system accountable for delivering the resources necessary to achieve them – teachers who know their subject and how to teach it to students; buildings that are welcoming and well equipped; additional instructional opportunities for students in difficulty, and the like – without those standards and resources, parents know the education system is denying their children what they need most – a first-rate education. *Now that's what the AFT calls unfair!*

10 Epilogue: Part 5 Response to Validity Standards and Principles on Equity (Robert Linn)

Donald M. Stewart

Obviously, the theme of this symposium is a critical one to the College Board, and to all of us personally. Assessment plays a key role in equity, and this meeting allows us to consider again how assessment can best serve educational equity at all levels. Robert Linn's presentation provides a number of provocative questions. I would like to suggest three points, ending with a recommendation for our joint action:

1. Validity is a powerful ally of equity; let's keep it so;

2. We must take a comprehensive, multi-faceted approach to "functional worth" or "test appropriateness"; and

3. We should agree, this morning, to mount a serious collaborative educational campaign regarding test score use.

VALIDITY AND EQUITY

Validity is a powerful ally of equity; let's keep it so: A great strength of Robert Linn's presentation has been to point out that validity has been enhanced by efforts to address equity, whether via DIF analysis, sensitivity reviews, and so on. Further, using validity as a lens through which to examine these nine equity principles seems a particularly effective approach for at least three reasons:

First, by speaking of how to "enhance equity by increasing validity," *equity is positioned as an ally of quality, as a necessary premise to sound assessment.* In the current climate, this seems a quite productive direction, as too many conversations appear to pit equity concerns against those of quality. Measurement provides an apt case for the opposite.

Second, given the rather wide-ranging definitions of equity that Dr. Linn has indicated – formal, compensatory, and democratic – *validity may, for all its evolution, be a more generally shared and intuitively straight-forward concept upon which to build common ground* And we certainly need, in regards to equity and many other issues these days, as much common ground as we can establish.

Third, *placing equity concerns within a comprehensive validity framework,* one emphasizing the "inferences and actions based on test scores," *makes equity a shared responsibility among test developers and test score users.* Not only is this more likely to produce the consensus needed for enhancing equity by increasing validity, it is also consistent with the efforts to integrate assessment instruments into the student's larger teaching/learning process, rather than treating assessment as an isolated event. For these reasons and others, validity – while not a sufficient framework for equity – does offer a very promising direction for addressing equity concerns in a sustainable way and one perceived as relatively objective. This is not a minor advantage.

Therefore, validity is a strong ally for equity, and we need to make sure it continues to be, that is does not lose its strength as a framework. My concern is that the "consequential basis of validity," if broadly used to include unintended and indirect consequences over time, might be used to so expand the meaning of "validity" that the term would lose its, albeit limited, ability to advance the interests of equity as it has in the past. That would be a loss far beyond a linguistic one in the current policy context, the loss of an analytical framework widely perceived as supporting "fairness" in educational opportunity.

Now, while we certainly need more research on the consequences of score use, so as to inform policy decisions, I think we should be careful to avoid placing this entirely within a "validity framework." Might this not be a slippery slope? What would be the time-frame in which consequences would be gauged? How many of the multiple causes involved in score use and interpretation would be included in our modeling? How would we separate out consequences resulting from assessment format, timing and purpose with those resulting from the nature of score reporting or their place in a larger reporting system? I am not sure if this would become so complex as to be of minimal guidance to policy, and susceptible to charges of bias and ideology. In addition, I think that we need to avoid any suspicion that we are hiding behind measurement terms in order to pursue a given social agenda behind closed "expert" doors, rather than face the difficult and risky challenges of public engagement. We need to keep the realms of measurement and policy decision-making distinct, in order to maintain their respective service to educational equity.

Further, we need the honesty and courage to look each other in the face and work out the values we will share and promote. We need to hash out publicly, openly and inclusively the standards we seek, the aims we want to fulfill through our assessment systems, and the uses that are appropriate to the scores that result. All of this should be well informed by the research Dr. Linn suggests, but it must never be seen as substituting for the messy but essential public discussion of our social values, our true educational agendas, the bedrock values we want reflected in the outcomes of schooling.

TEST APPROPRIATENESS ISSUES

This leads me to my second observation: We should take a comprehensive, multi-faceted approach to functional worth or test appropriateness. The late Sam Messick, in an excellent essay that Dr. Linn cites, states:

"... the functional worth of the testing depends not only on the degree to which the intended purposes are served but also on the consequences of the outcomes produced, because the values captured in the outcomes are at least as important as the values unleashed in the goals."

Even if we maintain the integrity of the term "validity," as I hope we do, we must still take into account these outcomes, as we care deeply about the values they reflect or unleash. Not to do so, declares Messick, is to take strong medicine without inquiring about its side effects. How should we do this? I suggest that a comprehensive approach would include at least the following four elements:

Seek clarity of purposes, and an ongoing mutual commitment to them

Developers and users must not only set out clear purposes from the start, they must commit themselves to maintaining and refining how the assessments serve the functions desired. An ongoing associational forum needs to exist as a basic infrastructure to that process, to that mutual developer-user commitment. Further, we need to be clear about not mixing inappropriately the various purposes for which educational assessments are designed. What we wish to infer from the whole exercise must be clear from the onset.

As those of us developing alternative assessments realize, the potential they have to support truly exciting changes in classrooms – not as any magic bullet, but in concert with all sorts of other supporting changes – that potential remains a powerful aim for all of us. However, the use of any assessment system in a high-stakes context can heavily damage validity as incentives for misuse of results increase. No matter how assessments develop, that context, those accountability purposes, and their direct effect on inferences made and actions taken, must be taken into account. Dr. Linn's paper is a valuable reminder. It is best, it seems to me, to keep the ends of classroom improvement and professional accountability quite clear, and generally, avoid aggravating the tension between them by forcing assessments to do both. Double-duty can damage validity too easily.

Follow the nine principles as they apply to test development

As my colleague Howard Everson stated, the assessments under development at the College Board seek to follow the nine principles to which we are a signatory, whether through our sensitivity review process, our use of test development committees comprised of a diverse group of teachers, faculty and educators, or our use of diverse samples of students during our field testing phases. This is true for work being done as a part of EQUITY 2000, Pacesetter and other programs. It is useful to keep in mind, in fact, that many of the techniques used to assure equity in assessment were pioneered through work at the College Board and ETS, such as differential item analysis, principled item writing and validity research. Even Sam Messick's research and writing on validity has been done with support, sometimes indirect, from the College Board.

Promote greater symmetry of information among end-users of scores

In other words, test scores should offer useful information not just to those in authority making decisions about the test taker. Such data should be balanced, depending of course on the purposes of the assessment, with information that assists the learning process and provides educational guidance to the test taker. The traditional tendency to provide much more of the former than the latter needs to be remedied.

Carry out systematic research on the contexts and consequences of testing, and disseminate results broadly

The nine principles indicate the need to take into account the varieties of contexts and consequences accompanying testing, and this is reflected in our own research efforts. For example, with funding provided by the Lilly Foundation, we have been conducting surveys, focus groups and interviews with various test takers to gather information about intended and unintended uses of our various testing programs. Our goal is to advance our understanding of the "functional worth" of our assessment programs, and to offer further guidance to the educational community on the appropriate use of College Board test scores. This information will be compiled and made available to policy makers, educators, students and parents. An earlier publication, Guidelines on the Uses of College Board Test Scores and Related Data, has been available since 1988. This, of course is in addition to such regular efforts as the board's Validity Study Service through which we work with colleges and universities to design and conduct validity studies and gather evidence on appropriate test score use.

In terms of longer-term consequences, we also hope to follow the students from our partner EQUITY 2000 districts over time, seeking, in part, to refine our understanding of the social consequences relating to use of various assessment programs. In terms of the larger context in which higher-stakes testing occurs, we have recently completed a brief study entitled *The Decision to Go to College*, an analysis of the attitudes and experiences associated with college attendance among low-income SAT Seniors.

While such a comprehensive approach is necessary, it will never be sufficient without greater attention to the wider audience, the public and professional users of test scores. This leads to my third general point, and an invitation, almost an imperative:

EDUCATION ON TEST SCORE USE

We must mount a serious, collaborative educational campaign regarding test score use. In order to take advantage of the fairness that valid assessments offer, we need to develop some enduring means to ensure that the uses and actions taken based on test results are appropriate to the assessment used. It is here, in the inferences and actions taken, that our social values, part of the "worth" Cronbach cites, are most likely to be reflected without the discipline of measurement techniques. How can we rectify this?

Given the unlikelihood that, in the context Dr. Linn describes so well, that we will see any single entity charged with the authority to enforce proper usage, I suggest we borrow a page from consumer education and develop a large-scale public service effort to educate test score users. It is long overdue, and the rising pressures on "meritocratic" approaches in this society urges us to act quickly.

It would seem apparent that the only enduring way to improve the appropriateness of inferences and actions taken based on score results – i.e., *improve validity* – would be a sustained effort on several fronts to educate continually the end-users of those scores. We at the College Board, as a membership association that both brings together many of the key score users and develops many assessment services, would be proud to help sponsor and host such an initiative, and I invite you to take us up on the offer.

Given the nature and scope of the task, I would suggest a broad collaborative effort, and given the nature of validity as a shared responsibility, a collaborative effort among both test developers and their primary users. Thus, we should bring together representatives from state and local education agencies, district offices, the admissions community, counseling organizations, teachers groups, parents associations, school boards, policymakers, schools of education, commercial and non-profit test developers and the media in order to develop a set of initial measures to educate end-users in the appropriate uses of various types of scores. This might feature public service cable ads in the Spring and Fall, regular workshops at professional conferences, regular press briefings, brief educational flyers to parents and professionals, and/or inclusion in teacher and counselor training requirements. We can start with modest cooperative ventures, funded broadly from among developers, users and concerned foundations.

In addition to a broad educational campaign, we might consider the following steps as well:

A guidebook for proper use of educational test scores, along the lines of what the American Psychological Association and others developed a few years ago entitled Responsible Test Use – We have in fact begun to develop some of the material for this, and welcome the chance to collaborate with others. The guidebook could serve as both a ready reference for practitioners as well as a useful element in professional education courses; an interactive web site might be developed for inquiries and case study generation.

Proper use or fair inference labels or insert cards: It seems that there is a need to accompany score results with clearer standard information regarding what uses are appropriate for the scores just received. Given that inferences depend on a variety of factors, this may not be a straightforward task. Yet, somehow end-users of test scores should have clearer guidance; we can say that scores are misused for only so long. We must figure out a practical way to inform users more effectively, and I would suggest that a label or insert accompanying all scores, with a message from a broad educational coalition, is worth investigating.

A regular conference on the social consequences of educational assessment: Educational assessments, particularly those involving high stakes, seem to bounce from being the salvation of our schools to being our ticket to the edge of Hades. All sides of the testing debate recognize that assessment operates within a larger context, and that the context and consequences of testing need to be taken into account. Let's do this, though, in a disciplined, public, peer-reviewed forum with an open invitation to all the stakeholders.

I do not pretend to suggest that this would solve the problems of invalid uses, nor resolve the equity concerns reflected in the principles. Yet, as Dr. Linn notes, the perfect cannot be the enemy of the good. So, as we continue to struggle to eradicate the tremendous inequities in education, we must maintain and improve the integrity – validity if you will – of the benchmarks used to mark our progress or our stagnation. Here is a partnership between the assessment community and the larger education world that promises powerful – if *measured* – advances.

We should also not forget that, in the final analysis, this is not just about testing, though the measurement field can offer a disciplined means of gauging our progress and keeping us honest. The tough political choices that need to be made, the social conscience that may need a good nudging, and the economic constraints that must be faced – these will not be solved by any formula of abstract mathematical hieroglyphics, any perfectly sensitive and equitable process of test development and score use. The ugly, bald-faced inequities in the school lives and lived experiences of our young people will all take a far more courageous stand than we can muster here this morning. It is to that crusade, to that campaign of equitable educational preparation, that this valuable national symposium can serve as loyal ally and sturdy rampart.

10 Epilogue: Part 6
At Risk and Unready?
African American Children
and Early Childhood Education

Arie L. Nettles
Kimberly Gene Browning
Regena Fails-Nelson

To be or not to be at risk and unready, is the question about African American children and early childhood education. Paraphrasing this famous Shakespearean quote is ever so timely today as educators, researchers, policymakers, and parents determine school readiness. Visibly distinct inequities at the earliest stage of development and various theoretical frameworks for early childhood education contribute varying levels of school readiness.

Many African-American children begin life precariously. For instance, low birth weight and other health problems, low socioeconomic status, family demographics, and the fact that the majority of African-American preschoolers are fed, clothed and sheltered at a subsistence level all contribute to this. The good news is that African-American parents believe in the importance of early education and send their children to preschool at higher rates than White parents and the overall population. In 1992, over one half of African-Americans 3- and 4-year olds (52.5%) were attending or had attended a preschool education program compared to 44.6% of the overall population (Nettles & Perna, 1997). The challenges these children will encounter during preschool and upon entry to public elementary education are numerous.

When we consider race and ethnic distribution of the U.S. population by household income in 1995, we see that 48% of the African-American children's household income is less than $20,000 compared to 27% for White s, 43% for Hispanics, and 25% for Asians. Twenty-six percent of the African-American households earn $20,000 to $39,999; 14% earn $40,000 to $59,999; 6% earn $60,000 to $79,999; and 5% earn $80,000 or more.

In 1993, the National Household Education Survey found that 67% of African-American males and 63% of African-American females, ages three and four, had no father represented in the home. By comparison, the same survey showed that for White three- and four-year-old males and females, 15% and 16% respectively had no father represented in the home.

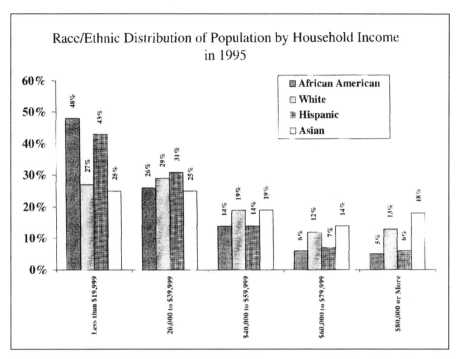

Race/Ethnic Distribution of Population by Household Income in 1995

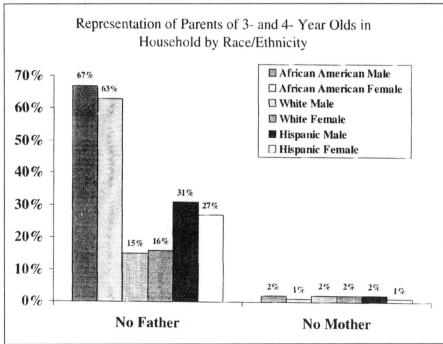

Representation of Parents of 3- and 4- Year Olds in Household by Race/Ethnicity

These early life challenges for African-American children are thus paired with varying definitions and theoretical frameworks for early childhood education. There are many definitions of readiness. As early childhood professionals attempt to define readiness, the most generally accepted definition is being prepared for school or being prepared for learning (Kagan, 1990). This definition assumes that there are criteria children must meet to be ready and readiness can be measured. If children do not meet these standards, they are considered not ready.

One concern raised by early childhood professionals is the reliance of public schools on testing and tracking to classify children in groups (Mitchell & Modigliani, 1989; Moore, 1987; Blank, 1985; Cummings, 1990; Moore, 1987; Zigler, 1987). The National Black Child Development Institute (NBCDI), in particular, has voiced concern about the reliance on group tests rather than individualized evaluation in public schools. With an emphasis on formalized assessment, African-American children potentially experience failure at a very early age. This has disastrous consequences for young Blacks, including low self-esteem, lowered expectations by teachers, and even earlier placement in lower tracks (Grubb, 1989; Moore, 1987; NBCDI, 1985). African American children have already suffered through the use of standardized assessments in public schools. For example, the overwhelming numbers of African-American children classified as educable mentally handicapped (approximately 40% of those classified) through the use of standardized assessments has had a deleterious effect on the Black family (Moore, 1987).

This section will begin by outlining and describing the history of the concept of readiness. It will look at the differences between readiness for learning and readiness for school, explore the relationship between educational ideology and readiness and educational practices, and then describe the beliefs and methods used to assess and measure readiness.

Historic Views on Readiness

The terms readiness and readiness testing were first used in the educational literature during the 1920s when educators became concerned about the number of children who were unsuccessful in first grade. Coinciding with the scientific measurement and testing movement of the early 20th century, instruments were designed and studies conducted to determine why some children failed in school (Dickson, 1920; Holmes, 1927; Monroe, 1932; Morphett & Washburne, 1931). Much of this research concluded that teachers could reduce the failure rate of students by waiting until children reached specified "mental ages" to begin formalized instruction. Mental ages were initially determined using IQ tests (Morphett & Washburne, 1931) and later by the use of readiness tests (Gates Reading Readiness Tests, 1939; Metropolitan Readiness Tests, 1933).

Buoyed by the research, and influenced by the work of G. Stanley Hall (1904) and his student Arnold Gesell (1925), educators during this period attempted to pinpoint mental ages – despite the fact that some researchers, citing little statistical relationship, objected to the concept of mental age as a determinant of educational advancement (Betts,

1946; Gates, 1937; Gates & Bond, 1936). As an alternative to a "just wait for development or mental age" philosophy, readiness tests were developed. These instruments were designed to predict the rate of development as well as measure the traits and achievements of young children – hopefully contributing to their readiness for first grade instruction (Metropolitan Readiness Tests, 1933). Readiness tests were perceived as a nonsubjective way to measure children's abilities, an important criterion in the scientific measurement movement which was dominant during this time (Stallman & Pearson, 1990).

Early readiness tests were paper-and-pencil, group-administered instruments that focused on skills that were thought to be indicative of mental maturity as well as physical development (Metropolitan Readiness Tests, 1933; Stallman & Pearson, 1990). As Stallman & Pearson (1990) discuss, while the intent of the tests were to diagnose the strengths and weaknesses of children so they could receive instruction in weak areas, the actual use of the tests was quite different. Schools tended to use tests scores as overall indicators of readiness and as a result many children were labeled as ready or not ready without any indication of what could be done to help them. Instructional decisions were left up to whatever educational program the school or teacher used (Durkin, 1989). Tests of this kind continued to be developed during the 1940s and '50s with relatively few changes in format, use, or underlying philosophy (Stallman & Pearson, 1990).

The 1960s brought about changes in educational instruction in the United States. The launch of Sputnik 1 by the Soviet Union in 1957 raised concerns about the quality of public school education. People began to feel that the schools should be teaching more and that basic skills should be taught earlier (Durkin, 1989). Researchers such as Bloom (1964), Bruner (1960), and Ausubel (1959) contributed to the discussion. Bruner contributed with his hypothesis that "any subject can be taught effectively in some intellectually honest form to any child at any stage of development (Bruner, 1960, p. 33). Bloom (1964) believed preschool age children have the ability to learn many kinds of skills, and intelligence develops most rapidly during the first five years of life. Ausubel outlined readiness as "the adequacy of existing capacity in relation to the demands of a given learning task" (Ausubel, 1959, p. 246). These perspectives jointly held that children had difficulty in school because of the quality of the instructional program, not due to their level of readiness or mental age. Each of these perspectives maintained that the child's early environment was extremely influential and that it was important to assist children in their educational endeavors rather than just wait for readiness to occur. This position was evident in the inception of Head Start program which aimed to provide an educational intervention for low-income children, thus increasing their opportunity for success in school (Durkin, 1989; Takanishi, 19677; Shonkoff and Meisels, 1990). In spite of all this, readiness tests of the 1960s reflected few of these philosophical changes and primarily remained the same.

Since the 1970s the educational climate in the United States has fostered the concept of readiness as well as the use of readiness tests because of a focus on mastery learning and skills management in curriculum (Stallman & Pearson, 1990). While current standardized readiness tests permit diagnosis of strengths and weaknesses, in practice only total scores are used and then usually as a basis for placement in educational programs (Kagan, 1990; Meisels, 1987; Shepard & Smith, 1986; Stallman & Pearson, 1990).

Let us examine the use of total test scores on Peabody Picture Vocabulary Test (PPVT) of African-American preschool children who participated in the 1986-1992 National Longitudinal Survey of Youth. African-American preschool children's PPVT scores averaged 75%, compared to 98% for White preschoolers and 91% for Asians. Hispanic children demonstrated about the same performance as African Americans, averaging 76%.

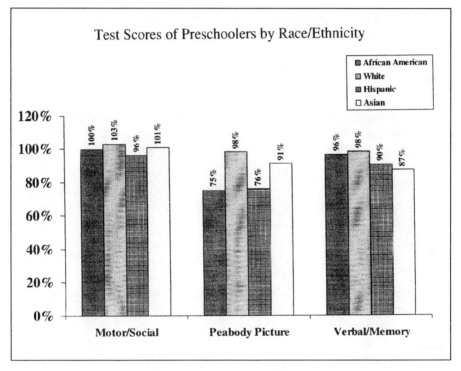

Table 3 also shows that African-American children differ little from these peers in other racial and ethnic groups. For example, African-American children's performance of motor/social skills and verbal/memory are comparable. Conversely some differences emerge when parents are asked about their preschoolers' skills. Approximately 83% of White parents report that their preschool children can identify colors compared to 62.9% of African-Americans. Twenty-one percent of White parents report recognition of letters and alphabets compared to 16.5% of African-Americans (Nettles & Perna, 1997).

Readiness thus remains a complex and controversial construct, poorly defined and open to different interpretations (Crnic & Lamberty, 1994). Recent history and empirical work in the area of readiness has been devoted to four major issues: 1) distinguishing between readiness for school and readiness to learn (Graue, 1993; Kagan, 1990; McGill-Franzen, 1993); 2) discerning differences between theories of educational psychology (primarily maturational and cognitive-development views) and the epistemological components and value systems which follow (Ellwein, Walsh, Eades, & Miller, 1991; Ilg, Ames, Haines, & Gilespie, 1978; Kohlberg & Mayer, 1972); 3) teachers' educational ideology and educational practices (Kagan, 1990; Smith & Shepard, 1988; Graue, 1993); and 4) assessment and measurement of school readiness (Ellwein, et al., 1991; May & Welch, 1986; Meisels, 1987; Porwancher & DeLisi, 1993; Shepard & Graue, 1993). Each of these will be examined in more detail.

READINESS FOR LEARNING VERSUS READINESS FOR SCHOOL

Readiness for learning is generally acknowledged as the level of development at which an individual has the ability to undertake the learning of specific material (Kagan, 1990). Readiness for school is a more finite construct usually characterized as characteristics, or specific skills or abilities that are necessary for success in school (McGill-Franzen, 1993). These can include items such as identifying four colors by name, copying a square, copying a triangle, repeating a series of four or five numbers, etc. These two concepts have often been explored and have occasionally intertwined (Kagan, 1990).

Although the meaning of readiness for learning is generally agreed upon by child development theorists, the mechanisms which affect readiness for learning are not. Constructivist approaches focus on the internal forces which allow children to construct their own knowledge through the process of equilibration (Piaget, 1970). Cultural-historical theorists place emphasis upon the cultural and environmental contexts of learning, proposing that learning takes place in a social and cultural context. The information to be discovered and the methods of discovery are products of human history and culture (Bodrova & Leong, 1996; Bruner, 1996). Motivational theorists suggest learning involves attention, motivation and development status (Brown, 1975; Gagne, 1970). What is clear from these varying perspectives is that multiple forces affect readiness to learn including motivation, physical development, intellectual ability, emotional maturity, and health (Kagan, 1990).

The construct of readiness for school has been historically equated with reading readiness (Kagan, 1990; McGill-Franzen, 1993), as well as with specific skills such as children's printing, drawing, self-concept, perceptual skills, fine and gross motor skills, school adaptation skills, and social skills (Gesell, 1940; Graue, 1993; Kagan, 1990; McGill-Franzen, 1993; Shepard & Smith, 1986). Some research associates school readiness and social and economic characteristics such as socioeconomic status, family size, and absent fathers (Gesell, 1940; Good & Brophy, 1986; Kagan, 1990; McGill-Franzen, 1993; Shepard & Smith, 1986). Other research maintains that readiness for school is directly related to the relationship between student backgrounds and the norms, values, and routines of school (Delpit, 1988; Heath, 1983; Ogbu, 1978). For many students (particularly non-White and low socioeconomic status) the knowledge base as well as the learning skills and strategies they developed prior to school entry, which are appropriate for their communities, appear to be ineffective in meeting the demands of school settings (Comer, 1988; Delpit, 1988; Heath, 1983; Ogbu, 1978). This, along with a lack of school-relevant experiences (e.g., exposure to books, opportunities to engage in cognitive processing), exacerbates the problems these students face in school. Whatever the cause, teachers (particularly in at-risk or readiness-based early childhood program) are believed to have a pivotal role in developing readiness by assessing readiness problems and providing experiences that help ameliorate the deficits.

EDUCATIONAL IDEOLOGY AND READINESS

Kohlberg and Mayer (1972) outlined three streams of educational thought that reflect different views of educational psychology and contain differing epistemological components and value systems. These streams are romanticism, cultural transmission, and cognitive development. These perspectives lead to different strategies for defining educational objectives and for evaluating educational experiences. Each of these articulates a theory of learning and development, which, when applied to risk status and readiness, has profound implications for the educational applications that follow.

Romanticism

Romanticism is a theory of development that reflects a maturational view of childhood growth. Cognitive, socio-emotional, and physical development are seen as primarily biological functions. It is the physiological unfolding of psychomotor, cognitive, and emotional structures which are the foundations of child behavior (DeVries & Kohlberg, 1987; Gesell, 1940; Graue, 1993; Kohlberg & Mayer, 1972). To maturationists, the environment is merely the setting for development; it contributes to or modifies development very little (Clarke-Stewart, Freidman & Koch, 1985). Educational interventions are delayed until the child is "ready" because it is believed that children will be unable to succeed if instruction is begun prematurely (Ellwein, Walsh, Eades, & Miller, 1991).

Arnold Gesell (1940) and his colleagues at the Gesell Institute (Ilg, et al., 1978) were the major proponents of this maturational approach related to kindergarten entry and readiness for school. As discussed earlier, Gesell (1940) argued that a major cause of school failure (as well as school problems such as emotional disturbance and learning disabilities) was a simple unreadiness for the work of the grade in which the child was placed. Indeed, Ilg et al., (1978) state that placing children in school based on their behavioral age rather than chronological age could prevent or cure 50% of school failures.

Cultural Transmission

Cultural transmission ideology (also known as a behavioristic perspective) forms the basis for the classical academic tradition of Western Education (Kohlberg & Mayer,

1972). This approach assumes that knowledge is internalized by children through explicit instruction and reward and punishment. Environmental arrangements of the classroom are paramount because they allow educators to employ basic behavioral principles to reinforce desirable behaviors; the environment is manipulated to build and elaborate on these behaviors (Neisworth & Buggey, 1993). The cultural transmission perspective is characterized by clear educational objectives, widespread of achievement testing and repetition and reinforcement as primary methods of teaching (DeVries &Kohlberg, 1987; Graue, 1993; Kohlberg & Mayer, 1972). To develop readiness skills, emphasis is placed on the acquisition of basic skills that children "lack" in their home and community environments. These can include the use of standard English, recognition of such symbols as letters and numbers, and the development of specific social skills such as sharing, etc. (Neisworth & Buggey, 1993)

Cognitive-Developmental Theory

Cognitive-developmental theory proposes that education and development are critically related to the interaction between the individual and the environment. From this perspective, readiness is not an important issue. Rather, development and education result as individual children construct knowledge while interacting with their environment (DeVries & Kohlberg, 1987; Forman, 1993; Graue, 1993; Kohlberg & Mayer, 1972). In these educational environments, ideas regarding readiness are manifested in the organization of activities, the manner in which the children are grouped, the pace of instruction, and the performance standards set for the children (Forman, 1993).

Definitions of risk status and readiness are believed to be constructed within a particular social or cultural system. These definitions are constructed in social interaction rather than being inherent in the nature of an institution, object, or characteristic (Graue, 1993). The effectiveness of early intervention from a cognitive-developmental perspective is shaped by the background and personal factors as well as past experiences a child may have had, as well as the interaction between a child and his or her teacher (s), other children and materials (Richardson, Casanova, Placier, & Guilfoyle, 1989).

EDUCATIONAL IDEOLOGY AND EDUCATIONAL PRACTICES

Researchers have examined the relationship between teachers' definitions of readiness, educational ideology, and their educational practices. It is clear that there is a lack of agreement regarding the definition of the qualities that comprise school readiness as well as lack of agreement about which experiences and abilities will facilitate success in classrooms. Kagan (1990) believes that readiness has been poorly defined and, as a result of subjective interpretations by practitioners and policy makers, has created conflict and confusion.

Smith and Shepard (1988) examined teachers' beliefs about how readiness develops. Over a one-year period, they interviewed teachers and parents, observed kindergarten classrooms and decision-making events, and analyzed important documents in a single school district. They found that individual teachers are, primarily, coherent and consistent in their views concerning the development of readiness and that there are variations in what teachers believe and how they act on their beliefs. They developed a scoring system based on beliefs about school readiness and the nature of child development. Four types of teachers were identified: nativist, diagnostic-prescriptive, interactionist, and remediationists. Nativists adhered to a view that children become prepared for school according to an evolutionary, physiologically-based unfolding of abilities. These individuals, similar to Kohlberg and Mayer's (1972) romanticists, hold the perspective that children not ready for school should be given more time to develop before being placed in a regular kindergarten classroom. Diagnostic-prescriptive teachers, like Kohlberg and Mayer's (1972) cultural-transmission theorists, ascribe to a philosophy that any inadequacies in school readiness occur because some specific trait (e.g., auditory memory, visual-motor integration) necessary for school learning is not intact. Deficits can be diagnosed and corrected through prescribed training programs. Interactionists, subscribing for example to Kohlberg and Mayer's (1972) cognitive developmentist perspective, adhere to a stage theory of development. They differ from nativists because they believe development is influenced by complex patterns of interactions between the child and his/her environment. Readiness is encouraged by providing children with a classroom that is sensitive to the developing child's needs and interests. Finally, remediationists subscribe to a theory that children of legal age are ready for kindergarten and can be taught. They believe that teachers need to break the curriculum into segments and give students extensive learning time. Generally, remediationists, like Kohlberg and Mayer's (1972) cognitive developmentalist perspective, believe that additional instruction can correct any readiness deficits children may have.

Smith and Shepard (1998) found that ideology appeared to be closely intertwined with the social climate and structure of the schools. Both formal rules/guidelines and informal rules existed in the district. Formal rules were stipulated at the district level for kindergarten curriculum. The rules were academic in nature and included prescribing the amount of time teachers should spend daily on readiness skills and outlining the academic abilities children should acquire by the end of kindergarten. Informal rules existed at individual school levels. Examples of informal rules included parental pressure on kindergarten teachers to spend more time on academic skills (i.e., curriculum issues) and first grade teachers' stipulations about the skills children needed upon entering first grade (i.e., letter-sound associations, knowledge of some sight words, ability to work independently). Smith and Shepard also found that teachers primarily believed that pupil careers should be based upon competence/readiness and not upon age and grade uniformity (1998).

Smith and Shepard concluded that teachers have strong beliefs about how children develop readiness for school and how development should best be dealt with. Teachers' perspectives were generally consistent and coherent. However, there were variations in what they believed and how they acted on those beliefs. The beliefs were strongly influenced by school structure and school climate and opposing views were given little attention or credence.

African American Teacher Beliefs

Graue (1993) examined meanings of readiness in three different kindergartens in three different communities. Using an ethnographic design, she engaged in participant observation, teacher and parent interviews, and analysis of documents such as lesson plans, curriculum guides, and home-school communications during a school year. As a participant observer, the researcher worked as a teacher aide once a week in the classroom. Teachers were interviewed prior to the beginning of school and at the end of the first quarter of school. Like Smith and Shepard (1988), Graue described teachers' ideology regarding readiness in theoretical terms. Of her three teachers, one held a maturational/ environmental model of readiness, one a more strictly maturational model, and the third postulated that low levels of readiness were the result of a lack of school-related activities in children's lives. Graue believed that conceptions of readiness were locally developed and used. Like Smith and Shepard (1988), she found that teachers' thoughts regarding readiness were comparable with school philosophy and structure. Teachers who worked together held similar beliefs and the structures in which they worked supported those beliefs.

Traditionally African-American teachers of children labeled at-risk have been strong proponents of skill-based instruction in early childhood education (Foster, 1997). African-American children need to be proficient in the core areas of the curriculum: reading, writing, and math. If young children have not been exposed to these concepts at home before entering school, then they will struggle in a class where the teacher assumes that they have background in these concepts and presents only high level tasks in core areas without reviewing the basic skills (Delpit, 1995). Many poor and minority children have not had exposure or explicit teaching of these skills prior to school entry and need time to study these skills in isolation before moving on to more complex concepts (Foster, 1997).

Most African-American teachers do not teach exclusively basic skills. They try to cover basic skills as well as higher level tasks to meet the learning needs of all of their students (Ladson-Billings, 1994). Minority teachers tend to present basic skills more explicitly than other teachers who prefer to embed basic skills in more complex tasks. Many teachers view this dilemma as different means to the same end. All teachers want their students to be critical and creative thinkers. However, each student requires a different strategy to reach that goal (Delpit, 1995). Some need explicit examples, modeling and basic skills review before they can engage in complex problem solving and others can only solve problems in the larger context and are confused when the skills are emphasized and isolated. Thus, it is important for all early childhood programs to present both strategies to reach all children. It is not developmentally appropriate to teach only one method to all children regardless of the method (Ladson-Billings, 1994).

ASSESSMENT AND MEASUREMENT OF SCHOOL READINESS

Reviews of readiness assessment instruments make clear that there are two primary problems inherent in the measurement of readiness. These problems are: (1)

there are few readiness tests which provide basic psychometric analyses and most have been unable to withstand rigorous reliability and validity assessment (Graue & Shepard, 1989; Kauffman, 1985; Liechtenstein, 1990; May & Welch, 1986; Meisels, 1988; Shepard & Smith, 1986); and (2) the instability of the developmental traits and skills being measured (Brooks-Gunn & Weinraub, 1976; Chase, 1985; Horowitz, 1982; Shepard & Smith 1986).

Psychometric Analysis

Shepard and Graue (1993) examined the technical validity of various readiness tests and found that readiness tests are not adequately reliable and that their predictive validity is not great enough to justify their use in making important classification decisions. They did believe that many tests could be used for instructional planning and possibly for initial screening. However, they felt that these purposes were rarely stressed in practice. Additionally, they emphasize that if a test is going to be used to segregate children into group A versus group B, it must be demonstrated empirically that these groups are better off in their respective educational experiences. They felt there is not enough evidence to support the use of readiness tests to delay entry to school, for the placement of children in readiness or developmental classrooms, or for assignment of children to segregated at-risk classrooms.

May and Welch (1986) examined the relationship between the predictive ability of school readiness testing and the influences of sex and age. Using 152 children whom they classified by birth date and sex, they compared their performances on the Gesell Screening Test (GSRT) and the Stanford Achievement Test. They found no significant differences between birth-date groups on the Stanford Achievement test and while there was some relationship between age and the Gesell measures, this relationship faded as the children aged.

Similarly, Ellen and others (1991) examined the technical characteristics of four readiness tests, the Brigance, the Daberon Screening for School Readiness, the Developmental Indicators for the Assessment of Learning-Revised (DIAL-R), and the Missouri Kindergarten Inventory of Developmental Skills. They found that boys, minorities, and low-socioeconomic children scored consistently lower on all four tests. While three of the four tests exhibited reasonable reliability, the fourth was highly inconsistent for minorities and children under 5 years of age. None of the tests they examined were excellent predictors of future test performance.

Porwancher and DeLisi (1993) explored the relationship between the GSRT and kindergarten placement for 119 families in three middle-class suburban elementary schools. They examined the connection between program placement, the GSRT, IQ measures (the Wechsler Preschool and Primary Scale of Intelligence-Revised (WPPSI-R), and academic achievement. Results revealed significant relationships among GSRT, IQ and academic achievement. The GSRT was highly correlated with IQ scores and achievement at the kindergarten level and there were no differences in achievement after first grade despite program placement.

Scientific knowledge underlying readiness assessment is such that none of the existing tests is sufficiently accurate to justify placement of children in special programs. Nevertheless, in 1988, testing was required for children entering kindergarten in four states. Six states mandate first-grade readiness testing. Twenty-six states allow local testing of entering kindergartners and 37 states allow first-grade readiness screening. The tests more frequently used were the DIAL-R, the Brigance, the Batelle, the Gesell School Readiness Screening Tests (GSRT), and locally developed tests (Gnezda & Bolig, 1988). A more recent example of the pervasiveness of the use of readiness assessment includes research by May and Kundert (1992a, 1992b, 199c), who surveyed school districts in New York and reported that 56% of the 260 responding districts used kindergarten screening results to make school readiness placement recommendations.

Instability of Development Traits

The frequent failure of readiness assessment to show high correlations between readiness assessment and later academic success is related to the instability of the developmental traits and skills being measured. The predominantly cognitive domains that are sampled in readiness tests are only moderately associated with later cognitive demands of reading and other academic tasks (Shepard & Smith, 1986). Readiness scores obtained in a brief single testing session may be inaccurate reflections of young children's functioning. Young children's development is characterized by rapid periods of growth as well as apparent plateaus and there is a strong instability in early categorizations (Brooks-Gunn & Weinraub, 1976; Chase, 1985; Horowitz, 1982; Shaywitz, Escobar, Shaywitz, Fletcher, and Makuch, 1992; Shepard & Smith, 1986). Additionally, the administration of readiness tests, often several months prior to school entry, exacerbates problems of inaccuracy (Porwancher and DeLisi, 1993).

SUMMARY

Scholars, parents and practitioners have been concerned about the concept of readiness for almost 80 years. While the term first appeared in print in the 1920s, it was not given serious attention until well into the 1930s. Since that time the educational and psychological literature on readiness has flourished. Much of the attention has focused on defining readiness for school, discerning differences between conceptions of psychological and educational ideology and educational practices, and effective assessment and measurement of school readiness. What none of these discussions address is the relationship between conceptions/definitions of readiness and the risk status of children. This is of particular importance since teachers in readiness-based early childhood programs are expected to encourage readiness by assessing readiness problems and providing experiences to ameliorate the deficiencies. The question remains, are African American children at risk and unready?

Bibliography

Ausubel, D. P. (1959). Viewpoints from related disciplines: Human growth and development. *Teachers College Record, 60,* 245-254.

Betts, E. A. (1946). *Foundations in reading instruction.* New York: America Book.

Blank, H. (1985). *Early childhood and the public schools: An essential partnership.* Young children, 40(4), 52-55.

Bloom, B. S. (1964). *Stability and changes in human characteristics.* New York: Wiley.

Bodrova, E., & Leong, D. (1996). *Tools of the mind: The Vygotskian approach to early childhood education.* Englewood Cliffs, NJ: Merrill Publishing.

Brooks-Gunn, J., & Weinraub, M. (1976). A history of infant intelligence testing. In M. Lewis (Ed.), *Origins of intelligence,* (pp. 25-66). New York: Plenum.

Brown, A. (1975). The development of memory: Knowing, knowing about knowing, and knowing how to know. In H. W. Reese (Ed.), *Advances in child development and behavior,* Volume 10. New York: Academic Press.

Bruner, J. (1960). *The process of education.* Cambridge: Harvard University Press.

Bruner, J. (1966). *The culture of education.* Cambridge: Harvard University Press.

Chase, J. B. (1985). Assessment of developmentally disabled children. *School Psychology Review, 14(2),* 150-154.

Clarke-Steward, A., Friedman, S., & Koch, J. (1985). *Child development: A topical approach.* New York: Wiley Publishing.

Comer J. P. (1988). Educating poor minority children. *Scientific American, 259 (5),* 42-48.

Crnic, K., & Lamberty, G. (1994). Reconsidering school readiness: Conceptual and applied perspectives. *Early Education and Development, 5(2),* 91-105.

Cummings, C. (1990). *Appropriate public school programs for young children.* (ERIC Document Reproduction Service No. ED 321 890).

Delpit, L. D. (1988). The silenced dialogue: Power and pedagogy in educating other people's children. *Harvard Educational Review, 58(3),* 280-298.

Delpit, L. (1995). *Other people's children: Cultural conflict in the classroom.* New York: The New Press.

DeVries, R., & Kohlberg, L. (1987). *Constructivist early education: Overview and comparison with other programs.* Washington, DC: National Association for the Education of Young Children.

Dickson, V. E. (1920). What first grade children can do in school as related to what is shown by mental tests. *Journal of Educational Research, 2,* 475-480.

Durkin, D. (1989). *Teaching them to read.* Boston: Allyn & Bacon.

Ellwein, M. C., Walsh, D. J., Eads, G. M., Miller, A. (1991). Using readiness tests to route kindergarten students: The snarled intersection of psychometrics, policy, and practice. *Educational Evaluation and Policy Analysis, 13(2),* 158-175.

Forman, B. D., & Hagan, B. J. (1983). A comparative view of total family functioning measures. *American Journal of Family Therapy, 11,* 25-40.

Foster, M. (1997). *Black teachers on teaching.* New York: The New Press.

Gagne, R. (1970). *The conditions of learning.* New York: Holt, Rinehart, and Winston.

Gates, A. I. (1937). The necessary mental age for beginning reading. *Elementary School Journal, 37,* 497-508.

Gates, A. I., & Bond, G. L. (1936). Reading readiness: A study of factors determining success and failure in beginning reading. *Teachers College Record, 37,* 679-685.

Gates Reading Readiness Tests. (1939). Teachers College, Columbia University.

Gesell, A. (1925). *The mental growth of the preschool child.* New York: Macmillan.

Gesell, A. (1940). *The first five years of life.* New York: Harper & Bros.

Gnezda, M. T., & Bolig, R. (1989). *A national survey of public school testing of prekindergarten and kindergarten children.* Paper commissioned by the National Forum on the Future of Children and Their Families of the national Academy of Sciences and the National Association of State Boards of Education.

Good, T. L., & Brophy, J. E. (1986). School effects. In M. L. Wittrock (Ed.). *Handbook of Research on Teaching* (3rd. ed.). New York: Macmillan.

Graue, M. E. (1993). Ready for what? Constructing meanings of readiness for kindergartners. Albany, NY: State University of New York Press.

Graue, M. E. & Shepard, L. A. (1989). Predictive validity of the Gesell school readiness tests. *Early Childhood Research Quarterly, 4,,* 303-315.

Grubb, W. N. (1989). Young children face the state: Issues and options for early childhood education. *American Journal of Education, 97,* 358-397.

Hall, G. S. (1904). *The psychology of adolescence.* New York: D. Appleton.

Heath, S. B. (1983). *Ways with words.* Cambridge: Cambridge University Press.

Holmes, M. C. (1927). Investigation of reading readiness of first grade entrants. *Childhood Education, 3,* 215-221.

Horowitz, F. D. (1982). Methods of assessment for high-risk and handicapped infants. In C. T. Ramey & P. L. Trohanis (Eds.), *Finding and educating high-risk and handicapped infants..* Baltimore, MD: University Park Press.

Ilg, F. L., Ames, L. B., Haines, J., & Gillespie, C. (1978). *School readiness: Behavior tests used at the Gesell Institute.* New York: Harper & Row.

Kagan, S. L. (1990). Readiness 2000: Rethinking rhetoric and responsibility. *Phi Delta Kappan, 72,* 272-279.

Kagan, S. L., & Zigler, E. F. (1987). Early schooling: A national opportunity? In S. L. Kagan and E. F. Zigler (Eds.), *Early schooling: The national debate.* (pp. 215-229). New Haven, CT: Yale University Press.

Kauffman, N. L. (1985). Review of the Gesell Preschool Test. In J. V. Mitchell (Ed.), *The Ninth Mental Measurements Yearbook,* Vol. 1, pp. 607-608). Lincoln, NE: Buros Institute of Mental Measurement.

Kohlberg, L., & Mayer, R. (1972). Development as the aim of education. *Harvard Educational Review, 42(4),* 449-496.

Ladson-Billings, G. (1994). *The dreamkeepers: Successful teachers of African American children.* San Francisco: Jossey-Bass Publishers.

Lichtenstein, R. (1990). Psychometric characteristics and appropriate use of the Gesell School Readiness Screening Test. *Early Childhood Research Quarterly, 19(4),* 323-329.

May, D. C. & Kundert, D. (1992a). Kindergarten screenings in New York State: Tests, purposes and recommendations. *Psychology in the schools, 29,* 35-41.

May, D. C., & Kundert, D. (1992b). Do extra-year classes pay off? *The Executive Educator, 14,* 25-27.

May, D. C., & Kundert, D. (1992c, November). *Identification of students for pre-first placements: A concern for school psychologists.* Paper presented at the annual meeting of the New York Association of School Psychologists, Bolton Landing, NY.

May, D. C., & Welch, D. (1986). Screening for school readiness: The influence of birthdate and sex. *Psychology in the Schools, 25,* 100-105.

McGill-Franzen, A. (1993). *Shaping the preschool agenda: Early literacy, public policy, and professional beliefs.* Albany, NY: State University of New York Press.

Meisels, S. J. (1987, January). Uses and abuses of developmental screening and school readiness testing. *Young children, 4-6,* 68-73.

Meisels, S. J. (1988). Developmental screening in early childhood: The interaction of research and social policy. *Annual Review of Public Health, 9,* 527-550.

Metropolitan Readiness Tests (1933). New York: World Book Co.

Mitchell, A., & Modigliani, K. (1989, September). Young children in public schools: The "only if's reconsidered." *Young Children, 56-61.*

Monroe, M. (1992). *Children who cannot read.* Chicago: University of Chicago Press.

Moore, E. (1987)., Childcare in the public schools: Public accountability and the black child. In S. L. Kagen & E. Zigler (Eds.), *Early schooling: The national debate* (pp. 83-97). New Haven: Yale University Press.

Morphett, M. V., & Washburne, C. (1931). When should children begin to read? *Elementary School Journal 31,* 496-508.

National Black Child Development Institute (1985). *Child care in the public schools: Incubator for inequality?* Washington, DC: Author.

Neisworth, J. Y., & Buggey, T. J. (1993). Behavior analysis and principles in early childhood education. In J. L. Roopnarine & J.E. Johnson (Eds.), *Approaches to early childhood education,* 2nd Ed., (pp. 113-135). New York: Merrill Publishing.

Nettles, M. T., & Perna, L. W. (1997). *The African American education data book,* Vol. II: Preschool through high school education. Fairfax, VA: Frederick D. Patterson Research Institute.

Ogbu, J. U. (1978). *Minority education and caste: The American system in cross-cultural perspective.* New York: Academic Press.

Piaget, J. (1970). *Science of education and the psychology of the child.* New York: Orion Press,

Porwancher, D., & DeLisi, R. (1993). Developmental placement of kindergarten children based on the Gesell School Readiness Test. *Early Childhood Research Quarterly, 8,* 149-166.

Richardson, V., Casanova, U., Placier, P., & Guilfoyle, K. (1989). *School children at-risk.* New York: Falmer Press.

Shaywitz, S., Escobar, M., Shaywitz, B., Fletcher, J., & Makuch, R. (1992). Evidence that dyslexia may represent the lower tail of a normal distribution of reading ability. *The New England Journal of Medicine, 326,* 145-150.

Shonkoff, J. P., & Meisels, S. J. (1990). Early childhood intervention: The evolution of a concept. In S. J. Meisels and J. P. Shonkoff (Eds.), *Handbook of early childhood intervention* , (pp. 3-32). New York: Cambridge University Press.

Shepard, L. A., & Graue, E. (1993). The morass of school readiness screening: Research on test use and test validity. In B. Spodek (Ed.), *Research on research on the education of young children,* (pp. 293-305). New York: Macmillan Publishing Co.

Shepard, L. A., & Smith, M. L. (1986). Synthesis of research on school readiness and kindergarten retention, *Educational Leadership, 44,* 78-88.

Smith, M. L., & Shepard, L., A. (1988). Kindergarten readiness and retention: A qualitative study of teachers' beliefs and practices. *American Educational Research Journal, 25(3)*, 307-333.

Stallman, A. C., & Pearson, P. D. (1990). *Formal measures of early literacy* (Contract No. G0087-C1001-90). Washington, DC: Office of Educational Research and Improvement.

Takanishi, R. (1977). Federal involvement in early education (1933-1973). In L. G. Katz (Ed.), *Current topics in early childhood education,* Vol. 1, pp. 139-163. Norwood, NJ: Ablex Publishing.

Zigler, E. F. (1987). Formal schooling for four year olds? No. *American Psychologist, 42(1)*, 254-260.

Index